The War That Wasn't
Canadians in Korea

By Les Peate

esprit de corps

ESPRIT DE CORPS BOOKS
OTTAWA, CANADA

ABOUT THE AUTHOR

Les Peate was born in England in 1929. He served six years with the British army, including service in Korea and the Far East as an infantry NCO.

Following two years as a police officer in the United Kingdom, he joined the Canadian army and served for a total of 31 years (regular and reserve service).

He has been writing for *Esprit de Corps* magazine for over 15 years. He is currently the national president of the Korea Veterans Association of Canada.

Copyright © 2005 by Leslie Peate

1ST PRINTING – NOVEMBER 2005

Library and Archives Canada Cataloguing in Publication

Peate, Les, 1929 -
The war that wasn't: Canadians in Korea / Les Peate.
Includes index.
ISBN 1-895896-34-7
1. Korean War, 1950-1953--Personal narratives, Canadian.
2. Soldiers--Canada--Biography. 3. Korean War, 1950-1953--Participation, Canadian.
I. Title.
DS919.2.P43 2005   951.9'042'092271   C2005-906717-9

Printed and bound in Canada
Esprit de Corps Books
1066 Somerset Street West, Suite 204
Ottawa, Ontario, K1Y 4T3
1-800-361-2791
www.espritdecorps.ca / espritdecorp@idirect.com
From outside Canada
Tel: (613) 725-5060 / Fax: (613) 725-1019

The War That Wasn't
Canadians in Korea

By Les Peate

ESPRIT DE CORPS BOOKS
OTTAWA, CANADA

FORWARD

Les Peate, who served as an infantryman in Korea, is a valued member of the veteran's community throughout Canada. He is currently serving as the president of the Korea Veterans Association of Canada (KVA). He has for many years been a valued vice-chairman of the National Council of Veteran Associations (52 member-associations).

The War That Wasn't is based on over a hundred *Esprit de Corps* articles linked with a running narrative. It describes major activities of Canadians and their allies in Korea, and gives a picture of the life of the sharp end soldier in and out of the line. Personal accounts of dozens of Korean War veterans add realism to the story.

All too little has been written about the dangers faced by the Canadian contingent in Korea. There were, of course, the fanatical charges by the communist Chinese army that supported the North Korean military.

Not enough has been said, notwithstanding, concerning the courage it took to fight against the "Commies" of China. Les Peate's book tells it like it was. It is a must read, not only for veterans, but for all Canadians.

Korea was a war – in every sense of the word!

Cliff Chadderton
Chairman,
National Council of Veteran Associations

Cliff Chadderton (above), a wounded infantry veteran of the Second World War, is probably Canada's most noted protagonist for veterans' rights and recognition.

AUTHOR'S NOTE

The war that (supposedly) wasn't.

Some called it a "police action." The Department of National Defence referred to it as a "United Nations operation." To many, it was a mere "conflict."

After 40 years of lobbying, the Canadian government agreed that it was, in fact, a war.

The 26,791 Canadians who served in the Korean War on land, at sea, and in the air, and the families of the 516 Canadians who gave their lives have never doubted that this, indeed, was a war!

*To Korean War veterans of Canada and our allies,
and the 516 Canadians who did not return,
this book is respectfully dedicated.
"They shall grow not old..."*

Contents

ABOVE: *On Sunday, June 20, 1950, waves of North Korean troops poured across the 38th parallel easily overpowering the South Korean border defences. As the communists advanced, the roads became clogged with anxious refugees. (W.H. OLSON)*

OPPOSITE PAGE: *In response to the growing humanitarian crisis, Canada was one of the first countries to begin airlifting supplies into embattled South Korea. (DND)*

ᔔ THE BLISSFUL SUMMER

IN 1950, CANADA, IN COMMON with many other nations, was like Minerva – "weary of war."

The Second World War had been over for five years and the nation was settling down to a peaceful existence. The veterans of the war were resettling into civilian life, many of them recent graduates of rehabilitation programs.

The armed forces had been drastically reduced. The army consisted of only three parachute-trained infantry battalions, supporting arms, and a number of administrative and training units. Their primary role was the defence of Canada. The Royal Canadian Air Force (RCAF) was little better off, even though Canada had entered the jet age with the production of the Avro CF-100 all-weather fighter aircraft in January 1950, and its transport potential had been enhanced by the first non-stop trans-Canada flight by an RCAF aircraft the previous year. The Royal Canadian Navy had been the fourth largest fleet in the world at the end of the Second World War, but rapid demobilization had left it just a peacetime shadow of its once mighty self.

Television was making its presence felt in Canadian homes, and Toronto was suffering from traffic snarls with the construction of an innovative subway system. For a quarter, Canadians could view the award-winning movie *All About Eve*, while errand-boys were whistling the popular hits from *South Pacific*.

To counter a possible threat from the Soviet Union, Canada and the U.S., together with their western European allies, had created the North Atlantic Treaty

Organization (NATO). External Affairs Minister Lester B. Pearson was a leading exponent. Louis St. Laurent headed a majority Liberal government that included, for the first time, Newfoundland, which had joined the Confederation the previous year.

The Montreal Alouettes were the 1950 Grey Cup champions, and the Detroit Red Wings had defeated the New York Rangers four games to three to win the Stanley Cup.

Canada's regular army, a little over 20,000 in strength, had been called upon in early May to assist in recovery efforts from disastrous flooding of the Red River in Winnipeg, which rendered over 100,000 Manitobans homeless.

Despite the Soviet threat, war was far from the minds of most of us. Young Canadians enjoyed the summer in the countryside and at city beaches. For some of them, it would be their last.

In an eastern nation that many had never heard of, events were taking place that would change the lives of thousands of Canadians forever.

AFTERMATH OF 1945

For centuries Korea, described by John Toland as "the crossroads of Asia," had been the scene of local wars by various warlords. The "Land of the Morning Calm" finally achieved stability under the benevolent protection of its Chinese neighbours for 12 centuries, acquiring a reputation for culture and, when occasion demanded, proving well capable of defending its borders against outside aggression. In the late 16th century, Japan attempted to invade China via Korea but was repelled, largely through the efforts of Admiral Yi Sun-sin, whose revolutionary "turtle boats" – the world's first "ironclads" – soundly defeated the Japanese fleet.

From the start of the 20th century, Japan exerted more control on Korea, until the latter became virtually a vassal state. Though Korea was nominally independent, Japan's sovereignty was evident in the 1936 Olympics, when Ki Jung Son, of Korea, won the marathon but was obliged to receive his gold medal under the Japanese flag.

Japan's protection was a mixed blessing. While some bright young Koreans were sent to Japan for education (many of them attained high rank in the Imperial military forces) other Koreans were treated as virtual slaves. Many were conscripted into the army (several of whom served as guards in POW camps). As well, 200,000 young women were abducted for use in Japanese army brothels.

During the Second World War, the Allies only briefly discussed Korea's postwar future. In 1943, Franklin D. Roosevelt, Chiang Kai-shek and Winston Churchill agreed in Cairo that following an Allied victory, the country would become independent, but this was almost an afterthought to other and more vital matters discussed. In July 1945, the Allied leaders – who now added Joseph Stalin to their group – again raised the issue briefly in the Potsdam conference, when it was decided that the Soviet Union, which was no longer threatened in the West, would join the war against Japan. Ironically, while division of the spoils was discussed, the fate of Korea was left to a comparatively low-level military group, whose main concern was to define a boundary determining where in the Korean Peninsula the surrender of Japanese troops would be accepted by either the Soviets or the Western allies. Eventually a U.S. colonel and his Soviet counterparts, with the blessing of Secretary of State Dean Rusk, arbitrarily drew a dividing line at the 38th parallel of latitude – a boundary which not only had no geographical significance, but which in fact isolated part of the southern zone from the rest.

In the North, the advancing Soviets – who had hardly fired a shot against the Japanese – were welcomed as liberators. The closest U.S. troops were a thousand miles away in Okinawa, and it was some time before they arrived. When they did so, it was as an army of occupation rather than restorers of freedom. Nevertheless, on August 15, 1945 Korea was again a free country, after nearly 36 years of subjugation to Japan. (This date is now celebrated annually as Liberation Day by Koreans.)

Political struggles, however, began soon after. In the North, the Soviets welcomed a reputed anti-Japanese guerrilla leader, Kim Il-Sung and when they left Korea in 1947, Kim became prime minister of the Democratic People's Republic of Korea in a manner familiar to many East European satellites – after an election during which his principal opponent had disappeared and in which only one name appeared on ballot sheets.

The South was politically active too. Against the wishes of the U.S. State Department, Gen. Douglas MacArthur (supreme commander of the Allied powers in Japan) brought in the aging Syngman Rhee, who had lived in exile in the U.S. for over 40 years. Another leadership contender was the head of the ad-hoc government-in-exile, Kim Kyu-Sik (the preponderance of "Kims" in the political and military field was due to the fact that about 25 per cent of Koreans from both areas shared that family name, which means "golden one").

For a time the political situation in the South was extremely volatile. At one point, over 140 "peoples committees" controlled various areas of the zone. The U.S. occupation forces antagonized many Koreans by restoring Japanese-organized administrative and police forces, and rioting and civil disorder occurred frequently. Problems increased with the arrival of over a million discontented refugees from the North, most of whom settled in or around the capital city of Seoul.

In 1947, the United Nations had voted for an "all-Korea" election, supervised by a supervisory commission (UNTCOK). Canada was represented in the nine-nation group. The North refused to admit the teams, but in the south Syngman Rhee eventually took office as president of the Republic of Korea on August 15, 1948 (the anniversary of Liberation Day).

There were now two Koreas – although both sides hoped for unification. The North (with about one third of the total population but almost all of the industry) would have liked a united Korea – under Kim Il-Sung. Not surprisingly, Syngman Rhee had the same goal, with himself as president. The Soviets evacuated their sector and two years later the Americans followed suit. The Communists were generous with military aid; artillery, aircraft, vehicles and hundreds of the famed T-34 tanks found their way to North Korea. The Western allies, who were afraid that the fiesty Rhee would invade the North if he had the resources, were more sparing. Only infantry small arms were allocated to the raw South Korean army, with an air force consisting of three elderly training aircraft.

Following the departure of the last U.S. occupation troops in 1949 – leaving behind a few hundred advisers – both sides began preparing defences along the 38th parallel. There were several border clashes and raids by communist guerrillas.

On June 19, 1950, John Foster Dulles addressed the Korean National Assembly and pledged U.S. aid, if necessary, in defence of South Korea. Meanwhile, North Korean armies, who hopelessly outclassed their southern neighbours in numbers, equipment and training, conducted exercises in the border areas. On the morning of Sunday, June 20, the roar of Communist artillery and the presence of hordes of T-34 tanks south of the parallel showed the world that this was no exercise. The rest is history.

MEANWHILE, IN EUROPE

In 1950, personnel-stretched Canadian Forces were presented with a double-whammy. Not only was Canada committed to a brigade-group sized contingent for Korea, but also the growing Communist threat in Europe resulted in an urgent call from the Allied Supreme Commander, Gen. Dwight D. Eisenhower, for Canadian support. In addition to RCAF fighter squadrons — equipped with the new Canadair-built F-86 Sabre — an infantry brigade group was to be raised.

The latter created problems. The Mobile Striking Force (MSF) was still tasked with the defence of Canada and 25 Brigade had absorbed most of the eligible volunteers. Once again, Canada turned to the militia. Under Operation PANDA, 15 infantry regiments were each tasked to provide a company for one of the three composite infantry battalions.

To maintain a degree of affinity they were grouped and designated according to their regimental traditions. Thus, the 1st Canadian Rifle Battalion consisted of companies from the Queen's Own Rifles, the Royal Winnipeg Rifles, the Regina Rifles, the Victoria Rifles and the Royal Hamilton Light Infantry. The 1st Canadian Highland Battalion came from kilted regiments, while other infantry units provided troops for the 1st Canadian Infantry Battalion. Most of the supporting elements were formed in the same way.

In the fall of 1951 the new formation, 27 Canadian Infantry Brigade, sailed for Germany. It was the first of many units to be rotated to Europe over the next four decades.

~ ~ ~ ~ ~ ~ ~ ~ ~ ~

While a large number of accounts have been written about Canada's entry into the Korean War, one of the most concise and coherent that I have researched was an analysis written as a doctoral thesis by Stephen Prince:

"When North Korea launched its invasion of the South on June 25, 1950 western leaders were universally dismayed. Most though, including Canada's prime minister, Louis St. Laurent, and the minister for External Affairs, Lester B. Pearson, were initially cautious in their reactions to the crisis as they knew only the United States possessed the military capacity to halt the aggression. This meant America must lead the response and determine the extent of active opposition to the invasion. When U.S. President Harry S. Truman committed increasing levels of American forces over the next three days, gaining approval for this assistance from the United Nations, Canada's leaders were both relieved and impressed. They felt his actions were important for the Cold War confrontation with the Soviet Union, which was thought to be the real power behind the North's attack, and also for the credibility of the UN, to which they also attached great importance.

"America, though, was only a decade away from the isolationist policies of the 1930s and Truman feared that if American opinion felt it was carrying the load of containing communism alone it would be unwilling to bear the burden. This apprehension resulted in strong pressure being placed on America's European allies and Canada to increase their defence effort before the NATO treaty was signed, committing the United States to their defence. It also meant that within days of the start of the Korean War America was pressing its allies for assistance.

"This pressure was particularly strong on the small circle of countries which America felt were its truly reliable allies: Britain, France, Australia and, of course, Canada. However, the Canadian government was resistant to this pressure. The general consensus was that Canada had relatively small interests in the Far East compared with the NATO area, the theatre which it felt would be decisive in the Cold War and where Canada's security contribution could best be made. In the background, there was also the ghost of the 1941 Canadian experience at Hong

Kong, when two ill-prepared battalions surrendered to the Japanese.

"On a purely practical level, Canada's response was also determined by the limited size of its armed forces. No allowance had been made for the early dispatch of forces overseas by 1950. Canada's army was designed to provide the framework for an expeditionary force of six divisions in a general mobilization for a major war. Its only active units in 1950 consisted of three infantry battalions, and two armoured and one artillery regiment. The infantry were assigned to the Mobile Striking Force, a brigade group designed as a response to Canada's new post-war danger, that of air or airborne attacks by the Soviets in the northwest. In June 1950, though the MSF was still more impressive in title than reality, its under-strength units were scattered across the country, it lacked a proper headquarters, and no exercise had ever been undertaken at more than battalion level. The chiefs of staff reported it would take six months to turn it into a battle-ready brigade group. Sending it to Korea would also leave Canada with no units at all for its own defence.

"Faced with this reality, the government limited its initial response to naval forces, ordering three destroyers to the Far East on June 30. Defence Minister Brooke Claxton, though, had few illusions about the usefulness of this relatively painless and risk-free contribution. He told the cabinet, 'While it was considered that more naval forces would probably be available than necessary, nevertheless a Canadian contribution might be a desirable gesture.'

"But as the crisis continued, with the North Korean forces making great advances, the issue had to be considered again. On July 19 the Cabinet Defence Committee decided that no Canadian ground force could be made available. It also failed to endorse Lester Pearson's suggestions that Canada might allow recruiting for 'some kind of international UN force' or send a medical unit. It did, though, recommend that a squadron of North Star transports be made available to the UN airlift. As such, the planes of No. 426 Squadron were the first Canadian forces actually in theatre. (Their comrades from 435 and 436 Transport Squadrons had been Canada's last operational units in the Second World War, through their flights over Burma in 1945.)

"However, it was ground forces America was really pressing for. Pearson described Canada's three destroyers as 'no mere token,' but an official of the U.S. State Department supposedly quipped back, 'Okay, let's call it three tokens.' When Britain, Australia, and New Zealand all announced they would be contributing ground forces on July 25, the pressure on Canada was greatly increased...

After a series of four cabinet meetings stretching over a week, St. Laurent announced on August 7 the decision to recruit a new infantry brigade group, the Canadian Army Special Force, for use by the UN or NATO, but in all probability for Korea.

"Much of the reluctance to mobilize such a force undoubtedly came from fears that it might not be possible to recruit and sustain it through voluntary recruiting, thus raising the divisive specter of conscription, particularly if other commitments arose, as indeed became the case when 27 Brigade was raised specifically for NATO. In a July poll of Canadians' feelings towards the war, two thirds of Quebecers were opposed to sending troops. However, the initial response was excellent, with the new battalion of the Royal 22e Regiment (Van Doos, from Vingt-Deuxième) swiftly brought up to strength. In fact, the numbers of volunteers were so overwhelming that the tiny army recruitment machinery, set up to cope with only a trickle of Permanent Force recruitment, was hard pressed to cope. The resulting mismatch between the eager queues and the small numbers actually led Brooke Claxton to reverse the normal procedures so that men were attested instantly, with checks and medical examinations coming later. In this way he hoped to capitalize fully on the initial enthusiasm.

"Captain Bill Sutherland of the Princess Patricia's Canadian Light Infantry (PPCLI) was seconded to the Royal Canadian Engineers as a recruitment officer. Suddenly confronted with 299 recruits for 59 Field Squadron, he only had time to ask them three questions: 'Have you ever been convicted of a criminal offence? Do you come from a broken family? Why do you want to go to war?' instead of the normal 40-minute interview. As he told me, his assessments had to 'rely a great deal on intuition.'

"Claxton's intervention in the recruiting has since been criticized for the many administrative problems and inefficiencies it later caused. Famously, a 72-year-old and a man with an artificial leg were enlisted. By the end of March 1951, when the bulk of the force went to Korea, over one third of the 10,000 Special Force recruits had been discharged or had deserted.

"However, the recruitment did quickly provide sufficient manpower for the 5,000-strong brigade and its support and reinforcement elements, as well as some of the manpower for the army's general expansion, despite all its losses while in training. Of the new recruits, 47 per cent were Second World War veterans. According to Captain Sutherland, only five of the 299 recruits for 59 Field Squadron were eventually rejected.

"Initial training quickly began at various bases throughout Canada and the army estimated a minimum of five months was required to achieve acceptable standards of readiness. Soon, though, the problems of concentrating the brigade and continuing its training through the winter were being considered. This issue was settled in the last week of October when it was agreed that 25 Canadian Infantry Brigade Group, as the force was now known, should use the U.S. Army's Fort Lewis in Washington State for advanced training."

~ ~ ~ ~ ~ ~ ~ ~ ~ ~ ~

One Fort Lewis trainee was Lieutenant (later Major General) Bob Ringma, who recalls:

"The move by train to Fort Lewis was another part of the adventure for the volunteers in the Canadian Army Special Force. Twenty-two trains, taking up to five days of travel time, carried the troops across Canada.

"Having disposed of surplus vehicles, weapons, and equipment after the Second World War, Canada now had to manufacture or buy replacements to equip 25 Brigade at Fort Lewis. The U.S. army agreed to sell vehicles, spare parts, certain wireless sets, rocket launchers, and rockets to Canada. It also agreed to maintain our force in the field with rations and gasoline. The cost of supporting our troops in Fort Lewis was calculated using a capitation rate of $2.46 per day per man. The total co-operation of the U.S. military in Fort Lewis and in Korea made Canadians feel that paying their own way was a buck well spent.

"Relations between the Canadian and American forces at Fort Lewis were good. The normal rivalry that exists between military units and foreign formations probably contributed to the high morale of the Canadians while in the U.S. The clubs, PXs, and other inexpensive amenities on the base were also appreciated, as were the contacts with civilians at Tacoma, Seattle, and Vancouver.

"Canadians enjoyed their stay at Fort Lewis and, from a training point of view, considered it a success. When the brigade left for Korea in April they were well prepared to meet the enemy. With the end of winter and the departure of the brigade, the remaining Canadians, now part of the Replacement Group, moved back up to Canada into Camp Wainwright, Alberta."

~ ~ ~ ~ ~ ~ ~ ~ ~ ~

In his thesis, Stephen Prince described the situation:

"For the new 2nd Battalion, PPCLI, however, the visit to Fort Lewis was in transit only as a result of the course of the fighting in Korea. By October, the war seemed to be almost over. General Douglas MacArthur felt he no longer required Canada's brigade for operations but did desire a Canadian presence to stress the UN character of the war. Thus, while the rest of the brigade continued training with its eventual destination — Korea or the Rhine — still uncertain, 2PPCLI was despatched to the Far East only three months after its formation. This was considered acceptable as it was thought the unit would be required for occupation duties only. The partly trained battalion sailed in the USNS *Private Joe P. Martinez* on November 25. This was the very day the Chinese launched their first major offensive in Korea.

"That intervention quickly called Canada's bluff over the deployment of 2PPCLI. The battalion arrived in Korea on December 18 and on the 20th its commanding officer, Lt.-Col. J. Stone, met his new American commander, Gen. Walton "Bulldog" Walker who headed the Eighth Army and wanted the PPCLI to immediately join Britain's 29 Independent Infantry Brigade in the line. Stone had to refuse, having been given a written order that his unit should not be engaged until he felt they had had sufficient training. While this was a reasonable order, especially remembering the Hong Kong experience [when two untrained Canadian battalions were virtually annihilated by the Japanese], the government had decided not to commit it to the UN command before Stone's arrival, despite the changed situation with Chinese intervention. Stone later praised the general's understanding over the issue, but the situation reflected little credit on the Canadian government.

"That Stone remained in an awkward position, training his troops while others, sometimes with less training, fought desperate battles against the Chinese, is shown by the battalion's war diary. The entry for January 5, 1951 shows Stone was once again asked to commit the battalion at once, and that the January 7 entry records: 'Lieutenant Colonel Stone is under heavy pressure to commit the battalion early.' The diary also reveals the level of preparedness at the time, with the entry for January 3 stating:

"'Questions were raised by platoon and company officers regarding the method and speed with which this battalion was raised, particularly when a battalion is sent overseas with some men who have never fired their weapons.'[3]

"It was to Stone's credit that the battalion was ready to move to reinforce the 27 British Commonwealth Brigade on February 15, a month before the Directorate of Military Training in Canada had thought it would be prepared. Their arrival meant 27 Brigade contained troops from five countries.

"Arrival of the remainder of the brigade was delayed both by the proper completion of training and vacillation over whether it was to go to Europe or Korea. Finally, on February 21, 1951 it was announced the brigade was to go to Korea, and on May 4 it arrived in Pusan. The last major UN reinforcement, it allowed the establishment of a proper three-brigade Commonwealth Division that July. The decision to group the brigade with the Commonwealth had originally been made strictly on practical logistic grounds, given the fact Canadian troops were still using British pattern small arms and artillery. By the time 25 Brigade arrived, Lester Pearson had also decided it would 'be safer and more efficient in a Commonwealth Division,' given the U.S. army's mixed record.

"Canada's response had been comparatively slow due to the lack of ready forces (a lesson for any government) and because of vacillation due to the unpredictable course of the war and [the concerns of] the still 'cold' conflict in Europe...

"It should also be remembered that once the Canadian troops were in position, they were kept fully up to strength in order to fulfil their role. By December

1951, Brig. John Rockingham had to tell the Canadian Liaison Mission in Tokyo that 25 Brigade was providing 'over half the infantry on the line [within the Commonwealth Division]' as well as undertaking 50 per cent of the service and engineering work, rather than the third which should have been their share. This was largely due to manpower problems among the other Commonwealth contributors, especially Britain. Ironically, given government worries at the outset, of all the problems associated with Canada's response to the war, quality and quantity of its newly recruited manpower was the one that had given it no real worries."

~ ~ ~ ~ ~ ~ ~ ~ ~ ~

Even before arrangements were being considered for the dispatch of land forces to Korea, the Royal Canadian Navy was ready to go.

At the end of June 1950, Rear-Admiral Harry DeWolf, the senior naval officer on Canada's Pacific coast, was ordered to prepare his three destroyers to join the United Nations effort. HMCS *Sioux* was just leaving dry dock (with more work to be done); *Cayuga* had also just left dry dock and had not yet been provisioned; and *Athabaskan*'s crew was on annual leave for another week. Nevertheless, after much hectic preparation, the trio of vessels sailed from their home port on July 5, on schedule. Barracks, other vessels, and storerooms in Esquimalt had been stripped of seamen and material to meet the challenge.

A seasoned veteran of the Battle of the Atlantic, Captain Jeffry V. Brock, DSC commanded the force, sailing in *Cayuga*. The destroyers were led into the Pacific by the cruiser HMCS *Ontario*, which departed home leaving a message from the chief of naval staff: "First at bat as usual. Good luck on your mission."

After a brief stay in Sasebo, Japan, *Athabaskan* was detached on July 31 to escort an American troopship carrying reinforcements to embattled Pusan. The Seventh Fleet command had decided that the Canadian vessels would operate individually, rather than as a Canadian flotilla, and *Cayuga* was the next to be detailed for escort duty.

The situation on Korea's west coast was uncertain. One British destroyer had suffered severe damage due to an air attack and, although North Korea had no submarines, the possibility of intervention by Soviet or (later) Chinese subsurface vessels was there. Ship-to-ship actions were rare, but mines were a constant threat.

~ ~ ~ ~ ~ ~ ~ ~ ~ ~

Although the navy lost no time in getting into action in Korean waters, the Royal Canadian Air Force was the first element to become operational in Canada's support of the United Nations.

Wing-Cmdr. C.H. Mussels, DSO, DFC, a Second World War Pathfinder veteran, commanded 426 Squadron, the RCAF's only long-range transport squadron. When the Korean War began, he envisaged the possibility of Canada's being called on for assistance, and with his senior officers began to formulate deployment plans just in case.

On July 19, 1950, the Canadian cabinet decided to offer the services of one air transport squadron to assist in supplying the United Nations forces in Korea, and the following day 426 Squadron was tasked to operate, under control of the U.S. Air Force's Military Air Transport Service (MATS). Six aircraft and 12 crews were to operate from McChord Air Force Base, near Tacoma (and Fort Lewis) in the state of Washington.

The preliminary planning and preparation paid off. On July 25, the first six North Stars sporting the UN flag on their tail fins lined up for inspection and departure at Dorval airport, in Montreal. As W/C Mussels took off in the leading aircraft at 1900 hrs, a rainsquall hit — perhaps a forewarning of some of the atrocious weather conditions 426 Squadron crews would encounter during the next four years.

The aircraft formed a double Big Vic formation and later that evening flew over Ottawa, dipping their wings in homage to former Prime Minister Mackenzie King, who was lying in state on Parliament Hill, having died three days earlier. (In a way this was ironic, as King had been far from supportive of the United Nations.) On July 26, the North Stars arrived at McChord.

The MATS commander had expected the Canadians to be operational after a week, but to the astonishment of the Americans, Mussels replied that 36 hours would be sufficient.

McChord was overcrowded; what was originally a fighter base had been "invaded" by four transport squadrons with three more expected at any time. Improvisation was the order of the day. When Mussels threatened to move his ground crews from inadequate barracks into civilian off-base accommodations, conditions improved.

At 1945 hours on July 27, less than 34 hours after the first Canadian North Star arrived at McChord, Squadron Leader Harry Lewis and his crew were airborne on the way to Tokyo with a full load of U.S. army reinforcements. Operation HAWK was underway.

Although 426 Squadron was Canada's only formedRCAF unit to participate in the Korean War, a number of fighter pilots served by flying Sabre jets in USAF squadrons. The first was Flight Lieutenant Omer Levesque, who had a distinguished Second World War record, including a lengthy term as a POW. In December 1950, while attached to a USAF unit, he became the first Canadian to engage in jet-to-jet combat in an action against Chinese MiG-15 fighters.

~ ~ ~ ~ ~ ~ ~ ~ ~ ~

TRAGEDY IN THE ROCKIES

Of the almost 22,000 Canadians who served in Korea and Japan, 516 Canadian servicemen gave their lives in the war. But not all of them saw Korea. Seventeen members of the Second Field Regiment, Royal Canadian Horse Artillery, died before they had even left Canada — more than the total number of gunners who were lost in the Far East.

During the months of October and November 1950, the soldiers of the newly formed Special Force travelled by rail from all parts of Canada to Fort Lewis to train and organize for their role in Korea.

One of the last of the 22 troop trains carried 340 members of 2RCHA. On the morning of November 21, the train had just crossed a trestle close to the Alberta-B.C. border, near the small community of Canoe River, B.C. As the train began the climb into a long curve, the eastbound Transcontinental Express sped into the same curve on the single-track railway. At 1035 hrs the trains collided.

The crash was catastrophic. The locomotive of the troop train was hurled into the air and landed on the coaches behind it. Several of the train's cars derailed, with some of them falling down a steep embankment. The wooden coaches twisted and shattered, and the bodies of dead and wounded soldiers and railroad staff were entombed in the wreckage.

At first, many of the soldiers thought their train had been caught in an avalanche or rockslide. Those in the rear of the train were horrified by the carnage they encountered when they ran forward. Several victims were trapped in one of the coaches beneath the remains of the two locomotives.

Rescue efforts were hampered by steam that gushed everywhere, eventually freezing in the sub-zero climate. A number of casualties, some of them fatal, were the result of scalding. Clouds of steam reduced visibility at the crash site, and rescuers were working in waist deep snow.

Most of the regiment's officers were in the rear of the train, and together with the NCOs, they quickly organized rescue attempts. To quote Jack Skinner, a former officer with 2RCHA: "Like good leaders, we had allowed the men to eat first and most of us were in the dining car."

The spirit and discipline of the gunners were exemplary. Although some of them were Second World War veterans, many had been in uniform for only a few weeks. A Transcontinental passenger recalled, "The first reaction of the injured soldiers was to ask if any of the women and children on our train had been hurt. They ignored their own injuries and, if trapped, waited quietly for their comrades

to come to their rescue."

The dining cars on the troop train became a makeshift hospital. An Alberta doctor, Patrick Kimmett, himself a Second World War veteran, was a passenger on the Transcontinental and, aided by his wife and a nurse whose name he never knew ("We were too busy to get acquainted then"), took charge of the injured until the arrival of a medical team from Jasper several hours later. Fortunately, in addition to the regular first aid supplies carried on the trains, the unit equipment included medical items such as bandages, morphine, and antiseptics. These were put to good use.

Meanwhile, many of the troops injured or scalded themselves, but worked feverishly to extract their dead and living comrades from the wreckage. One NCO recalled that he saw a shoe with a foot in it, a severed head, and part of a torso pulled out of the wreckage; another gunner helped to remove six bodies but had to leave three others pinned under the locomotive boiler.

Although first reports denied this, it was later confirmed that fire had broken out in two of the shattered wooden coaches, adding to the difficulties.

Some soldiers were lucky. Gunner Boutillier, slightly injured by flying wreckage, credits his survival to the fact that at the time of the crash he was purchasing

ABOVE: *Gunners of 2RCHA view the damage and attempt to assist their less fortunate comrades. The November 21, 1950 Canoe River, B.C., train wreck killed 17 Canadian soldiers and seriously injured another 50. They were Canada's first casualties of the Korean War. (DND)*

a pack of cigarettes from the news vendor, whose portable cart provided a few square feet of cover. James Thomas recalls that he was pinned to the floor by a detached upper berth, but his car was less battered than those in front; he survived without serious injury.

Improvisation was the order of the day. Somehow the news vendors were able to produce a little coffee to warm the rescue workers. Towels, table linen, and even white seat covers were pressed into service as improvised bandages and dressings.

Even in the midst of the tragedy, Jack Skinner recalls there were lighter moments. He remembers that while most of the passengers and train crews were busily engaged in rescue operations, a number of the dining car staff were frantically searching the wreckage and the surrounding area for dining room silverware. When he tried to remove a fire axe from its clips to help free his troops from the wreckage, he was severely chastised by a trainman who told him to leave it alone as "it was for emergency use." His reply was not recorded.

Eventually help arrived. The train crew had hooked in to the telegraph lines, and a relief train arrived from Jasper. The serviceable cars of the troop train were hauled to Edmonton, arriving early in the morning of November 22nd. A special train containing military medical staff met the train at Edson, where the redoubtable Dr. Kimmett and his family left for a well-earned respite. On arrival in Edmonton the dining car windows were smashed to allow the removal of the stretchers with over 50 injured soldiers. More quietly, 12 blanket-wrapped bundles were carried off, the bodies that had so far been recovered from the wreckage. Every available ambulance in the city was pressed into service to convey the injured to military and civilian hospitals.

Meanwhile, the less damaged Transcontinental, was towed into Kamloops. Ironically, of the only two casualties on the train requiring hospitalization, one was an army staff sergeant posted east with his family.

There are sequels to this tragic story.

2RCHA arrived in Korea on May 5, 1951 and served with distinction in support of Commonwealth Division units. The first Canadian artillery shell fired in the Korean War was from one of the 25-pounder guns of "E" Battery. Five more members of the regiment lost their lives before the unit returned, a year later. While in Korea they were redesignated Second Regiment, Royal Canadian Horse Artillery. During their tour, members of 2RCHA received 25 awards for gallantry and distinguished services.

Canadian National Railways eventually attempted to pin the blame for the disaster on a young telegrapher, Alfred Atherton. CNR officials alleged he had omitted part of a message ordering the westbound train onto a siding to permit the passage of the Transcontinental. Atherton was tried for manslaughter in Prince George, BC. He was defended by the lawyer and upcoming politician John Diefenbaker, who was admitted to the B.C. bar for the occasion by passing a simple, one-question oral examination. Atherton was acquitted. And Diefenbaker, of course, went on to greater things, including, unfortunately, the scrapping of the Avro Arrow program.

Gunners Atchison, Barkhouse, Carroll, Conway, Craig, George, Levesque, Manley, McKeown, Orr, Owens, Snow, Stroud, Thistle, Wenkert, White, and Wright became the RCHA's first casualties in the Korean War.

~ ~ ~ ~ ~ ~ ~ ~ ~ ~

GETTING THERE WAS NO FUN AT ALL

While the rail accident was tragic, the suffering on the sea passage was universal. One famous steamship line, to encourage travel on its vessels, coined the motto "Getting there is half the fun!" The thousands of Canadians who traveled from Seattle and other North American ports to Korea between 1950 and 1953 would certainly disagree. Most Korean War veterans have horror stories of their three-week transit to Pusan or Inchon.

Visions of luxury cruises soon dissipated when the members of the Second Battalion Princess Patricia's Canadian Light Infantry (2PPCLI) set eyes on the *Private Joe P. Martinez* in the United States Army Transportation Corps Ocean Terminal, Seattle, on a rainy November 25, 1950. The *Martinez* was one of the Kaiser Corporation's Liberty and Victory ships that were built by the hundred during the Second World War; these vessels were so cheaply constructed that if a craft made a single transatlantic crossing it was considered to have paid for itself. *Martinez* was a typical example. The vessel was rusted and battered, the cargo space replaced with four-tiered bunks. Conditions were cramped, privacy non-existent and, later, as the voyage progressed, the effects of seasickness added the stench of vomit to the miseries. Altogether, 900 Canadians and about twice that number of U.S. servicemen endured this 20th century Noah's Ark on the voyage.

On another ship, Bill Turner, a former Strathcona, recalled that the shock set in even before leaving the dock. As part of a draft on the *Balue*, he had been herded aboard the vessel "like so many sheep" when a hubbub occurred on the dockside. In Turner's words:

"What happened next no Canadian would understand. A convoy of three buses escorted by MPs in jeeps turned onto the dock. The MPs surrounded the buses, with shotguns at the ready. An officer and senior NCOs marched the soldiers from the buses up the gangway, onto the ship, and down to the bottom deck. The Canadians couldn't understand what was happening — we were already three hours late in leaving.

"The MP officer and his staff explained that these soldiers had been court-martialled and already had served some of their sentences for AWOL, desertion and other, more serious, offences. They were called into court again and told that the rest of their sentence would be served in Korea — the more serious the offence, the worse place in the front lines they would be serving."

Besides the cramped, unsanitary conditions, one of the biggest gripes concerned the food. Despite the ever-present mal de mer, some troops made a point of attending every meal. In his memoir, *The King's Bishop*, John Bishop recalled that "the dirty weather was exceeded only by the foulness of the food, and only a few soldiers were able to keep their food down. I threw up every meal that I ate during the three worst days."

Menus included watery soup with a few crackers, skinny slices of poor-quality beef, an occasional potato and, on one vessel, dinner consisted of a few turnips. Only two meals a day were served; with the large number of passengers, the mess was forced to operate on a 24-hour basis.

As members of formed units, the Canadians probably fared better than their U.S. travel companions. Reluctant soldiers were driven from their stinking troop-decks and made to participate in physical training. That, and the enforced exposure to fresh air, may not have been appreciated, but in retrospect helped to keep them in a little better condition. As the chief (and almost sole) form of recreation was gambling, several members who may not have suffered physically no doubt suffered financially.

Some were lucky. Bill Olson, a photographer, was able to assist the ship's X-ray technician and, in exchange, had a cozy berth in the medical quarters. Don Eager, on the *Marine Adder*, developed a toothache and was sent to the sick bay. Although his dental abscess disappeared, he remained quiet and spent the rest of the trip in comfort.

The journeys were broken by a run ashore in Honolulu. This turned out in most voyages to be a short march around the dock to restore land legs. However, with the typical ingenuity of the Canadian soldier, a few enterprising troops somehow managed to acquire a bottle or two of liquor while ashore.

Some troops were lucky enough to spend a few hours sampling the delights of Yokohama, where they were at last able to let off a little steam. As booze, hookers, and just about anything else could be obtained by barter, many Canadians returned to their vessels lacking many items of their uniform. Then it was on to Pusan, disembarkation, and the comparative comfort of the Korean railways.

Surprisingly for once, the underpaid, underfed British troops had a better time on their trip to Korea. The troopships (such as *Empire Orwell* and *Empire Fowey*) were especially designed for this purpose. Space was far more adequate (double bunks were the norm on the troop decks) and well-run mess halls served three good meals daily. Shore leave in Port Said, Aden, Columbo, Singapore, and Hong Kong made the voyage a luxury cruise compared to the Seattle-Pusan trip.

Responsibility for the shipping of troops and material from North America to Korea fell to the U.S. Army Transportation Corps, which not only organized cargoes of unwilling troops but about a million tons of freight monthly. It quickly developed from a makeshift, no-warning operation to an effective system of logistics. About half a dozen Canadian vessels from our rapidly shrinking merchant navy participated in the sealift.

However, dreams of an exotic Orient were soon dispelled when Pusan came into sight or, more specifically, smelling range. Smoke and fumes from a million cooking fires, open sewers, fields that had been fertilized for centuries with human feces, and the over-riding vapour of cabbage and garlic from the Korean staple (kimchi) heralded the presence of the port. In the early stages, an influx of hundreds of thousands of refugees had added to the problem.

The musical greeting by a U.S. army band, which welcomed the Canadians with *If I Knew You Were Coming I'd Have Baked a Cake!* did little to conceal the disappointment of the new arrivals. Nor was their journey over. After a truck ride through streets teeming with starving refugees to the almost-wrecked rail station, the soldiers embarked on yet another uncomfortable leg of their trip to the forward area.

~ ~ ~ ~ ~ ~ ~ ~ ~ ~

IT'S GOING TO BE A BUMPY RIDE

The heavy "coming-and-going" fighting of the first year of the war took a toll on an already inadequate railroad system on both sides of the 38th parallel.

At the start of the war virtually all of the locomotives in Korea were steam-powered and most of them were of Russian design and reminiscent of the turn of the century. Many of them were destroyed by mines, artillery, sabotage, air strikes and, in the case of North Korea, by naval gunfire. The South Korean railways lost many locomotives. Indeed, bullet- and shell-riddled trains lying off the embankments were so common that after a time they attracted little attention from the troops moving up into the line.

It was there that most of us made our first acquaintance with the South Korean railroads. After disembarking at Pusan, we were trucked to the train station. This shattered cavernous structure was a scene of disorder. While U.S. Red Cross ladies distributed coffee and doughnuts, harried rail transport officers attempted to assemble the heavily laden soldiers on the right platforms and ultimately on the right trains. The confusion was compounded by many unattached multilingual individual servicemen and hosts of Korean refugees, who had arrived from the north and now had nowhere to go and no means of support, save whatever food or other items they could beg from the troops.

Eventually the train arrived. In the early days, it was usually pulled by one or two ancient-looking locomotives, leaking steam from several places. The engine crew was Korean and despite calumnious rumours that sometimes they would refuse to drive north and had to be replaced by UN drivers, I have yet to hear of this actually happening. Meanwhile the troops would be assigned to passenger cars.

Mike White, a former gunner with 2RCHA, described the scene:

"The train, when it arrived, reminded me of one of the old wood-burners of the Wild West which Jesse James used to hold up. We were seated in pairs, facing each other, on carriage seats that were wooden slats, with our bags (of which we had two) piled high down the gangways and everyone clambering over them when leaving the compartment.

"The dining car consisted of an M-37 field cooker, on which two large vats of water were boiling. One contained heated C-ration cans, the other we used to make our instant coffee. Meals were handed out haphazardly, and a great deal of swapping took place (few of us liked the ground meat and spaghetti).

"Most of us spent the trip reading, playing cards or trying with little or no success to sleep. Until the novelty wore off, we got a kick out of receiving a present arms from the ROK sentries who were posted on every bridge — a necessary precaution as guerrillas were still active. Many of our younger troops who had not seen the effects of war before were sobered by the sight of wrecked locomotives and rolling stock in sidings or off the track, as well as the stations that we passed through. The Pusan-Seoul trip could take between 15 and 24 hours. Fifty years later I did the reverse trip in under four hours, in much more comfortable conditions."

Moving people was only one function of the railroads. Ammunition, equipment, supplies and rations all had to be shipped to the railheads for onward distribution to units by truck.

In less than 12 months, civilians in a peaceable Canada had been converted to soldiers, and more were about to experience the horrors of war in a far-off land.

OPPOSITE TOP: The airlift mounted by 426 Transport Squadron was one of Canada's first demonstrable responses to the Korean War. (DND)

OPPOSITE BOTTOM: HMCS Cayuga was hastily provisioned after leaving drydock and she set sail for Korea on July 5, 1950, along with HMCS Sioux and Athabaskan. (DND)

ABOVE: *The first army unit to deploy to the Korean Penninsula was the Second Battalion, Princess Patricias Canadian Light Infantry. Hastily established, 2PPCLI continued to train after they arrived in theatre. (DND)*

OPPOSITE PAGE: *As well as preparing to fight in Korea, the Canadian army simultaneously mobilized 27 Brigade to deploy to West Germany. Supreme Allied Commander (NATO) General Dwight Eisenhower reviews Canadians upon their arrival in Rotterdam. (DND)*

❧ FIT TO FIGHT

*"An ounce of sweat lost in training may
save a pint of blood lost in battle"*
~ Military axiom ~
*"A gram of common sense spent in planning
may save both."*
~ Les Peate's corollary ~

THE RECRUITMENT, ORGANIZATION, and training of the Special Force for Korea provides an excellent example of a transformation from chaos to the establishment of an effective fighting formation.

The problems encountered with the hasty and unexpectedly heavy response to Canada's call for volunteers to serve in Korea were overcome by a combination of strong leadership, energetic staff work and, in many cases, by turning a Nelsonian blind eye to regulations and established procedures where appropriate.

By November 1950, basic training had been completed – for the infantry units, conducted by the regular force parent battalions. The newly designated 25th Canadian Infantry Brigade Group (25 CIBG) was preparing to move to Fort Lewis for unit and formation training. Many of the unsuitable recruits who had been so hastily enlisted had either been weeded out or had deserted, and the wartime veterans and the younger enlistees were developing *esprit de corps* and regimental pride.

Meanwhile, in Korea the situation had changed. Following the Inchon landing and the breakout from the Pusan perimeter, the North Korean armies were now in full retreat. General Douglas MacArthur's pressing need for reinforcements no longer existed. MacArthur felt that the war was as good as won, and that token forces only from the other UN participants would be required for occupation duties. With this in mind, and perhaps to ensure that at least some Canadians might be able to see action before an enemy capitulation, the Canadian government decided to send one infantry battalion directly to Korea.

They need not have hurried. By the time the brigade arrived in Korea there was enough fighting for all. While the other units in 25 CIBG were assembling in Fort Lewis, 2PPCLI had a much shorter stay there. After four days, during which they paraded with the other units for the minister of National Defence, they sailed for Korea on the USNS *Private Joe P. Martinez*. Although they had only received a little over two months training — mostly at an individual and sub-unit level — they were further advanced than the other two battalions, as well as being located in Alberta and thus closest to Seattle, the port of embarkation.

On arrival in Pusan, they were transported to the island of Yongdo, on the outskirts of the city. Here they recovered their land legs after the 23-day voyage and began to unload and sort out their equipment. Thanks to a plentiful supply of material from their U.S. allies, this was generally adequate, although there were a few shortages, such as tentage and cooking equipment.

General "Bulldog" Walker, commander of the U.S. Eighth Army, had ordered the Canadians to join the British 29th Brigade in the line. However, Lt.-Col. "Big Jim" Stone refused to commit his troops until they had received more training, and Walker agreed. Accordingly, following a brief Christmas break, the Patricias left for a training area in Miryang-chon, where they were fortunate enough to locate in an orchard. Despite severe cold — and a constant shortage of fuel for the few heaters — intense training began. Here the battalion became familiar with their new U.S. support weapons, such as the 81-mm and 60-mm mortars and the 3.5-inch rocket launchers, as well as sub-unit and unit operations and general toughening-up.

While their comrades in the other two infantry battalions (as well as their successors in what would become 3PPCLI) were training in the Fort Lewis area with simulated enemies, Colonel Stone's battalion had a real enemy to deal with. There were a number of enemy guerrillas in the Miryang area (estimates ranged from a few dozen to thousands) and anti-guerrilla patrols were part of the routine.

The enemy presence was made very clear when two New Zealand gunners were ambushed, tortured, and killed in the area, and on January 17, Lieutenant

H.T. Ross became the first PPCLI battle casualty when he was wounded by sniper fire. The next day the RSM, Jim Wood, died following an accident while demonstrating an enemy mine.

The presence of Korean civilians inevitably led to minor military transgressions such as breaking of bounds and drunkenness. Colonel Stone found a solution: his pioneer platoon constructed a crow-bar hotel detention facility, where miscreants were subjected to rigorous and uncomfortable disciplinary measures. Surprisingly, perhaps as a result of their exposure to intense training and discipline, many of the inmates later became exemplary NCOs. At Miryang, too, many of the hurriedly recruited, but unsuitable, members were weeded out. For medical and other reasons, 60 of them were returned to Canada and by the end of March 1951, a further 88 would been sent home.

Following a final five-day exercise — MAPLE LEAF — the unit left the comparative comfort of Miryang to join the other infantry battalions of 27 Commonwealth Brigade, the Middlesex Regiment, Argyll and Sutherland Highlanders, and the 3rd Battalion of the Royal Australian Regiment. On February 19th they were given their first objective: the capture of Hill 404.

BAPTISM OF FIRE

The move forward was a sobering one. En route, the battalion passed the bodies of 60 U.S. soldiers who had been caught by the Chinese in their sleeping bags and shot and bayoneted to death. From then on it was a policy of 2PPCLI (and indeed, of the whole Commonwealth Division) never to sleep inside sleeping bags in forward areas. The initial advance met with no opposition, although LCpl. John Bishop later recalled a scary moment when, advancing through a disused rail tunnel, his section saw a group of enemy at the exit. Charging the enemy, they found to their relief that the Chinese were, in fact, all dead. These soldiers were probably victims of an air attack and had presumably taken cover in the tunnel before expiring.

The next objective, Hill 444, was taken after a difficult approach through rugged terrain. Casualties were incurred by falls on the slippery slopes, and four Patricias were killed by enemy fire as the unit encountered its first real resistance.

After having dug in in the snow-covered ground, the unit awaited orders for its next objective. This was to be the commanding position of Hill 419. The promised preliminary napalm air strike was misdirected, the hills were steep and covered with heavy undergrowth, and the Canadians were unable to reach their objective. Six more were killed in action. The following day, preceded by more accurate air support and softening up by the 16th New Zealand Field Regiment, "D" Company was able to establish positions on the adjacent Hill 614. Under

The Monument for the Hongchon Region Combat honours ROK troops, the U.S. First Marine Division, and soldiers of Canadian and New Zealand units. It reads: "The Canadian 2nd Battalion on March 7, 1951, launched an offensive to obtain the Hongchon Region and repelled Chinese forces, contributing to securing the middle front. This monument was established to commemorate this military achievement and to respect those soldiers who were killed during the combat." Fourteen were Canadian.

pressure from 2PPCLI and the Australians, the enemy eventually withdrew and the Canadians took possession of the hill on February 28.

On March 7, the Canadian battalion was given the task of clearing the Chinese from Hill 532, near the village of Hagal-li. Air strikes, artillery and mortar fire had failed to dislodge the enemy. After a series of bitter section-level fights, most Canadians were stalled and forced to dig in. Later, "D" Company reached its objective only to come under fire from a higher point; and could advance no further. In the early hours, frustrated by mocking calls and a continual rain of grenades from the Chinese, the exasperated Canadians fixed bayonets and charged, to find that most of the enemy had pulled out. By 0900 hours, the objective was secured. 2PPCLI suffered 34 casualties, seven of them fatal.

In his memoir, *The King's Bishop*, John Bishop recalls the battle. He describes how his "A" Company achieved its objective with few incidents. He remembers that after siting his section, he took over a large enemy slit trench. When daylight came he found that what he had thought was a bed roll, and used as a pillow, was in fact the dismembered thigh of an American soldier, and that he had been sharing his bed with a dead Chinese soldier.

As battles go, Hill 532 may not have been considered a major action. Nevertheless it proved that Canadians were a force to be reckoned with.

~ ~ ~ ~ ~ ~ ~ ~ ~ ~

THE BATTLE OF KAPYONG

Probably the most written-about Canadian event of the Korean War, the following account on the Battle of Kapyong was compiled by Terry Loveridge, a latter-day member of 2PPCLI:

"By April 1951 the Korean War was into its tenth month. The dramatic manoeuvre battles of the Pusan Perimeter, Inchon and the Chosin were history. Seoul, the capital of South Korea had been captured and liberated twice. The

United Nations navies, including Canada's three destroyers, controlled the waters on both sides of the Korean peninsula and the UN air forces dominated the skies. The armies of the UN who had advanced north beyond the long, high ridges of the old border along the 38th parallel, were now being pushed back by the hordes of fresh Chinese troops who had entered the war. The Chinese Communist forces (CCF) and the North Korean army were contesting every ridge and fold along the rocky spine of that country.

"Second Battalion Princess Patricia's Canadian Light Infantry had been in the van of the UN advance with 27 Commonwealth Brigade since February and were quite content to be placed in Corps reserve when the 6th Republic of Korea Division moved forward to take the lead. The battalion, with its comrades in 27 Brigade, were placed in the Kapyong River valley. The valley seemed like a good place to be, since the town of the same name was a road and rail centre with easy access to anywhere in 9 Corps. The positions straddled one to two main routes to Seoul.

"However, any thought of decently cooked meals and dry blankets was short-lived as one quarter of a million Chinese soldiers from 27 divisions burst into the unconsolidated UN lines on April 22nd.

"Early on the 23rd the battalion found itself rousted from bivouac. The inevitable grumbling from the troops was tempered by the rumble of massed artillery to the northeast. As battle kits and ammunition was stowed, fragments of orders and rumours painted a bleak picture: The 6th ROKs had been crushed, the roads were jammed with retreating troops, refugees and infiltrators, ammo dumps had been ordered blown, the CO was forward recceing a battle position and the Aussies were already on the move. The worst of the gossip, this time, was true.

"By afternoon the battalion was headed along the valley toward Hill 677 and the mile long ridge extending from it. The Australians were already climbing the slopes of Hill 504 across the river. Just one look at those two hills told the story: the Princess Pats and the 3rd Royal Australians would be the cork in the Kapyong bottle.

"The unit guides paused in the village of Tugmudae at the foot of 677. In the gathering darkness Tugmudae soon became a cacophony of sound and light as ammo depots and fuel dumps exploded; machine guns splattered tracers from the ROK checkpoint; houses flamed into bonfires and snipers bullets cracked through the night air.

"By last light the rifle companies were digging shell scrapes into the hard contours of Hill 677. Battalion headquarters and Mortar Platoon were jockeying their vehicles toward the ravine that was to be Lieutenant-Colonel Jim Stone's battle headquarters. At about 10 p.m. the sounds of mortar and small arms fire could be heard from Hill 504. The Australians were into the thick of it. Not all the shadowy figures in the valley were retreating ROKs. Shell scrapes rapidly became trenches.

"Line communications went out. Radio traffic reported the Australians fighting off successive waves of enemy troops, hand-to-hand fights in their headquarters, and the U.S. 72d Regiment tanks carrying out the wounded. Toward dawn machine guns spluttered periodically along the Patricia front and mortar rounds began dropping in the battalion area. "B" Company reported masses of troops crossing the Kapyong while the fire on the Australian position intensified.

"After more than 16 hours of fighting, the Australians were ordered off. Smoke drifted across 504 as small groups fought a rearguard action under its screen. Darkness crept along the ravines of the Kapyong valley and the Patricias now stood alone.

"A new sound soon punctuated the mortar and machine gun fire along the company perimeters – bugles. With a bugle and whistle fanfare, they came out of the darkness. Six platoon was hit first. Then all of "B" Company found itself firing at hundreds of cotton-clad figures scrambling up the slopes and through the brush. The night became a confusion of strobing muzzle flashes, blinding bomb blasts and grenade thumps. Each attack was followed by another – the infamous CCF waves. Sections were overrun and men grappled in the dark with bayonets and fists. About 100 enemy troops skirted "B" Company and swarmed into the headquarters ravine where they were met by point blank machine gun and mortar fire and blasted back out.

"An even larger force hit "D" Company on the battalion's left flank. By now, the whole battalion was firing. The CCF broke like a wave over a rock in "D" Company, reformed and came again. This time, they went for the deadly machine guns and came fast enough and in sufficient number that the guns were overrun as they fired. In 12 Platoon the gunners died firing their guns to the last and the platoon was forced back into the company area. Six Platoon in "B" Company, by now almost out of ammunition, was also forced to leapfrog back. Private Wayne Mitchell and Private Ken Barwise were conspicuous that night for keeping up the fire and extricating buddies. They fired Brens, threw grenades until they were all gone, fired CCF machine guns and used empty weapons as clubs until they got their sections out.

"Ammunition was becoming a problem across the battalion. "D" Company was now crawling with Chinese and so desperately short of grenades that Captain Wally Mills called artillery down on his own positions. Platoons were isolated. Companies were separated by groups of tenacious CCF. The battalion, by now, was surrounded. Colonel Stone requested air resupply of ammunition.

"Some 40 miles to the west the other prong of the CCF offensive was overwhelming the Gloucester Regiment in its epic last stand. The crisis of the offensive was at hand for the UN command, and only the selfless gallantry of many small units would stem the Chinese tide.

"At first light on April 25th the battalion reoccupied its lost trenches. The light now allowed better artillery shooting and air strikes. The New Zealand Artillery Regiment would fire 14,500 rounds before this battle was ended. The Middlesex began clearing the enemy from the road to Hill 677. The 5th U.S. Cavalry had arrived from Seoul. At 11 a.m. C-119 "Flying Boxcars" dropped ammunition into the Patricia lines. The CCF, sensing the moment had passed, gradually drew in its horns. It would take the rest of the day to clear the snipers, but by 1400 hours the road was open and the UN line secure.

"In recognition of the stand at Kapyong and its importance in preventing the loss of two UN corps and Seoul, 2PPCLI was awarded the United States Distinguished Unit Citation, the only Canadian unit to be so honoured. Captain Mills, Wayne Mitchell and Ken Barwise were decorated for their bravery."

~ ~ ~ ~ ~ ~ ~ ~ ~ ~

A KOREAN MYSTERY

One of the strangest recollections of service in Korea was a patrol experienced by Patricia Lieutenant Hub Gray:

"My patrol was ordered north of the burned out rail station of Gumcochyi. Our battalion position was in the general vicinity of Tokso-Ri. 2PPCLI, "D" Coy in reserve, dug in on Line Golden. We remained here for about three weeks. Virtually every day our patrols would foray into enemy territory. We had fought the enemy's spring offensive to a standstill at Kapyong, April 23-25, 1951. We reorganized to develop a stationary line, from which we were probing the enemy positions preparatory to taking the offensive. On occasion there were company and battalion thrusts, the latter having both armour and air support. This platoon patrol boarded U.S. army Patton tanks, of the 72nd U.S. Heavy Tank Battalion, which took us to the burned out rail stop, Gumcochyi; we then patrolled north on foot.

"About an hour and a half later, roughly five to seven miles from our forward defence line, we were advancing along a trail through the middle of a broad valley, when we spotted an enemy force exposed some distance in front. We deployed, whether for defence or offence, yet as we changed formation something strange occurred, the enemy remained motionless, as if frozen in time. Was this a trap? We checked our flanks, the valley appeared clear, we advanced cautiously. It became evident the enemy were squatting on their haunches, positioned upright in four columns of 14 to a row. The group consisted of two officers, a few NCOs and the troops. They were all dead. Strangely dead.

"I had never seen the enemy so well equipped. Recent prisoners had one rifle to three men, three days rations with instructions to secure weapons from us and take food in Seoul. This lot had powerful binoculars, a variety of automatic weapons, pistols and grenades, compass light mortars and all were weighed down with ammunition. It was a morbidly curious sight. Instead of the usual green uniform, they were attired in a khaki summer dress. The equipment, arms, ammunition and uniforms were totally out of keeping with our experience in Korea. Where did all of this originate? And who occupied this area 20 to 30 days ago?

"A soldier inquired, could they liberate souvenirs. I concurred. He stepped forward to retrieve binoculars from an officer's chest; they remained attached to the body. The soldier pulled harder, the binoculars came free in his grip but adhered to them were the front of the uniform along with the officers' crumbling ribs. Thereupon there erupted from the empty shell of the corpse a dark cloud of bugs...maggots! Our soldier was frightened – he leaped backwards with a start, flailing at the mass engulfing him. Having devoured the entire innards of the corpse, the maggots descended en masse upon a warm body!

"Some of us laughed, momentarily. One or two had retrieved other items such as family photos, searching terminated. Though they were the enemy we were suddenly compassionate for the terrible injustice that had been inflicted upon these unfortunate human beings. The sight of the photos of loved ones impacted upon all of us in a form of personal awareness.

"The sight of 56 decaying corpses, as if positioned and pleading in vain, even begging for mercy from an unknown and unseen deity of death, became a source of nausea.

"On returning to our battalion I delivered a detailed report to D Coy acting OC (officer commanding), Captain Wally Mills.

"In 1997 at the Museum of the Regiments in Calgary, I went through the War Diary of Second Battalion PPCLI in Korea. I was mystified as to why there was not a reference to this 12 Platoon patrol.

"This event has been engraved on my memory. For many years I experienced waves of nausea when dwelling upon it. Historians may ponder the potential implications of the intent of the perpetrator of this action, whoever it may have been."

~ ~ ~ ~ ~ ~ ~ ~ ~ ~

SETBACK AT KAKHUL-BONG

In May 1951, the 25th Canadian Infantry Brigade Group was formed under Brig. Gen. J.M. Rockingham. It consisted of the 2nd Battalion, Royal Canadian Regiment; 2nd Battalion, the Royal 22e Regiment; "C" Squadron, Lord

Strathcona's Horse; 2nd Field Regiment, Royal Canadian Horse Artillery (RCHA); and the 57th Independent Field Squadron, Royal Canadian Engineers. The 2nd Battalion, Princess Patricia Canadian Light Infantry, joined on the 27th of May, but was regrouping after its incredible stand at Kapyong.

Beginning with Operation INITIATE, the 25th Brigade moved up the P'och'on valley on the May 25th. The Royal Canadian Regiment was detailed to clear the heights on the left flank, with the Van Doos on the right. This advance continued for 30 miles, over the 38th parallel, with only minor resistance.

Operation FOLLOW-UP began on May 29th and saw tanks of "C" Squadron, in conjunction with Philippine troops, overtake Chinese soldiers still in retreat. The Royal 22e occupied a burnt-out village at the foot of a mountain barrier called Kakhul-Bong. The next day, the Canadians discovered that they had struck a raw nerve in Chinese communications and the easy advance was at an end.

On the morning of May 30th, the RCR found Kakhul-Bong along their axis of advance and four companies were assigned to capture this feature and the village of Chail-li, which lay beyond.

Lt. Col. R.A. Keane ordered "A" Company under Major Medlands DSO to push up the road to Chail-li. "B" Company under Major Duncan was to cover the left flank by occupying Hill 162 with "C" Company under Major Peterson DSO taking Hill 269 halfway between Chail-li and Kakhul-Bong. The main effort was directed at Kakhul-Bong or Hill 467. "D" Company under Major Boates was given the honour.

The first three companies, ignoring a driving rainstorm, reached their objectives with little resistance. Boates' command, however, found itself faced with a steep slope and stiffening resistance from an organized and vigorous defence.

As it turned out, Kakhul-Bong represented a primary feature in the Chinese defensive position for the entire area. From its peak one could look south nearly to the 38th parallel. To the north, the Hantan valley spread panoramically to the Chorwan plain 32 kilometers away. This plain was a main supply centre and a hub for lateral communications across that sector of the Korean peninsula. The Chinese had no intention of giving this up, even to a company of Canadians.

"D" Company struggled into the teeth of a defence featuring extensive trenches and camouflaged bunkers. Increasing mortar and machine gun fire failed to stop the RCRs as they cleared the western peak and advanced to the main feature still some 300 meters away. However, this pinnacle was surmounted by a determined enemy machine-gunner who was able to survive artillery, mortar and 3.5-inch rocket fire. Lieutenant John Woods of Ottawa assigned his ace bazooka-man Pte. H.B. McCutcheon to take out the stubborn Chinese and a well placed shot quieted things down. For a short time the Canadians were in possession of Hill 467.

Unfortunately, they were a depleted company, under artillery fire, and in the path of a great number of very displeased Chinese soldiers.

While "D" Company's efforts on Kakhul-Bong grounded to a halt, the other companies of the RCRs found themselves in increasingly untenable positions. Company "A", occupying the village of Chail-li, noticed soldiers in ponchos on its flanks, but due to poor visibility, could not determine their nationality. Their identity became apparent very quickly when small arms fire and mortars rained down on the Canadians. The guns of the 2nd Royal Canadian Horse Artillery attempted to relieve the pressure on the left flank, but the Chinese infiltration persisted. By 1300 hrs, it became obvious that the enemy was growing in strength on both flanks and Major Medlands came to the unhappy realization that he was being surrounded.

"C" Company on Hill 269 was finally able to identify enemy forces by late afternoon and attempted to engage with rifles and Bren guns. Unfortunately, the ranges were extreme and with too few troops, the unit found itself hopelessly watching Chinese forces moving against brother companies across the valley.

Back at Brigade Headquarters, Rockingham had to make a decision soon. With "A" Company surrounded, "D" Company pinned down, and "C" Company unable to support either, the time to withdraw or reinforce was fast approaching. The Brigade's advance had created a salient that left its flank protection eight kilometers behind on either side. It was decided that this offensive had achieved enough. At 1430 hrs, the units were ordered to disengage and fall back.

"A" Company placed its wounded on tanks and worked its way out under the cover of artillery and tank fire. Gunner K.W. Wishart of "D" Battery, 2RCHA, stood by his radio under intense fire and continued to direct his guns against enemy counter-attacks. Private P.A. Sargent of "A" Company wielded a Bren gun with such skill and courage that he, along with Wishart, was awarded the Military Medal. "B", "C", and "D" Companies, thanks to the excellent work of the mortar and artillery observers of the Royal Canadian Horse Artillery, managed to retire with a minimum of casualties. Complete withdrawal was not achieved until 2100 hrs on May 31st. Some equipment was left behind although the RCR, with help from the Royal 22e Regiment, did retrieve two tanks that evening and a third the following day. Withdrawing under fire is the most difficult of military operations and the Canadians handled it with great skill.

In three days of contact, the new brigade had learned that Korea was going to be a battlefield quite unlike northwest Europe. New tactics and lessons would have to be absorbed. This one cost six Canadian lives and 54 wounded.

~ ~ ~ ~ ~ ~ ~ ~ ~ ~

PREPARING FOR THE ADVANCE

After acquitting itself with distinction at Chail-li, 25 Brigade was withdrawn into a corps reserve, 15 miles south of the Imjin River. If they had hoped to re-acquaint themselves with the 2PPCLI, last seen leaving Fort Lewis in November 1950, they were in for a disappointment. On June 2nd, the PPCLI were ordered to the Imjin to establish a patrol base on its northern side. Patrol bases were a way for the UN (read: U.S.) command to execute forward-oriented operations without committing itself to major offensive actions. At this point the political will necessary to achieve victory was tempered by a reluctance to risk a wider, general war with the Communist world.

On the eastern flank of the Korean front, the Communists showed less reluctance to attempt a battlefield decision. An offensive against Republic of Korea forces shoved a ROK Corps southward and the UN felt compelled to advance on the western flank to relieve the pressure. The advance, or rather series of advances, were largely uncoordinated and met resistance in varying degrees.

Control of the Imjin River valley was vitally important as its wide valley and principal tributaries all offered invasion routes into South Korea. In the next few months the crossing would form the base for operations against enemy forces in the elbow of the river.

On June 3rd, Major H.D.P. Tighe reconnoitered the site of the bridgehead; about 4.6 km from the junction of the Imjin with the Hantan River. The propensity for these mountain streams to flash flood led to a 48-hour delay and a host of other difficulties. On June 6th the crossing was affected without opposition, although there was some harassing mortar fire. However, at the end of the first day, the bridge was incomplete and patrols scrambled along the bank searching for fords in case of emergency. Fortunately, the operation was completed without incident. On the 11th, the Patricias were replaced by the Royal 22e Regiment, who anticipated a Chinese offensive that never came.

The 25 Brigade was placed under the command of the American First Cavalry on June 18th and was detailed to take over 7500 yards of front on the Wyoming Line. The brigade left its reserve area south of the Imjin and travelled by its own wits to its new area of operation near the Ch'orwon plain. With no help from I Corps, Brigadier Rockingham was forced to execute the 25-mile movement with himself and his staff as scouts. Reconnoitering two hours ahead of his unit, he sought out the best route and directed their movement by radio.

2PPCLI were on the left flank with 2RCR on the right and the Van Doos joining in reserve. On the morning of June 21, the RCRs with a troop of tanks and a troop of artillery, advanced toward the first patrol objective 12 miles to the north. Late in the afternoon, after breaking up small enemy units with tank fire, the RCRs were informed that a strong enemy force was occupying a nearby hill.

True to the nature of the war at this point, artillery was called down on their position and the patrol returned to friendly lines by 1900 hours.

The patrolling of the Ch'orwon plain went on through the height of summer and 38 degree Celsius days sapped men's strength. The flanking units did not seem so predisposed to vigorous patrolling as the Canadians and battalions had to assign pickets to prevent patrols being encircled. At first, the Chinese were content to observe from a distance but by mid-July their strength and resistance was increasing.

On July 9 the Royal 22e lost Maj. Gosselin and two others when his scout car ran over a mine. On July 11 "B" Company of the Patricias took six casualties when another patrol was ambushed. On the 18th the Patricias were relieved by the Turkish Brigade. By August, the 25th Canadian Infantry Brigade would be back on the Imjin while Communist and UN negotiators tried to outwit each other at the conference table. From now on, the fighting would reflect the resolve of the political masters.

~ ~ ~ ~ ~ ~ ~ ~ ~ ~

ACROSS THE IMJIN

When the Commonwealth Division was formed on July 28, 1951, it was holding a front of about nine miles on the south bank of the Imjin River, with the U.S. First Cavalry Division on its right flank and the First ROK Division on the left. Opposing the Commonwealth Division (COMWEL) was the 64th Chinese Communist Army – a misnomer as it was actually a corps-sized formation of three divisions. The Chinese held a light forward screen about 1-1/4 miles north of the river, with strong main defensive positions a few miles beyond them

In Operation SLAM, on August 4th, two British, one Australian and the attached Belgian battalion crossed the Imjin and advanced over three miles to the north. Little or no resistance was met in what was in essence a reconnaissance in force. What the Chinese didn't achieve, nature did. During the two days of the operation, the Imjin rose to a depth of five metres, and the troops were cut off. At some risk, light liaison aircraft dropped food (which was welcomed) and boxes of Bren magazines (which were not, as hardly any ammunition had been expended and it was just more to carry). The Commonwealth troops were accompanied by the ubiquitous Korean porters, and many of the British soldiers had given cans of ground meat and spaghetti and other less popular C-rations to their allied helpers to reduce the weight in their own small packs. They now tried with varying degrees of success to recover them when hunger struck. The troops were finally ferried back across the river in the evening of August 5th.

Meanwhile the 25th Canadian Brigade had been placed under command of the First Cavalry, replacing the 5th U.S. Cavalry (despite their title, these regiments served in an infantry role). The U.S. troops, moving on the right of the COMWEL force, encountered some resistance before returning from their foray to relieve the Canadians, who had been holding their positions.

Next came Operations DIRK and CLAYMORE. This time it was Canada's turn.

~ ~ ~ ~ ~ ~ ~ ~ ~ ~

DIRK AND CLAYMORE

They called it routine patrolling, words that sound as though life at the front was humdrum and the enemy nowhere to be seen. That was not the case.

Furthermore, when Brigadier John Rockingham issued orders on September 8, 1951 for his 25th Canadian Infantry Brigade Group to begin Operation MINDEN, codename for activities across the Imjin River, his troops had been in reserve since the end of June. "In reserve" gives the impression of operational inactivity. However, military terminology often has a tendency to be misleading.

What is considered routine patrolling by those far removed from the battlefield often means bloodshed and death for troops doing the patrolling. Being in reserve doesn't always mean being freed from dangerous employment. Far from it.

During the two months of high summer in 1951, the Commonwealth Division was formed under British Major-General A.J.A. Cassels and 2PPCLI rejoined Rockingham's brigade. The Patricia's had seen 18 weeks of active operations as part of 27th Commonwealth Brigade following its sailing for Korea the previous December.

While technically in reserve, both 2RCR and 2R22eR, with a squadron of Lord Strathcona's Horse and 2RCHA in support, had been involved throughout August in routine patrolling, which actually meant carrying out deep penetrations across the Imjin River to ensure that the enemy was not building up his strength or jockeying into positions from which he might later threaten Canadian and American security. Several small hit and run clashes with the enemy's outposts took place, but casualties on both sides were minimal.

These August patrols were codenamed DIRK and CLAYMORE. The first was a battalion-sized patrol by 2RCR north of the Imjin, hopefully to capture a prisoner, clear the enemy away from any possible outpost line along the river and discover main positions. Major C.H. Lithgow, the battalion second-in-command led this patrol, as the CO Lt.-Col. R.A. Keane, was temporarily in command of the brigade. A troop of Lord Strathcona's tanks accompanied Lithgow. "C" Company, under Capt. L.W.G. Hayes came under fire and Lt. A.P. Rankine's platoon charged with the bayonet, capturing what appeared to have been a platoon position. They found seven dead Chinese, apparently victims of the artillery shoot which preceded their assault. Two others were dying, the rest had fled. Rankine's platoon had two men wounded, one Pte. G.G. Rowden who won the Military Medal for his dash.

Having achieved all three of its aims, albeit their prisoners were dying, the battalion returned to base under heavy fire from another enemy position and a half-hearted counter-attack, which Pte. CO. Bell turned back with his accurate Bren gun fire, thereby earning himself the Military Medal.

Operation CLAYMORE, a two-battalion patrol featuring 2PPCLI and 2R22eR was less exciting. These two battalions patrolled deep into enemy territory across the Imjin between August 22-24, but were met with only a few scattered shots and, unable to locate any definite enemy positions, returned to base without casualties. September's operation was designed not just to cross the Imjin and play hide-and-seek with the enemy, but also to occupy vital ground in the area and keep the enemy off it. The enemy's main position was now known to be some three miles north of the Imjin and his activity in the area jeopardized an important UN supply line from Seoul to Ch'orwon. August's patrolling had de- termined the enemy's approximate positions. September was to see the achieve- ment of "defence in depth" along the front and the provision of flank protection to the supply route.

On September 8, the 28th Commonwealth Brigade launched Operation MINDEN, which established a firm bridgehead in the no man's land north of the Imjin. Three days later, the other two brigades of the Commonwealth Division, the British 29th and the Canadian 25th, broke out of the bridgehead and ad- vanced to a selected line. Meanwhile, the engineers put in two bridges over the Imjin to connect the rear maintenance areas with the forward troops.

September 11 saw the two forward brigades move north with South Korean troops on one flank and U.S. troops on the other. By September 13 the operation was complete and casualties were few in all formations. Most of the enemy evapo- rated before the advancing UN forces and until the end of the month activity once again was confined to routine patrolling.

The Canadian part in MINDEN had not been particularly exciting, the only casualties being three killed and ten wounded. However, on September 12 "B" Company of 2R22eR had a sharp fight when it attacked a triple-hill objective supported by tanks and following an air strike. The enemy were quickly put to flight, but not before several stubborn machine-gunners were killed by a platoon under Lt. J.P.A. Therien, whose leadership was rewarded with the Military Cross, as was that of his company commander, Capt. J.P.R. Tremblay. Two of Therien's men, Cpl. J.G. Ostiguy and Pte. R. Gagnon both received Military Medals for their part in the action.

OPERATION SNATCH

During the so-called routine patrolling which followed, 2RCR had a brief, but spirited fight on September 22. This was a planned venture and was codenamed Operation SNATCH. The aim was to capture one live Chinese prisoner. Capt. E.K. Wildfang's "B" Company, plus an "A" Company platoon were given the job. For several days those concerned studied maps, aerial photos and the weather forecasts.

SNATCH was supported by 2RCHA and was a complete success. Assembling just before dusk, Wildfang brought his little force back in three and a half hours. During that time he had three men wounded, which was light since they ran into considerable mortar and small arms fire. It was reported that Wildfang's men killed 18 of the enemy and possibly seven others. The patrol captured two live Chinese soldiers – double the requirement. Strangely enough, neither Wildfang nor any of his men were decorated. Presumably, such a patrol action was categorized as "routine." One wonders how routine one can get.

The tactical stage was now set for October's Operation COMMANDO, designed to gain more important ground and keep the enemy in retreat. Although September's fighting was not heavy it allowed battle procedures to be further tested and developed, so that the Canadian brigade's hitting power was measurably enhanced and its skills improved. This paid off in the weeks to come.

While Rockingham's men, with their British, American, Korean and other UN comrades, were pressing forward across the Imjin and beyond, truce talks were already going on at the higher levels. Although these talks began at the request of the Communists they dragged on for two years. Despite the UN forces' hopes for a ceasefire, it appears that the enemy never intended the talks to produce an early peace, but were using them as a sort of smoke screen to gain military advantage.

~ ~ ~ ~ ~ ~ ~ ~ ~ ~

FRIENDLY FIRE: A MILITARY OXYMORON

However, as Canadian troops were busy warding off the Communists, not all opposition was coming from the enemy.

Casualties of so-called friendly fire have occurred almost as long as warfare. From the Roman catapults that collapsed or projected their missiles short, through the premature ignition of Greek fire and later, with the advent of artillery, the "drop-shorts," soldiers have succumbed to the well-intentioned efforts of support weapons crews. The introduction of air power increased the risk, as many Second World War veterans would attest.

The Korean War was no exception. By the 1950s, high performance piston-engined aircraft and jet-propelled ground attack planes were used extensively in support of the United Nations forces. Air support by land- and carrier-based Mustangs, Corsairs, Sea Furies, Meteors, Phantoms, F-80s and other allied aircraft was highly developed, and calls for attacks on enemy troops and positions were quickly answered. Rockets, bombs, cannon shells, machine guns, and napalm were quickly brought to bear on the Chinese and North Koreans, with deadly effect. For example, in late 1950, virtually the whole of the North Korean armour was eliminated, almost entirely by air strikes.

Unfortunately, some of the U.S. Air Force (USAF) ordnance fell on friendly forces. Two significant incidents could have turned the outcome of the action. In both cases, the USAF accidentally unloaded on allied soldiers.

In September1950, the 1st Battalion, Argyll and Sutherland Highlanders, who had arrived in Korea less that a month earlier, were part of the advance north, following the breakout from the Pusan perimeter. On September 23, "B" and "C" Companies were tasked with the capture of two features in the Songju area. The first, Hill 282, was consolidated in the early morning, but increasingly strong enemy infiltration made the position hazardous. Heavy mortar and shell-fire, and a scarcity of ammunition caused problems, but the Scots held.

The enemy's dominance of the adjacent feature, Hill 388, was an obvious threat, and "C" Company was ordered to attack and secure the hill. To soften up the enemy, an air strike was called for.

Allied units were normally equipped with air recognition panels, which consisted of florescent panels in bright colours, which are laid out in specified patterns such as Ts, crosses, or parallel bars to indicate the presence and location of friendly troops. "B" and "C" Companies laid these out to mark their positions on Hill 282.

Promptly at 1215 hours the air strike came in. Three Mustangs accurately dropped their napalm – but on the wrong hill. The effects of the enemy's opposition and the friendly fire resulted in a reduction of the fighting strength of the two companies to less than 40 men. At this stage, the battalion's second-in-command, Major Kenneth Muir, made history. Rallying the small force, he regained the hill crest and held the position while the wounded were evacuated. As ammunition ran out, he personally took over a two-inch mortar, encouraging his men and holding on until he was finally mortally wounded by automatic fire. His last words – which today would probably have resulted in accusations of political incorrectness – were "The Gooks will never drive the Argylls off this hill!" They didn't. Major Muir became the first Korean War recipient of the Victoria Cross.

The British were not the only victims of the attentions of the USAF. In 1952, the Greek Battalion suffered a similar experience. On September 27, the First Company of the Greek Battalion was tasked with the mission of securing two Chinese strong-points, "Big Nori" and "Little Nori," close to the Imjin River.

They were successful in their mission and held fast against four enemy counter-attacks, in increasing strength.

As the final enemy effort was beaten off, two heavy bombs were dropped on the Greek position by an allied aircraft. This time the enemy was able to take advantage of the confusion, and re-take the position. The Greeks suffered 36 casualties during the action. The following day, "Big Nori" was retaken, but because of its vulnerability and proximity to enemy fire, was eventually abandoned.

Interestingly, Eighth Army Headquarters announced that UN air forces had "misbombed" on "Big Nori" Hill, held by the Greek unit. However, three days later the Fifth U.S. Air Force stated that the report was "groundless and far from the truth" as a result of fact-finding investigations through aerial photographs. In my opinion, the experience of those on the receiving end of the ordnance outweighs the evidence of subsequent air photography.

Perhaps one of the reasons that such incidents were comparatively few is the use of the Tactical Air Support Groups – the de-mothballed AT-6 (Harvard) trainers that carried army officers as observers. While the faster strike aircraft had little time for target identification, and air recognition panels could be obscured by smoke or dust, the target identification and marking by these slow but rugged aircraft usually ensured that the fire and napalm were aimed at their intended targets.

In the early summer of 1951, a company of the King's Shropshire Light Infantry (KSLI or "Shropshires") conducted a reconnaissance in force north of the Imjin River. Accompanying them was a group of U.S. Rangers. As was their wont at the time, the U.S. troops preferred to use the roads, while the British (used to skipping around the hills like mountain goats) foot-slogged it along the adjacent high ground.

The Rangers suddenly observed the movement in the nearby hills and opened up with the .50-calibre machine guns mounted on their half-tracks. One KSLI officer was able to halt the fire before any serious casualties occurred by dancing onto the forward slopes, displaying the appropriate air recognition panels with a flourish and taking a bow from the astonished Americans. The U.S. troops were sufficiently impressed to include the incident in their record, *U.S. Rangers in the Korean War*. Sadly, on a similar patrol a few weeks later, a KSLI sub-unit was mistaken for an enemy patrol and artillery fire was called down, resulting in one death and three wounded.

~ ~ ~ ~ ~ ~ ~ ~ ~ ~

BACK ACROSS THE IMJIN — FOR GOOD

On August 4, 1951, 25 brigade units had adventured across the Imjin River and made their presence felt. When the peace talks at Kaesong collapsed a need to straighten the UN line became evident and it was apparent that hostilities would continue for some time.

As mentioned earlier, the first phase of this operation was MINDEN. 28 Commonwealth Brigade was now established north of the river and set up two bridgeheads – Teal and Pintail to support two pontoon bridges. On September 11, the other two Commonwealth brigades, the Canadian 25th and the British 29th, crossed and advanced northwest to a new line some five kilometres from the river which was called the Wyoming Line.

Although opposition was relatively light, the Canadians suffered several casualties, including three killed. By the morning of September 13, the Commonwealth brigades were in place on the Wyoming Line. One of the hot spots was Hill 172, from which Captain J.P.R. Tremblay's company of the Van Doos launched a successful attack on three enemy positions that could have threatened his own troops. "Pat" Tremblay was awarded the Military Cross for this action and for another act of courage and initiative as an observer in an AT-6 Harvard aircraft. Other awards to "B" Company include the MC to Lieutenant J.P.A. Therien and Military Medals to Corporal J. Ostiguy and Private R. Gagnon.

Operation COMMANDO was a Corps operation with the aim of establishing a new line (the Jamestown Line). Five divisions were involved, including the whole of the Commonwealth Division. 28 Commonwealth Brigade would conduct Phase I, which included the capture of Hill 355 (well known to Korean War veterans as Kowang-San or Little Gibraltar). Face-off time was first light on October 3rd.

One advantage of the three-stage attack was that in each phase the attack would receive the support of the entire divisional artillery, as well as heavier support from the 8-inch Persuaders and 155-mm corps artillery. The supporting tanks of the King's Royal Irish Hussars played a significant supporting role, despite the unsuitable terrain.

28 Brigade (augmented by the Royal Northumberland Fusiliers) had reached their objectives by the following afternoon. The King's Own Scottish Borderers (KOSB) seized Hill 355 after a fierce battle (the first of many which the Commonwealth troops were to experience over the years on that particular piece of real estate).

Now it was Canada's turn. While the Scots were still battling for Little Gibraltar, the second battalions of The RCR and PPCLI moved forward on the morning of October 4. The Patricia's, on the right, were tasked with taking the formidable Hill 187 (another future hot spot). After two hours of desperate fighting, the Canadians gained their objective. "A" Company was able to relieve the KSLI on Hill 210, enabling the Shropshires to occupy another critical position, Hill

227, where they were subsequently relieved by 2R22eR. A few days later the Van Doos held this feature against overwhelming odds, in what was arguably the hardest battle fought by 25 Brigade.

To the left (and southwest) of 2PPCLI, the Royal Canadian Regiment encountered little infantry opposition, but came under very strong artillery fire. "B" Company, in particular, encountered heavy fire, and was able to move aided by fire support from 2RCHA, typified by the forward observation officer (FOO) who continued to direct fire despite severe wounds, and his signaller, Lance Corporal Mort Dorman, who carried on with the work under heavy fire. (Dorman received a well-earned Military Medal.)

The intensity of the fire was evidenced by the experience of Baker Company. The Canadians were not only on the receiving end of heavy artillery and mortar ordnance, but the terrain was atrocious – steep slopes and heavy tangled brush.

By October 5, the Canadian brigade was in place on the Jamestown Line, between Republic of Korea troops on its left and 28 Brigade on the right flank. They faced a valley to their northwest, varying from over a mile in width to the south and about half a mile in the north. This terrain was to become very familiar to succeeding battalions of the three infantry regiments. While the Canadian casualties were lighter than the other Commonwealth brigades (four killed compared with 54 British and Australian dead), this is not necessarily a true reflection of the intensity of the battle.

COMMANDO was not quite over. On the right, 28 Brigade still had to take Hills 217 and 317. The former was taken, lost and recaptured by the Australians (3RAR) and the Fusiliers (a well-controlled airstrike was an important factor in the final success). Meanwhile, the Royal Ulster Rifles, who had earlier distinguished themselves on the Imjin in April, left Korea and 2R22eR moved into the line in their place – leaving all three Canadian battalions in forward positions.

Phase Three was euphemistically described as exploitation, meaning adjusting and improving defences. The positions taken on COMMANDO were, with very minor adjustments, to become home for COMWEL Division for the next two years. Almost 400 Canadian lives would be sacrificed on or around the Jamestown Line over the future months, but all three infantry battalions as well as the supporting arms would distinguish themselves in holding their hard-fought gains against a numerically-superior and aggressive enemy.

Ironically, British and Australian units were awarded battle honours for their role in COMMANDO. Submissions for the Canadian battalions, whose part was just as hazardous and vital, were rejected by the Canadian Battle Honours Committee.

~ ~ ~ ~ ~ ~ ~ ~ ~ ~

THE LAST "BIG PUSH"

During the early days of the Korean War there was a great deal of coming and going. The North Korean army was slowly being rolled back from the Pusan perimeter, and the first Commonwealth land forces (27 Brigade HQ, the Middlesex Regiment and the Argyll and Sutherland Highlanders) moved into the line on September 5, 1950. Following the Inchon landings, the jubilant UN troops pushed into North Korea. The tables were quickly turned. In October patrols reported contact with Chinese troops south of the Yalu River, and soon the United Nations forces were forced to withdraw under heavy pressure.

The Chinese offensive finally petered out some miles north of Seoul, where four Commonwealth units, including 2PPCLI, earned U.S. Presidential Unit Citations for their part in the battles.

By the end of the summer the Commonwealth Division was established more or less on the line of the Imjin River. In September a bridgehead was established north of the river, and it became the jumping-off point for Operation COMMANDO. This was to be an advance of 6,000-10,000 metres, with the intention of securing the left flank of the U.S. I Corps.

On October 3, 1951, 28 Commonwealth Brigade reached its objectives on the right flank after a desperate battle. The next day, 2PPCLI captured Hill 187 following heavy fighting and 2RCR seized neighbouring high ground but was very heavily shelled. "B" Company of the Royal Canadian Regiment, in particular, came under especially heavy fire. It was not until four days later that the British and Australian units achieved their final objectives.

Eric Devlin, a former platoon commander with 2RCR, later recalled that "'B' Company was committed to a leading role. We reached our objective successfully. In the second phase my platoon was in reserve. I learned that [the 6 Platoon Commander] had been wounded and his platoon had suffered a good many casualties. My platoon lost two wounded at this time." Lt. Devlin said that the company medic, Cpl. Ernest Poole, was in the thick of the action. Cpl. Poole's participation was of such a high standard that I can only quote the words of 2RCR Commanding Officer LCol. Bob Keane:

"On October 3, 1951, the 2nd Battalion, The Royal Canadian Regiment, was moving forward against enemy opposition as part of a general attack launched by our own forces.

""B" Company was ordered forward from the NAECHON feature, an intermediate objective, to the final object on the right flank of the battalion, the feature Nabu-ri.

"At 1745 hours, No. 6 Platoon came under very heavy and accurate enemy small arms and mortar fire from the left flank and intense machine gun fire from the right flank. Within a few minutes, a dozen casualties had been suffered by the platoon, some of them critical. Because of the steep slopes and thick underbrush it was not possible to determine precisely the nature and location of all the casualties, and there was a real danger that some of them would be lost to the enemy where they fell.

"Corporal Poole, RCAMC was the NCO in charge of stretcher-bearers with "B" Company during this operation; his actions in dealing with the casualties suffered gave evidence of courage of the highest order under enemy fire and contributed very markedly to the ultimate success of the operation.

"Cpl. Poole proceeded forward through intense enemy mortar and shell fire to render first aid and arrange for the evacuation of the wounded. He was warned that he could be killed but he insisted, 'I have a job to do and I am going to do it.' He searched meticulously the whole area and did not stop until satisfied that all casualties had been accounted for. Enemy artillery and mortars were harassing the area, and enemy snipers and machine gunners made any movement hazardous, but nothing could deter him in his search for the wounded. Two of the casualties were again hit while he was tending them, but he continued with unruffled calm to render aid.

"While still under fire Cpl. Poole improvised stretchers from rifles and branches of trees; he bound the casualties securely by using thick vines. He moved from man to man with complete disregard for his own safety; his steady hand and quiet courage brought relief to all the wounded. No. 5 Platoon was ordered to pass through No. 6 platoon in order to maintain the momentum of the attack. They, too, came under heavy fire and suffered serious casualties. Corporal Poole was on hand at once and urged the platoon commander, 'Go on, I will see that your men get good care.'

"When the wounded had been prepared for evacuation, Corporal Poole led his party of bearers back some 3000 yards in the dark to the Regimental Aid Post. The route was subjected to continuous shell fire. Enemy patrols had infiltrated along both sides, the area was heavily mined, and even the natural hazards were enough to deter any but the very brave. But Corporal Poole led his party with confidence and all the casualties were borne safely to the Regimental Aid Post. Undoubtedly his leadership and the persistence with which he carried out his duties against any odds was vital in saving the lives of one officer and three other ranks and in preventing two of the wounded from falling into the hands of the enemy.

"Throughout the day of October 3, all that night and the next day, Corporal Poole continued his task of attending the needs of the wounded. Whenever first aid was required, he was present to administer it. He was utterly tireless in his work. During the operation one thought only dominated his action: That his duty was to tend his wounded comrades. No obstacles, no hazard, no personal danger, was allowed to stand in his way; his selfless devotion to his work was in the highest traditions of military service.

"Corporal Poole's conscientious determination to carry out his duties, his complete disregard for his own well being, his exemplary conduct under the most adverse conditions and his outstanding leadership resulted not only in saving the lives of five men and making possible the evacuation of and treatment of many others, but, even more, inspired his comrades to maintain the fight and contributed largely to the successful attainment of the objective."

Lieutenant-Colonel Keane recommended Corporal Poole for the Victoria Cross. This was concurred with by Brigadier John M. Rockingham, but Corporal Poole was covertly awarded the Distinguished Conduct Medal.

ABOVE: *After the sweeping offensives and counteroffensives in 1950, the Korean War settled into a relative stalemate along the 38th parallel. (DND)*

OPPOSITE PAGE: *The mountainous terrain favoured the defenders, and both sides settled into the routine of trench warfare. (DND)*

✑ THE DEFENSIVE WAR

"I have the sea on my left flank, the
Commonwealth Division on my right, and
when I go to bed at night I sleep well because
I know that when I wake up in the
morning, they'll both still be there."
~ Commander, I U.S. Marine Division

THE COMMONWEALTH DIVISON WAS now established on the Jamestown Line, north of the 38th parallel between the Imjin and Sami-ch'on rivers. For the remaining 21 months of hostilities this would be home to the Canadians, British, Australians, New Zealand and Indian troops of the division.

At times positions had to be tenaciously defended against heavy enemy attack. It was during this phase of operations that most casualties were incurred. While the war was mostly static, it was never dull.

As 1951 was drawing to a close, the war on the Korean peninsula showed no signs that it would be doing the same. In July, at Kaesong, peace talks had begun in an air of comic opera that would have invoked hilarity had not the subject been so serious. The UN negotiating team, led by Admiral C. Turner Joy, was treated to an endless series of staged scenes and settings that were intended to present them in the worst possible light in the public forum. Kaesong was inside Communist lines which provided their side with the opportunity to manipulate the media and position the delegates for maximum propaganda effect. The Americans were paraded before the Communist press as if they were the vanquished, suing for peace. They were provided with uncomfortably low chairs facing north; the direction of the defeated. For ten months Joy jousted with General Nam Il, while young men fought and died to re-adjust the lines on the map.

United Nations forces controlled the surrounding seas and the air. On land, they were no longer threatened with expulsion, but neither could they think of evicting their Chinese foes. At best the war was now being fought for political gains, and in such a way as to minimize the expenditure of lives and resources. Battles were fought by platoons and companies with one eye on the next hill, and one on Kaesong (later Panmunjom) with a hope for peace.

Offensively, elements of the Commonwealth Division engaged in raids and feint attacks from their Jamestown Line positions. On October 23, Operation PEPPERPOT sent "D" Company of the 2R22eR, "D" Company of the 2RCR, and "A" Company of the PPCLI, with tanks of "C" Squadron, Lord Strathcona's Horse across the valley of the Sami-ch'on. The objective was to take Hill 166, and some smaller features, long enough to destroy the Chinese bunkers found there and return to the start lines.

The RCR company under Captain R.J. O'Dell reached its objective within an hour causing 17 Chinese casualties against five of its own. The Patricias rushed Hill 156 while the Van Doos advanced on 166. Despite the concentration of artillery fire and the destruction of four out of five enemy machine gun emplacements, Brigadier Rockingham felt that Hill 166 was not worth further trouble and ordered his companies to return.

Winter was fast approaching the Korean hills, but the Chinese appeared to be turning up the heat on the Commonwealth front. The enemy's reaction to Operation COMMANDO was to continue their probing attacks into November. In the early part of the month the enemy began a series of attacks in an attempt to drive the Australians, British and Canadians from their newly-won positions. On the night of October 31, a small attack was launched against 2PPCLI, who were due to be relieved by the regiment's First Battalion in a few days. Artificial moonlight was used to good effect and the Chinese were repulsed. On the second of that month, the 568th Regiment, 190th Chinese Division, tested the RCR at the Songgok spur. This feature, held by "A" Coy, 2nd RCR and Hill 187, held by "C" Coy, was attacked in the evening and again the next morning. At 0840 three dozen Chinese floundered into a minefield and left wounded and dead behind. At 2230 another probe was stopped by mortar and small arms fire, but at 0245 a more serious threat fell upon "A" Coy. The forward platoon fought a successful delaying action (Lt. E.J. Mastronardi won the Military Cross) and divisional artillery smashed the remainder of the attacking force, leaving 35 enemy dead on the battlefield.

While the 28th British Commonwealth Brigade was having a rough go on the flank (losing Hill 217 and 317 on November 4), the Canadians were not to be left out. The newly arrived 1st Battalion came under increasing mortar and artillery fire at 1420. By 1815 infantry were attacking from across the valley, but UN artillery and Canadian Bren guns broke this up. Two hours later, the enemy waves came on again with bangalore torpedoes. The forward platoon was out of ammunition and forced to withdraw to company positions, but hand grenades and rifles stopped any further progress. At the cost of three Canadian dead, the Chinese lost three dozen.

Far from taking this stinging rebuke as a definitive answer, Communist forces prepared another series of attacks intended to push the lines further south.

On November 22, the 2nd Van Doos were repositioned in a general movement to shorten the front of the Commonwealth Division. They relieved units of the 28th Brigade and found themselves with the Patricias on their left and the 2nd Battalion, 7th U.S. Infantry Regiment on their right flank. The Yanks held Hill 355 (Little Gibraltar), while the four companies of the Van Doos were deployed over two hills and the saddle between. "D" Coy was up between Hill 227 and 355, "A" was on a spur pointing at "C" Coy on the forward face of Hill 210, and "B" Coy held a ridge running west from 210.

Captain (Acting Major) Réal Liboiron of "D" Coy was very dissatisfied with the positions he had inherited. The King's Shropshire Light Infantry had recently lost Hill 227 on his left flank, though at this point it was unoccupied. Too many fire positions were built up with sand bags, rather than dug down to give better protection. As a consequence, his platoons were crowded and not in proper position to support each other. Given time the Canadians would have applied their skills at defensive preparation, but within hours, Chinese artillery and wet snow began to fall on the UN front.

The next day, the shelling continued although the sun appeared to melt away the snow. The Van Doos struggled in mud to dig in their tactical headquarters, as the 57th Field Squadron pushed a road around 210 to the forward companies. The Chinese began probing Hill 355 as their guns increased the tempo. Little Gibraltar seemed to be the focus of the Communist efforts, but Liboiron's men shot up patrols on their left as they offered support on the American front.

By 1730 hrs, two companies of the U.S. 7th Regiment were in trouble, while a third, directly opposite the Canadians, had been overrun. The Americans were preparing a counterattack by their 15th Regiment, but contact had been lost and the infantry had to move cross-country before they could begin their attack. With the Chinese momentarily in possession of Hill 355, the Van Doos found themselves in an extremely dangerous position and badly in need of some friendly support.

Three field regiments of the Commonwealth forces answered the call – the 2nd Canadian, 14th British and 16th New Zealand pounded enemy movements from greater range, while tanks of the Strathcona's and mortars of the Van Doos and Patricias brought it up close and personal. Liboiron coolly coordinated all this firepower as the Chinese attempted to drop in from unexpected quarters.

To quote 11 Platoon's commander "the Chinese began running down the hill towards the platoon position in twos. They were like sitting ducks and the men shot them down…with ease." Later, it was the turn of 12 Platoon, on the right, who were able to bring effective fire into the rear of Chinese troops attacking the Americans on Hill 355.

Meanwhile, the centre platoon, commanded by Lieutenant Mario Côté, was under heavy attack by at least two enemy companies. The Canadians held, and the Chinese were brought to a halt just short of the Van Doos' lines. For more than a hour, Corporal Earl Istead, although wounded, held a critical point of the line with a Bren gun, while another corporal, Joseph Harvey, also under heavy fire, used a pick-axe to destroy fortifications left by previous tenants that had become a danger to the defenders.

The battalion was now exposed on both flanks, as the enemy had taken over the unoccupied Hill 227 on the left, and had driven the Americans from 355. The R22eR commanding officer, Lieutenant Colonel J.A. Dextraze had a choice – to hold firm or to withdraw, perhaps jeopardizing other UN troops. "Jadex" was a tough, experienced soldier who had already earned a DSO in Europe, there was no question, the troops would stay put.

At 1930 the 2nd Royal Canadian Horse Artillery drew a curtain of fire around "D" Coy's position as the Brits and New Zealanders fired into the enemy rear. Some Chinese managed to fire into the right hand platoon, but they were driven off by small arms and mortars. Probes of the Patricias flanks were given a similar welcome.

Within an hour an attack developed on the left flank from the top of Hill 227. Through the night the enemy shouted, blew bugles, and infiltrated the platoons as the shells crashed among them. The concentrated enemy made an ideal artillery target, but they still kept coming. In the words of Lt. R. MacDuff of 11 Platoon "the first row was armed with burp guns, the second with heavy matting carpets and the third with bayonets on sticks… They came over the wire like buffaloes over a ridge." When more Chinese approached from another flank, MacDuff ordered his men to pull back. When Major Liboiron heard of the situation, he immediately called down tank, mortar and artillery fire on 11 Platoon's position. Meanwhile, MacDuff and the few survivors of his platoon had reached 12 Platoon's positions. They were assisted by the indomitable Corporal Harvey, who had been dispatched by his platoon commander to their rescue.

The left forward platoon found itself surrounded, but mortars and artillery, nearly on top of the position, eventually managed to restore the situation. The American counterattack on Little Gibraltar was proceeding well, but had the effect of pushing many Chinese down into R22eR positions. Throughout the morning of November 24th, successive waves of enemy troops washed up against the Canadian right flank only to be dashed by grenades and mortars. Strathcona tanks and regimental artillery fired on enemy concentrations and, along with air strikes, provided counter battery fire to the Chinese guns.

The enemy ignored great losses to form up for further infantry attacks. Three hundred came over Hill 227 to push in the left flank. Lt. MacDuff found his forward platoon overrun, but reassembled the remnants further back while Commonwealth guns hammered the vacated position. On Hill 355 Chinese and American regiments ground past each other as they reached for hilltop objectives only hundreds of yards apart.

Another decorated Second World War veteran now entered the picture. Cpl. Léo Major had already earned a Distinguished Conduct Medal in Holland with Le Régiment de la Chaudière. His part in the fight that night was to win a bar to that coveted decoration – one of only two awarded in the whole Korean War (the other recipient was Sergeant Bill Rowlinson of the Royal Australian Regiment who was awarded both the Medal and the Bar in Korea).

Corporal Major commanded a platoon of 18 scouts and snipers. Colonel Dextraze ordered him to recapture the ground lost by 11 Platoon and to restore the defences. The history of the Commonwealth Division simply states, "One platoon position was overrun, but was recaptured soon after midnight."

The citation for Corporal Major's award is a little more explicit. It reads in part: "Although he had no previous knowledge of the ground, Corporal Major led his platoon in the dark over the wind and snow swept hills firing his Sten… as he advanced. Dugout by dugout, slit trench by slit trench, using grenades and bayonets the platoon cleared the enemy from the position. By sheer determination and courage and because of great confidence in their leader, this small group overran an enemy six times their number causing them to fall back. Corporal Major hastily organized the defence. So expertly did he direct fire of supporting mortars and artillery that the platoon was able to repulse four separate enemy counter attacks.

"Running from one point of danger to another under heavy small arms fire from his flank he directed the fire of his men, encouraging them to hold firm against overwhelming odds. While under a heavy attack a part of his platoon was overrun. Corporal Major left his wireless set… to fire his personal weapon to assist in restoring the situation. He was credited with killing four enemy during this attack.

"Against a force superior in numbers Corporal Major refused to give ground. His personal courage, coolness and leadership were an inspiration to the men of his platoon."

The long battle was not quite over. Lieutenant Nash, commanding the right-hand platoon, recalled that the Americans were counterattacking and forcing the enemy down the west ridge of Hill 355 into his position. At one time the company commander had to order artillery and mortar fire onto 12 Platoon position. The Van Doos could see the Chinese on 355, but could not get clearance from the Americans to fire on them. Nash was short of water and ammunition. One unnamed soldier typified the fighting spirit and tenacity of the troops. In Lieutenant Nash's words, "[Three soldiers] left the company supply point to carry ammunition and water to the platoon position. Shell fire wounded one man and the other took him back… The other soldier picked up both his loads and continued on his way. His load consisted of 10 loaded Bren magazines, two boxes of grenades, a 4-gallon jerrican of water, a can of oil, a large can of four by two flannelette cleaning strips, a rifle and two bandoliers of .303. He arrived at my position… after taking nearly four hours to crawl half a mile under heavy shell fire… right through the Chinese… who had the platoon surrounded. He then helped to man the position and then carried one of our dead part way out until he was forced by heavy shelling to leave the body."

Incidentally, during the attacks, several members of 12 Platoon claim to have encountered the "Dragon Lady," a legendary exotic Chinese woman who inspired her troops in attacks.

On the evening of November 25, the Chinese attacked again. They swarmed towards the left and centre platoons, and Lt. Côté called for immediate artillery support. Colonel Dextraze ordered all the UN artillery within range to bring down fire and very shortly afterwards 3500 artillery shells broke up what was to be the last large-scale attack against the Van Doos.

By now, "D" Company had been without sleep for four days, and had undergone atrocious weather conditions in addition to their other privations and dangers. Food and water were in short supply. Nevertheless, Col. Dextraze's advice to have the troops shave was a real morale-booster and helped to sustain the regimental pride which so far, had not been lacking. Just before dawn on November 26, the weary members of Dog Company were relieved by Baker Company and were able, at last to rest and lick their wounds.

There were no battle honours for the Van Doos. During their six days of battle, they had 16 killed, 36 wounded and two captured. However a number of participants received individual awards. Corporal Harvey received a DCM – this was the only Canadian action for which two DCMs were awarded. Major Liboiron was awarded the DSO – one of the only two such awards to a sub-unit commander in the Korean War. Colonel Dextraze added the Order of the British Empire (OBE) to his DSO and went on to become chief of the defence staff. Lieutenants MacDuff and Nash, together with corporals Istead and Prud'homme were Mentioned in Despatches.

For six days the Van Doos endured everything that the enemy could produce and held their own. Perhaps their regiment's fighting prowess is best typified by Corporal Major's laconic response to his CO's request for a situation report when his newly-won position was being heavily attacked – "No Problem!"

~ ~ ~ ~ ~ ~ ~ ~ ~ ~

GRINDING ROUTINE PIERCED BY EXCITING MOMENTS

A defensive war has been described as "long periods of boredom punctuated by moments of extreme terror."

March 1952 was far from a pleasant month for Canadian servicemen serving in Korea. Officially, fighting had died down as Communist and United Nations negotiators met at the Panmunjom bargaining table. But Chinese delegates seemed more interested in stalling, than negotiating a peace treaty, and shooting continued.

March provided plenty of hard work and a little excitement for Canadians. This sort of monotonous, demanding work separated true professional soldiers from short-term servicemen.

At the beginning of March, the 25th Canadian Infantry Brigade was in reserve north of Seoul. They passed the time improving defensive positions along the Wyoming Line.

During the second week of March, Canadians moved in to the front lines. The PPCLI and R22eR took over British positions over-looking the Sami-Ch'on River during the evening of March 9. Foot soldiers of the 2RCR occupied the trenches on Hill 163. First Battalion, Princess Patricia's Canadian Light Infantry were to their immediate right on razor-backed Hill 132, which was otherwise known as "The Hook."

Meanwhile, 2R22eR took over similar positions on the eastern side of the valley. Sherman tanks of Lord Strathcona's Horse provided close support while 25-pound guns of 2nd Royal Canadian Horse Artillery provided heavy supporting fire.

Canadian soldiers overlooking the Sami-Ch'on River settled in to a grinding routine. During daylight, they shivered in muddy trenches trying to dodge the rain, snow, sleet, high winds and Communist artillery.

Infantry being infantry, they soon tired of shoring up trenches and began looking for excitement. Forbidden to scrap with the United States Marines to their left or British troops to their right, Canadian infanteers turned to fighting with Communists across the river. The Chinese, being excellent night fighters, obliged with nightly clashes in no man's land.

The routine varied. Some nights, Canadian soldiers laid mines and ambushes. Other nights they snatched prisoners or did a little sniping. RCR snipers killed a dozen enemy troops in only three days.

Some nights, with nothing better to do, they set out to annoy the Communists across the valley. If the enemy stirred, Canadian patrols called down artillery fire on Chinese trenches. When the dust settled, the enemy could be heard digging new trenches a few hundred metres further back.

Night patrols were dirty, exhausting affairs. They often resulted in short, sharp skirmishes between opposing infantry sneaking around no man's land.

Corporal K.V. McOrmond and Corporal Delphis Cormier both earned Military Medals during clashes with Chinese troops.

When Cpl. McOrmond's "C" Company, 2RCR patrol was ambushed in no man's land, he shot the first Chinese soldier who broke cover. McOrmond fought his way clear and led the rest of his men back to Canadian lines. He fired directional flares until the last three patrol members returned in the morning.

Some patrols produced nothing more than casualties. Lt. R. O'Donnell (2R22eR) was unlucky. When his patrol fell into a mousetrap ambush on the enemy side of the barbed wire, they suffered several wounded. It was only with great difficulty that a wounded Lt. O'Donnell led his patrol back to Canadian lines.

Four Patricias were wounded on the night of March 24, when Lt. H.E. Gauley (PPCLI) led a fighting patrol against Chinese positions.

That same night, the Van Doos proved they were still masters of their sector. Lt. P.E.C. Charland's patrol was attacked from behind as it snuck down a small stream. The Van Doos responded with small arms and bayonets. After killing eight or nine assailants, Cpl. Delphis Cormier led his men back to Van Doo lines. Three of them were wounded.

Late March brought warmer weather with a hint of spring. But spring was never a pleasant season for soldiers in Korea. Snow turned to rain and frozen ground turned to a quagmire. Bunkers collapsed and trenches caved in. Streams became torrents overnight, washing out roads and sweeping away bridges. Royal Canadian Engineers laboured long and hard to keep primitive roads open.

The Chinese launched their biggest attack on the night of March 26th. Eighty Chinese soldiers attacked Canadian positions west of the Sami-Ch'on River.

Chinese artillery opened up at 20 minutes past midnight. Five minutes later Chinese troops swarmed over "C" Company, RCR on Hill 163. Cpl. Gilmore's section was cut off. Four of the five RCRs were killed.

The attack on the RCR was only a diversion. The main attack was directed against the Princess Pats on Hill 132. No. 7 Platoon, under acting platoon commander Sgt. R.G. Buxton, was 400 yards ahead of the main position. Chinese troops snuck through minefields on both flanks to attack "C" Company PPCLI from the rear.

Sgt. Buxton redeployed his men for all round defense and kept on firing. After Chinese troops infiltrated barbed wire and knocked out a machine gun covering the rear of the company command post, Sgt Buxton took over the gun and killed the intruders.

The bunker containing their ammunition had collapsed under the weight of the incoming fire. By 0230 hours Sgt. Buxton's platoon was cut off and running low on ammunition. A relief party, which was advancing single-file through a minefield, took almost two hours to reach the isolated platoon. They finally reached the beleaguered platoon as the Chinese began withdrawing at 0430 hours. Thirty-one dead and one wounded Chinese were found on the battlefield.

Patricia casualties included four killed and nine wounded. Despite his wounds, Sgt Buxton remained in command until ordered out of action the next morning. Buxton was awarded a Distinguished Conduct Medal for his leadership and stubbornness.

The RCRs suffered four killed and six wounded that night; the sole survivor of Cpl. Gilmore's RCR section crawled back the next morning. Some wounded Canadian soldiers were treated by Canadian medics serving with the 8055 Mobile Army Surgical Hospital.

Throughout the attack, "D" Company 1PPCLI poured heavy fire on the Chinese. Despite heavy counter-battery fire, PPCLI mortars hung protective curtains around the beleaguered platoon. Even though he was knocked off his feet several times, Cpl. J.E. Rimmer continued firing illumination rounds from his 60-mm mortars.

Divisional artillery, including 2RCHA, did a terrific job laying down covering fire.

After having their noses bloodied on March 26th, the Chinese didn't launch any more attacks against the Canadians. Both sides settled down to patrolling. 2RCR's last brush with the enemy occurred on March 29, when an ambush patrol returned with a prisoner. As March 1952 ended, Canadian soldiers in Korea looked forward to rotating home.

~ ~ ~ ~ ~ ~ ~ ~ ~ ~ ~

PATROLLING

One of the principles of war constantly drummed into junior tacticians was "maintaining the offensive" – in other words, forcing the enemy to act in a responsive way rather than letting him determine the conduct of operations. During the lengthy static period of the Korean War, UN policy was to maintain the initiative, and hopefully dominate no man's land, by intensive patrolling.

Eighth Army planned to conduct at least one major patrol every 24 hours by each battalion-sized unit. The Commonwealth Division commander, however, felt that this practise would result in unnecessary casualties with doubtful results, and the British, Canadian and Australian infantry were reluctantly exempted from this order. Nevertheless, units sent out nightly ambush and standing patrols, and every few days fighting patrols were ordered, usually for the purpose of capturing prisoners or destroying enemy installations.

Fighting patrols were usually at platoon strength — about 25 men — and according to the rules, were to be commanded by an officer. This was not always the case, as evidenced by a fighting patrol conducted by the 1PPCLI in October 1952.

The patrol was commanded by Sergeant John Richardson, who had enlisted in 1945, soon after his 18th birthday, and remained in the army after the Second World War. The night's activities can best be described in the citation for the Distinguished Conduct Medal awarded to Sergeant Richardson:

"On the night of October 15, 1952 a fighting patrol of 25 men was sent out from the 1st Battalion, Princess Patricia's Canadian Light Infantry, the task of the patrol being to search out the enemy and capture a prisoner. The patrol limit was the base of a strongly held enemy feature some 2800 yards by patrol route from our forward defended localities over very rough, broken terrain. The patrol was commanded by Sergeant Richardson. Having established a firm base, this non-commissioned officer with the assault group of 16 men proceeded a further 150 yards. He then, with two snipers, detached himself from the main group and reconnoitred forward searching out the enemy.

"Having observed a small party of enemy digging, Sergeant Richardson withdrew to the assault group, where he called for supporting artillery fire to cover the sound of his intended attack on this enemy party.

"Suddenly, in pitch blackness, Sergeant Richardson and his men were assailed on two sides, over-run and cut off from the firm base by an enemy force estimated at 35 to 40, which apparently had been lying in wait. Eleven of his men were wounded by the first volleys of small arms and grenade fire, and the patrol wireless set was destroyed. However, the enemy were beaten off temporarily and heavy casualties were inflicted.

"Sergeant Richardson, himself severely wounded in five places, reorganized his group and began a withdrawal with his wounded in the face of continuous enemy small arms fire. Although pursued by the enemy, this courageous non-commissioned officer personally carried Sergeant R.A. "Rocky" Prentice, a seriously wounded comrade, a distance of over 100 yards to the firm base. Despite the severity of his own wounds, on regaining wireless communication at the firm base Sergeant Richardson called down artillery, mortar and machine gun fire on the pursuing enemy while supervising and encouraging his men in the difficult task of carrying back the wounded a further 800 yards where they were met by a carrying party sent out from the battalion."

The official patrol report paints an even more vivid picture, parts of which Richardson refutes. According to the report "both sides used a number of automatic weapons" in the firefight; in fact, all the Canadians had were a Bren, a Sten machine carbine, a Thompson submachine gun and two U.S. semi-automatic carbines. The rest of the patrol carried standard .303 rifles. The Chinese assailants were, however, equipped with several Soviet-made submachine guns, which were also known as burp guns.

The report also stated that the Chinese attackers employed concussion grenades — to which Sergeant Richardson replied, "Concussion grenades my ass! They were all the standard Chinese potato-masher type. I have the marks to prove it!"

Two members of the patrol were reported missing — later to be presumed killed in action. One was seen to fall, and the other was hit by a burst of fire and went down close to Sergeant Richardson. To quote the Patrol Report, "L/Cpl. Hastings was being carried back by Sgt. Richardson [who] saw Sgt. Prentice, also wounded and unable to move. Though Sgt. Richardson had now been wounded in the stomach and leg... He began to carry them both back, Prentice by his left arm and Hastings by his right, when (he was again wounded) by a concussion grenade."

Richardson disputed this — in fact, after ascertaining that Hastings was apparently beyond help, he was firing his carbine at the enemy and attempting to half-carry Sgt. Prentice to safety at the same time.

While he is justifiably proud of his award, one of the last DCMs presented to a Canadian, Richardson's personal account gives credit to others whose part went unrecognized.

"I tried to pass the word that my Bren gunner, Pte. Chute from Nova Scotia, should get at least a Mention in Despatches," he said. "He'd taken over the section and done a fine job from start to finish!" Pte. Chute was wounded in the action.

Richardson also acknowledged the part played by his unit's pioneer platoon commander, who on his own initiative, organized a stretcher party to bring in the wounded. Sergeant "Rocky" Prentice survived a broken hip, and was himself a recipient of the Military Medal a few months later. Richardson recovered from his wounds, completed a second Far East tour, and retired from the PPCLI as a sergeant-major some years ago.

The PPCLI museum has Sergeant Richardson's olive drab field service cap with a bullet hole in the peak. He still regrets that his U.S. carbine which he had borrowed for the patrol was not returned to its owner, 2Lt. (now MGen.) Herbert Pitts who later became colonel of the regiment.

Another particularly creditable operation took place in September 1952, when members of "B" Coy, 1RCR, carried out a daring snatch patrol. What was less publicized was a preliminary "pre-patrol patrol" carried out a few days earlier, which paved the way for the exploit.

In September 1952, Major E.L. Cohen, 'B' Company Commander of 1RCR, had asked Lt. Russ Gardner to form a patrol to go behind enemy lines to gain some intelligence of the enemy's position. Besides Lt. Gardner three others volunteered: Cpl. Karl Fowler, L/Cpl. "Scotty" Mannion and Pte. "Duke" Moodie. Mannion later recalled the actions of that night:

"When the patrol passed through the outpost Little Gibraltar, around 0100-0200 hrs, Lt. Gardner was carrying a Thompson machine gun and pistol, Cpl. Fowler a U.S. carbine and pistol. I was the 'B' Coy signaller, and was carrying the radio (300 set), a carbine and pistol, Duke Moodie was carrying the 88 set and a carbine. Lt. Gardner was a tall athletic individual and with his familiarity with that sort of terrain was ideally picked for the patrol; his father was a game warden in one of the large parks near Arnprior. Cpl. Fowler was a well-liked fellow, enthusiastic and a trifle gung-ho, who often stated he would become RSM of the battalion. My function was the company signaller with the knowledge of radio and the connection between the patrol and Company HQ. Duke Moodie, a rifleman, was to be the contact between another off-shoot patrol of Gardner and Fowler.

"The patrol travelled well into the valley, approximately one mile from Hill 355 and had advanced to about 200-300 yards into the rear of the Chinese forward positions. We were on a finger of a forward enemy slope where we were able to observe the rear slope of their position, and when one looked back at the very impressive Hill 355 it seemed a long, long way off.

"At first light the patrol commander felt that we should lay low during the daylight, and of course use the radio as little as possible. So, the patrol hid in the dense brush. Gardner and Fowler later devised a plan to recce the Chinese positions. On two successive mornings they had observed two of the enemy coming down for water near a bunker at the base of the rear slope, so off they went. Duke and myself lay in waiting for hours, and what seemed like an eternity, only whispering in low syllables for fear of being overheard by a Chinese patrol.

"Finally Gardner and Fowler returned. It was decided if possible the waterhole would be the ideal place to take a prisoner. Fowler had sketched the area and also the surrounding area. Karl Fowler wanted to try it then, but Lt. Gardner saw the futility of it at that time. We were a little too far from our positions on 355 for back-up, but before we left, the patrol commander decided to call in a shoot on the Chinese kitchen area. The RCHA gunners were right on their mark and after the first round hit Gardner called, 'Repeat, repeat, repeat.' Then this lone aircraft flew overhead. It was a U.S. Navy Corsair. It strafed the Chinese positions then dropped a napalm bomb that didn't go off, but he returned firing his guns and blew it up. Lt. Gardner informed us that he was actually sent over to see if he could spot us.

"On the third night we waited till dark then set back to return to our positions. As we grew closer to our own positions the patrol members joked about remembering the password and hoped that it hadn't changed and none of our guys got trigger-happy!"

The following morning all four went down to Tac HQ where Lt. Gardner along with Maj. Cohen reported to the CO, Peter Bingham. It was this meeting and the response to the enthusiasm that a capture could be made that actually gave birth to a snatch patrol. While the officers went to their mess to congratulate Lt. Gardner on the success of the patrol, Col. Bingham paid his compliments to Fowler, Mannion and Moodie, and gave a case of Labatt's beer with the comment "Drink up lads, you've earned it." In the early hours of September 24th, a snatch patrol led by Lt. Gardner left once again through Little Gibraltar.

The kidnap party consisted of Gardner, Fowler and Moodie. Scotty Mannion was left behind, but the patrol included a backup group consisting of Cpl. Leroy Faulkner and Privates Ed Mathews, Ed Knight and Chuck Bowden.

After establishing a firm base, codenamed PANSY, the group was given a shot of rum to stave off the chill and the snatch group left for the waterhole. It was now past first light, but no one came down for water. Leaving Moodie at the waterhole, Gardner and his corporal located and cut a nearby signal cable. By now it was broad daylight.

In about 20 minutes, as they had hoped, an enemy signaller came down to check the line. They jumped him and hit him twice on the head with pistol butts, but the thick-skulled enemy continued to resist.

Wasting no time, Gardner and Fowler dragged their noisy, reluctant guest to PANSY where they were joined by Moodie whose withdrawal was well covered by the alert Cpl. Faulkner and his team. To add to their problems, the return spring on the Bren gave out after one burst was fired. The patrol radioed back for smoke on PANSY to cover their withdrawal and all returned safely, including, in Scotty Mannion's words, a "stunned and bewildered prisoner."

The patrol was rewarded with copious shots of rum both at the platoon CP, where they arrived back in the RCR lines and later at "B" Company HQ. The prisoner, less fortunate, was passed back for interrogation – there is no record of the RCR hospitality being extended to him.

Lt. Gardner received a Military Cross for his efforts, while Karl Fowler was awarded a well-deserved Military Medal. Cpl. Faulkner was Mentioned in Despatches for his part in the action. Sadly, Chuck Bowden and Ed Knight were both killed in action a month later during a heavy attack on Hill 355.

A PRESENT FROM SANTA MAO

Christmas Eve, 1951, somewhere in the Yongdong area just north of the 38th parallel in Korea. It was a bitterly cold night, and the infantrymen in the forward positions were waiting for the dawn stand-to and after that stand-down, so most of their number could return to their warmer hootchies brew up and dig into their breakfast meal of C-rations.

The slit trenches contained small charcoal burners, but they were there to keep the working parts of our automatic weapons – Brens and section commanders' Stens – from freezing up. The cold feet of the infantrymen were of secondary importance.

As it grew lighter we saw something new a few yards in front of our outer wire apron. It was a wooden box, a little larger than an Asahi beer crate, and above it a banner which read "Merry Christmas Gifts From the Chinese Peoples Volunteers. This is not a booby trap." We called the company CP and heard that other platoons in our area had reported the same thing. It says something for the field-craft ability of the enemy that these had apparently been deposited close to our forward positions without detection!

"Take two of your section and bring the box in!" A very reluctant section commander lashed two squad tent side poles together and from the shelter of four sandbags, gingerly maneuvered the box into cover, where we just as carefully opened it. Fortunately, the lid was not fastened shut and we were able to do this from a distance with our tent poles.

The remainder of the platoon, who had been conspicuously absent during the poking and shoving stages, now reappeared. We found that the box contained a treasure trove of souvenirs such as imitation ivory rings, brooches, cigarettes holders, silk scarves and a number of Christmas cards. The knick-knacks all carried emblems of the dove of peace.

When we reported the particulars of our find, the word came down from Company Headquarters to collect all these and pass them back for intelligence purposes. Most of the goodies were reluctantly returned by their possessors and sent to Company HQ. It goes without saying that most of us never saw them again. (I did, in fact, encounter some of these items years later in London's Imperial War Museum — no credit, of course, was given to the forward troops who recovered them.)

I was able to retain a Christmas card, which I eventually donated to the Canadian Intelligence Corps museum. The verse read:

> *Whatever your color (sic), race or creed*
> *Frontline soldiers are brothers indeed*
> *We are your friends, and we want peace*
> *If you go home, the war will cease.*
> *Christmas greetings from the Chinese Peoples Volunteers*

The design of the card and the paper used were identical with those produced for our own regimental greeting card, by a Hong Kong printing company.

Besides the gifts, a Christmas message on the theme of "Go home, don't fight the Americans' war" was included. These were nothing new. Leaflets comparing our hardships with the activities of a clearly Semitic "Mr. Moneybags in Florida" were common – indeed many of the graphic illustrations of Mr. M's erotic activities with the forlorn grass widows of Korea servicemen were prized as pornographic art. However, no doubt in keeping with the spiritual nature of Christmas, our Chinese friends did not see fit to include any of this material in their gift boxes.

It would seem that Mao Tse-tung's volunteers considered this seasonable gesture a propaganda success. In any case, this was repeated the following year, and it appears that the variety and quality of the gifts had improved.

Well-known writer-publisher Peter Worthington wrote in his entertaining autobiography *Looking for Trouble* of his experiences as a junior officer with the PPCLI in Korea during Christmas 1952. He recalled there were several enemy in front of our positions, and our troops put down flares and artillery in anticipation of a Christmas Eve attack.

"At first light," he said, "we were startled to see shapes looming in front of wire… they seemed giant figures – the troops called them Manchurians for some inexplicable reason."

"When the sun came up we saw that the shapes were actually Christmas trees. The Chinese had spent the night putting them up in front of our wire and decorating them with gifts and packages. A huge banner was also stretched along the front, urging us not to fight the Yankees' war."

This time the caution seemed to be on the side of higher command as despite the Brigadier's instructions to keep off, the forward troops descended through the wire and minefields to get at the goodies. Worthington reports that the troops returned laden with gifts of glass animal figurines, anti-war diaries, tea, postcards, stamps and propaganda items including safe-conduct passes for use in the unlikely event that any Canadians may have wished to surrender.

Again higher command asked that the stuff be turned in and their platoon commander was instructed to not let the troops read the propaganda. Worthington (a somewhat unconventional soldier) felt that it would be a good idea to return the enemy's generosity with gifts of C-ration ham and lima beans which our troops detested. This was vetoed by his commanding officer. However, the young subaltern conveniently turned a Nelsonian blind eye when that night, following the return of a PPCLI patrol, several gallon cans of beans and ham chunks turned up in the Chinese lines.

Any doubts that the headquarters staff may have had regarding a possible softening of the Patricia's aggressive attitude were dispelled when, at about 1100 hours on Boxing Day, two Chinese soldiers were seen in the open.

"The effect on the platoon was instantaneous and electric," Worthington wrote. "The men roused from their bunkers and within moments it was like a shooting gallery with everyone trying to knock off the two Chinese running and ducking along the hillside. So much for pacifism or reluctance to shoot those from whom you'd just received Christmas gifts and to whom you'd just given a gift of ham chunks!" (Incidentally, there is no accounting for tastes; the British troops, perhaps less choosy due to austerity conditions at home, considered the ham and lima one of the better C-ration options.)

IMPROVISATION AND AUGMENTATION

A meticulous inspecting officer in Korea would probably throw up his hands in disgust when he encountered the variety of unofficial weapons carried by Canadian troops in the line.

Sharp-end soldiers augmented their armament for a number of reasons. One of these was undoubtedly what would now be referred to as the gung-ho or macho effect. Many an infantryman, in addition to his rifle, carried a sidearm. The most popular of these illegally acquired weapons was the U.S. 1911 model .45 automatic. Not only did it have a respectable stopping power, but was relatively easy to obtain from the "dry" Americans in exchange for a bottle of NAAFI liquor. A few other ranks were able to get hold of .38 Webley revolvers. However, ammunition for these was harder to come by and owners were forced to use rimless 9-mm rounds which would not extract, so that the cases had to be tapped out with the cleaning rods every six shots. (Fortunately, mine was not put to the test in battle – the only targets I engaged were a snake which proved to be non-poisonous and bottles floating in the Imjin River during a shooting contest with a bored MP while waiting for Pintail bridge to reopen.)

Another status symbol was the possession and conspicuous display of a former enemy weapon – especially the Russian-made PPS 43 burp gun. While this was undoubtedly an effective close-quarter weapon, it had its drawbacks. In one case a group of British troops, proudly but illegally carrying captured burp guns were hitchhiking when they were passed by a truckload of U.S. infantrymen. The Americans didn't recognize the different combat uniforms, but did recognize the distinctive PPS. Fortunately for the Brits, their U.S. allies were poor shots!

In November 1951, two companies of the 1RCR occupied a spur and hill feature (Hill 187) in the Sami-ch'on area of Korea. During the night of November 2nd, they were attacked by a strong force of Chinese troops. In the early morning hours several enemy penetrated the point position held by 2 Platoon of "A" Company. Platoon commander Lieutenant Ed Mastronardi recalled that his position was virtually overrun and over half of his platoon was killed or wounded. The Canadians were out of grenades and had very little small arms ammunition left. The platoon commander's efforts to provide illumination were hampered when the firing pin of his mortar failed after the first round. He resorted to the use of a Verey pistol which, after his issue 9mm Browning pistol was empty, was utilized to good effect as an anti-personnel weapon. (Mastronardi referred to this stage of the battle as "the cowboys and Indians stuff.") When the flare pistol was shot out of his hand, he picked up a fallen burp gun and continued the fight.

Improvisation was evident everywhere and Mastronardi paid tribute to the spontaneous adaptation of other weapons when the need arose. He later recalled one soldier using a pickaxe to attack and drive off an enemy, while another killed a Chinese by bashing him on the head with an unprimed grenade. Several Royals distinguished themselves in the action. Private Eddy Bauer, a Bren-gunner, broke up an enemy breach literally at muzzle-point. Bauer had already improvised an effective night-aiming device for his weapon by using two bayonets and a piece of wire. Private Jack Johnson had arrived in the line the previous day – when the section Brens overheated he coolly collected them, stripped and repaired them and returned them to their users – all under heavy fire.

The ferocity of the action can be judged that at least 35 enemy dead were found in and around 2 Platoon's position, as well as by the award of the RCR's only Distinguished Conduct Medal in Korea to Eddy Bauer, and the Military Cross and Military Medal to Lieutenant Mastronardi and Private Johnson. Three gallantry decorations to one platoon for one night's action was not a common occurrence!

The most popular reason for augmentation of the "Scale of Issue" in Korea was the improvement of firepower. Having witnessed the effectiveness of the U.S. 60-mm mortar compared with my platoon's own handy but eyeball sighted and short-ranged 2-inch model, I can now plead the statute of limitations and confess that following the passing of two bottles of appropriate beverage, a 60-mm came into the possession of my platoon.

Perhaps the most popular innovation was the Browning MG which was used to boost platoon firepower or, in some cases, to form additional machine-gun sections.

Sergeant "Jigger" Lee, of the Welch Regiment, later recalled his first encounter with the Canadians in Korea, in this case 1PPCLI, on Umdalmal, a spur of the notorious "Hook" feature, in April 1952: "When they were close enough... my first impression was 'My God – professionals!'... They were all sporting a great beard and wearing camouflage smocks and para wings. Almost every other one seemed to be carrying a Browning machine gun with belts of ammunition around their necks."

A few days after their relief of the Welshmen, the Patricias' platoon was attacked by the Chinese in company strength. The PPCLI platoon commander, by skillful use of his assorted weapons, enabled his men to repulse the enemy with heavy losses, while keeping his own casualties to a minimum. Jigger Lee recalled that enemy mortars and artillery caused several casualties among the South Korean porters bringing up desperately needed ammunition to the PPCLI. As Jigger says, "Probably the reason why the platoon's ammunition went so quickly was due to carrying too many unofficial Brownings."

Former Corporal Danny Bordeleau, a member of 7 Platoon, PPCLI agreed with the Welshman that the additional firepower probably carried the day. Bordeleau also recalls that in addition to the .30-calibre weapons, his platoon had two .50-calibre machine guns, which had not been emplaced due to their size and unwieldiness. He remembers that a group of enemy had been cut down by one of the platoon's Brownings, but not before they had caused further confusion by setting alight the .50-calibre ammunition supply.

Bordeleau was full of praise for the leadership ability of Sergeant R. Buxton, his platoon commander. This opinion was shared by the authorities and recognized by the award of the DCM to Buxton, who eventually became a regimental sergeant-major before losing his life in a parachuting mishap.

Perhaps the most odd-ball of the buckshee weapons were those invented or adopted by the troops, partly in an attempt to carry out the offensive action principle of war, and partly out of boredom or inquisitiveness. Such items as a grenade launcher was made from a shell casing and PIAT spring or various booby trap devices. (The Chinese had a particularly effective one. It consisted of a grenade packed in clay, the pin then being removed from the baked product and the clay-wrapped grenade left on a well-travelled path where it would either be trodden or rained upon. In either case, the clay holding down the striker lever would dissolve, resulting in at worst a serious leg wound and at best a night disturbed by disconcerting explosions all around one's positions.)

Tales were told in the wet canteens of a marvelous innovation produced by the sappers or pioneer sections known as the "Ooflungdung." This consisted of a 40-gallon oil can buried in front of our wire and packed with sundry explosives, No. 80 phosphorus grenades, scrap metal, and various other unpleasant surprises (one of which gave the contraption its name). The whole thing was supposed to be electrically detonated should we have surprise visitors on the doorstep. I have yet to hear of any actual instances where this deadly (and possible illegal weapon) had been actually activated.

~ ~ ~ ~ ~ ~ ~ ~ ~ ~

CHANGE OF VENUE AND ROLE

Korea, May 1952. The Warning Order sounded ominous. "'B' Coy 1RCR will proceed to an unidentified destination on an unspecified mission. Transport will be by truck, train and boat. Extra Brens will be carried." Speculation intensified when the Royals arrived at Tangkok railhead and joined a green-bereted British contingent. Rumours of island raids, and even a second "Inchon landing" spread, before the destination was finally announced as the troops had boarded the train. We were going to Koje-do.

The island of Koje-do, off the coast of Pusan, held over 150,000 North Korean and Chinese prisoners of war. The North Koreans, concerned over the number of defectors to the South and seeking to gain a propaganda victory in the truce talks under way at Panmunjom, infiltrated the camps with hardcore political officers to encourage resistance to the U.S. and South Korean guards. They were very successful.

After a number of bloody riots, the prisoners gained complete control within the compounds. Finally, on May 7, 1952, they seized the camp commander, Brigadier-General Dodd and held him hostage; they presented a series of demands, including confessions of ill treatment, to which General Dodd's successor acquiesced. General Dodd was then released.

The UN Commander, General Matthew Ridgway, and his successor General Mark Clark, were appalled and reacted promptly.

The former camp commanders were removed and summarily demoted, to be replaced by an experienced veteran of the Far East service, Brigadier General H.L. "Bull" Boatner. The guards were replaced or reinforced by field troops from the United States and other national UN contingents.

When Prime Minister Clement Atlee's British government went along with the UN Command's request, Canadian Prime Minister Louis St. Laurent was less willing to accede. While admitting that this was perhaps a legitimate military order, he felt the request should have been made through diplomatic channels rather than presented as a *fait accompli*.

The Commonwealth Division was represented by "B" Coy, 1st Battalion, The Royal Canadian Regiment, commanded by Major Ed Cohen, and "B" Company of the King's Shropshire Light Infantry. Despite the secrecy accompanying the move, Peterforce, (as the group was known) was greeted on Koje-do on May 25 by POWs brandishing welcome banners and singing a very catchy song, later identified as "The Big-Nosed American."

Following a speech of welcome by General Boatner, the troops received a few days training from the Americans. The "Bull" cautioned the newcomers against indiscriminate use of firearms, although advocating us to "slash them, use the rifle butt or knee in the groin" if necessary.

To the Commonwealth soldiers, used to weapon training conducted in small groups, the U.S. method of teaching the use of shotguns, tear gas grenades, riot drill, and other subjects was a startling contrast. The Americans adopted an en masse "lecture-demonstration" approach. The Military Law lectures were particularly disappointing: a U.S. officer read for hours from a manual, and even the explicit descriptions of sexual offences failed to keep the troops awake.

After a week Peterforce took over guard duties on Compound 66, which held about 3500 prisoners. No one was sure of the exact number, because during the period of misrule prisoners had moved fairly freely between compounds.

The compound was surrounded by double-apron wire and seven two-storey watchtowers alternated with sandbagged guard posts. Roving guards patrolled the area between the two barbed wire fences, while the towers and ground posts held light machine guns (including the extra Brens we had brought).

The guards' orders were unusual. Besides keeping the POWs in order, they were instructed to assist, where possible, any prisoners trying to escape. To discourage defectors, hardcore Communists guarded the inner perimeter and used all means – including killing – to stop prisoners from leaving. In fact, most of those defecting to Peterforce did so by quitting working parties, mostly the "honey-bucket" latrine emptying details, outside the compounds.

The North Koreans were most ingenious. From ordinary materials such as ponchos, tent fabric, food products and scrap lumber they fabricated national flags, realistic UN uniforms and badges, dummy firearms and real lethal weapons. Compound 66 even had a functional ironworker's shop created from misappropriated U.S. materials. Colourful female costumes surfaced in a corner of the compound, worn by soldiers who were variously identified as either amateur actors, potential spies, or inmates of a homosexual brothel.

Alarms and excursions were frequent. The POWs drilled with dummy rifles and bayonets, and from time to time would charge the perimeter guards, stopping just short of the wire. A report of a tunnel system between compounds resulted in the arrival of a large mechanical shovel, which dug a large trench round the compound. It attracted many interested spectators, but revealed no unauthorized excavations. (Later, when the compound had been evacuated, the beginning of a large tunnel *was* discovered.)

Less amusing was the discovery, following a foray by the UN troops into the compound, of a number of dismembered bodies, presumably of potential defectors. A number of vicious–looking spears, hatchets, and other weapons also came to light.

There was a bright side. To quote one Peterforce member: "It was a hell of a sight better than the sharp end. The Airborne (187 Regimental Combat team) had loads of beer and gave it away freely. The Dutch had gin in their canteen for ten cents a shot and the Red Cross clubs and PX had all the coffee, donuts and ice cream you wanted." Peterforce long remembered the hospitality of the U.S. troops.

In early June the prisoners were moved into new, smaller compounds. A few days earlier, attempts by the U.S. troops to clear another compound resulted in strong resistance and several casualties. This time, there were few problems. Tear gas effectively removed the hard core prisoners, and the compound was surrounded by tanks, half-tracks mounting heavy machine guns, and what seemed like a whole regiment of U.S. troops in full battle order, supervised by the "Bull" himself. (The Commonwealth troops were particularly intrigued by one hefty second lieutenant whose sole function appeared to be to photograph the general giving orders.)

In contrast, when the prisoners had marched to the halfway point, they passed between a double line of lightly-armed and equipped Shropshires and Royals, spaced at intervals of about 20 yards.

On arrival in their new compound the prisoners' representatives were advised by the Peterforce commander, Major D.R. Bancroft of the KSLI, that they would be treated fairly but that no misconduct would be tolerated. Major Bancroft had already gained the respect of the prisoners, if not his allies, when he forced an American driver to return a homemade cap badge which the latter had ripped from a North Korean's cap.

The rest of the tour passed smoothly. Our riot drill training proved unnecessary — while our American allies would enter the compounds in a "flying wedge" of troops with fixed bayonets, visitors to the Commonwealth compound would be escorted by an unarmed NCO – a practise which discouraged visits from our allies. One minor rebellion was quickly quashed when the instigators were forced to remain outside on parade during one of the frequent rainstorms. An RCR member successfully removed a rebellious prisoner from a hut roof with a charge of birdshot.

The prisoners ate well, receiving an issue of vegetables and rice supplemented by time-expired K-rations. As cigarettes could be used as currency they had to be removed from K-rations before the meals were passed to the POWs. The removal and theoretical destruction of the smokes was a chore which never lacked volunteers, especially among the British, whose daily pay was roughly the cost of thirty cigarettes at home.

With the pacification of the prisoners, Peterforce's work was done. On July 12, the Commonwealth troops left the island — following farewell parties hosted not only by the UN troops, but by our involuntary North Korean guests, who held a sports meet in our honour.

En route back to rejoin our units at the sharp end, derisory calls from passing troops, no doubt envious of our stay in the island paradise, gave us our new nickname – "The Koje Commandos."

The Koje–do saga was not quite over. In *Strange Battleground*, LCol H.F. Wood's official history of the Canadian army in Korea, the author reports that Chinese interrogators singled out 1 RCR prisoners for special attention, and those identified as "B" Company members were unsuccessfully pressured to give details of U.S. atrocities on Koje-do.

~ ~ ~ ~ ~ ~ ~ ~ ~ ~

A NIGHT TO REMEMBER

Although the 1952 action at Hill 355 was a hard-fought defensive battle for the Royal Canadian Regiment, the most costly battle for Canadians was Hill 187 in May 1953. Second-Lieutenant Ed Hollyer was on the ground in charge of 7 Platoon. He later recalled the action that took place:

"It was April 19, 1953 when we moved into our position… We went in that night and in the morning the platoon sergeant and I toured the site and checked through all the weapons. The morale of the troops was pretty good and I had some mortars in my position… I was happy to see them because I had been a mortar officer. Because I had those mortars there the sergeant and I decided to fire them off and see what was happening. So we shot off a few and the one landed and must have struck an ammunition dump because there were great big puffs of smoke and almost immediately after that mortars and artillery fire started coming in on us so we took shelter in our bunker. But they continued the next morning after we'd been there that night and they started really shelling us… This harassment continued for 13 days until the 2-3 of May – firing through the daytime hours and in the night we spent trying to restore our positions because we were getting beaten pretty bad in the daytime. During this period, at nighttime a Chinese Lady over a loudspeaker counselled us Americans, not Canadians, but

Americans, to sit on the edge of our foxholes and that we wouldn't be fired upon. This went on every night.

"On the night of 2-3 May we hadn't stood down. It was very dark and this night we were told to stand to until the moon came up, which was at least until midnight. That night I wasn't quite happy with the way the patrol was laid out. I could see there were command and control problems with it because my bunker was on the river side of the slope and there was no way of getting to the forward sections without being observed—the control was very difficult.

"During these 13 days of shelling we didn't see anything of the Chinese, but 8 Platoon was always talking about the Chinese being on their wire; we figured they were just jumpy because we didn't see any. We owned the gap in the minefield— that's a path through the minefield where all the patrols had to go out, on that side of the hill so we were the last ones they saw and all patrols exiting had to go through our piece of real estate. This gap consists of a path with fences on both sides, free of lines, and it wound from the platoon position down into the valley — no man's land. So every patrol had to go through that area.

"What I did was I sent back and asked for the signals officer and the pioneer officer… I figured if I could change my command post on top of the hill where I could see everything and have tunnels down to my former position I could get back and forth more easily and have more control. They both said they'd come up for the 2-3 of May and 'A' Company was also being sent up with a patrol of 16 men.

"From the top of the hill we were fairly close and we could see the Chinese positions across the valley. More importantly, we could see the way they could get from their place up to our position easier and how it would be much easier for me to direct the fire from this position.

"As usual, I guided the patrol up to the gap and watched it safely through, after which I returned to my CP for a cup of coffee with my two guests; and as I mentioned we had not stood down — we were waiting for the men to come up. About two hours after this patrol was sent out firing was heard from the valley. The next thing you could see was the Chinese running across the minefield. The fact that it was a minefield didn't even bother them — I always figured that probably that minefield had been cleared for quite some time, maybe before we had even taken over Hill 187.

"So I rushed back to my command post and informed my company commander and commanding officer. I was told that a patrol from '8' Platoon—the platoon immediately behind me—was on its way forward and I should try to stop it. So I took my signaler and went forward to stop the patrol; however, I was too late as this rescue patrol from 8 Platoon had passed through the wire and was itself being ambushed. I reported this to the commanding officer and at the same time called for DFSOS tasks to be fired.

"I requested the artillery fire be moved in closer to cover all the approaches on the slope of the hill I was on. I found out that the artillery regiment that was supporting us had been firing on these various targets earlier than that and they had fired the DFSOS tasks even before I asked for it — so there was lots of fire coming down even before I requested it.

"In the meantime, I had six Bren guns and a .30-caliber American machine gun, and we were providing pretty devastating fire on all sides of the hill. At this time I lost contact with battalion headquarters and I returned to my CP and, aided by the signals officer, re-established communication.

"And then all hell broke loose. Our position was being pounded by artillery and mortar. I went forward to observe the action and direct as necessary. The Chinese had continued to move up the side of the hill and the troops threw grenades and yelled back and forth as much as they could and fired magazine after magazine of Bren gun and belts of ammunition at the approaching Chinese. The attacking force moved up to the edge of our defences during this bombardment and they appeared to enter our trenches before the artillery fire was lifted. But that's not exactly what was happening; the fire had been lifted but those who were at the edges of the trenches were firing all kinds of grenades while in the meantime the others came right on to our trenches closely followed by those who were throwing the grenades.

"We had bolt-action rifles and we're dealing in close quarters with Chinese because they were right in our position and in some instances the rifles were being used as clubs. I could see we were fighting a losing cause and something had to be done to get the Chinese to back off. I ordered the section commander of the right flank to pass on to the rest of the platoon that in five minutes I would call for artillery on our own position.

"As I fought my way back to the CP, I was stopped by two Chinese who weren't interested in letting me advance. I was armed with a Sten machine gun, a pistol and a primed hand grenade that hung from my belt. So you can imagine my surprise when I tried to fire my Sten to find that I had failed to put a magazine on it. The Chinese shouted at me and motioned me with their weapons to indicate that I should surrender. There was a little trench nearby and when I threw my Sten on the ground, I think they thought I was giving up. I jumped into the trench and at the same time grabbed the grenade on my belt, pulled the pin and threw it. They left me alone then—one guy was hurt a bit, he let out a scream, and the other guy pulled him off.

"I made my way back to the command post. At this point I told my signaler to contact battalion headquarters and request artillery fire on our hill. At that point the radio operator informed me that the battery commander wanted to speak with me. I had explained what the situation was and requested he bring down fire on my position. He told me that a concentration of proximity infused rounds would be fired.

"During this period some remnants of the patrols that had gone forward started to make their way back while, at the same time, 'A' Company sent out a small stretcher party to evacuate the wounded. One of the guys that did this came into my command post at the time; this was a chap I had served with as a corporal. I told him we didn't have time to talk, to get out and do his job and we'd talk later. I saw him in a hospital after the war was over and he told me the story that after I chased him from my CP he went out to discover an Oriental in a padded suit. He had assumed it was one of our Korean service corps struggling with a stretcher and soon realized his mistake when he was hustled by another Chinese into the enemy lines where he spent the remainder of the war. The pioneer officer was also captured that night and he was held prisoner until the end of the war.

"When the first of the artillery came down it was an intensive bombardment that sounded like the worst thunderstorm one can imagine. After some time I asked for it to be lifted and I went forward with a soldier from the bunker to appreciate the situation. As we exited a round came in and I hit the ground. The shrapnel from the round landed right beside me and went over my body and punctured all these water cans I had and they poured all over me. I wasn't sure if it was water or blood.

"So the soldier and I went forward and found the position was still overrun. The Chinese were everywhere with lots of dead and wounded. They were rolling the bodies over the sides of the hill so they could be carried away. We made our way back towards the command post, but as we were passing a bunker we were jumped by three Chinese. Somehow we managed to get away from these guys and jumped over a sandbag wall and returned our assailants' fire. The chap I was with raised himself for a better shot and was immediately cut down with a whole magazine of fire. So there I was all by myself.

"I noticed a box of grenades in the corner and started lobbing them at the Chinese, but it was just like throwing rocks because none of the grenades exploded. Finally, I reached at the other end of the box, pulled the pin, threw it. There was an explosion and a shout of pain and then the three guys took off. My escort was dead. I made my way back to the CP and called for the continuation of artillery support.

"When it finally lifted I returned to the position gathering what troops I could still locate. There was scattered enemy, but most had returned to their lines. Besides artillery support from our own regiment, there was fire from two other field regimental divisions and all medium and heavy guns were supporting this little action I had that night.

"We had 26 killed, 27 wounded, and seven were taken prisoner. The 81st Field Regiment alone fired 4,300 rounds. In addition there was four Korean corps soldiers killed. The official estimate for the Chinese was 80 casualties, but according to the people that came back there was many more than that."

For his bravery and leadership in this battle, 2nd Lieutenant Ed Hollyer was awarded the Military Cross. The signals officer that night was awarded one as well, and three soldiers were given Military Medals.

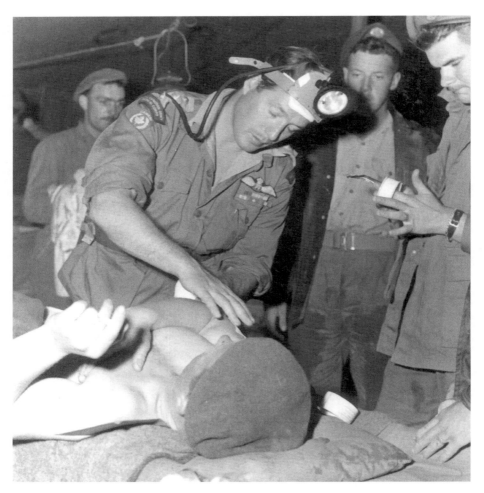

ABOVE: *Over 1600 Canadians were wounded in Korea – a number of those were casualties on more than one occasion. That they survived was due in large part to the diligence and courage of the Medical Corps. (DND)*

OPPOSITE PAGE: *Although the terrain did not facilitate major armoured trucks, Canadian tanks were used on many occasions to provide fire support to the infantry. (DND)*

☙ ALSO PRESENT WERE...

Korea was an infantryman's war.
Objectives had to be taken and held by the
foot soldiers. We could not achieve this aim
without the support of other arms and
services.

CODE WORD: IRONSIDES. Anyone who used a radio set in the Korean War era will recognize the appointment code designation for armour.

Although Canada's part in the Korean War was primarily an infantry role, the tankers of Lord Strathcona's Horse were an important element of 25 CIBG.

Unlike previous (and subsequent) wars, the fairly static situation in Korea following the formation of the Commonwealth Division, and the very nature of the terrain, neither called for nor favoured the tanks' greatest asset: mobility. Their other characteristic – firepower – was often put to better use.

In initial stages of the Korean War, with successive advances and withdrawals for the whole length of the peninsula, both sides made good use of armour. Russian-built T-34s, arguably the most effective all-round AFV of the Second World War, spearheaded the North Koreans' invasion. With over 200 of these formidable machines, against four U.S. companies equipped with light Chaffee tanks, the North Koreans had a fairly easy ride at first. Not only were the outnumbered UN and ROK forces hopelessly outmatched in armour, but the refusal of the U.S. to provide the South Korean armies with anything but small arms before 1950 meant that other anti-tank weapons were few and far between.

Eventually, the beleaguered Pusan perimeter troops were substantially reinforced with more tanks, until the UN forces outnumbered the North Koreans by five-to-one in armour. The bulk of it was in the form of M4A (Sherman), Pershing and Patton tanks, which proved more than a match for their opponents. By late 1950, the North Korean 105th Armoured Division was no more. After the Inchon and Pusan perimeter breakouts, 239 destroyed T-34s were found, with aircraft having knocked out almost half of them. Only 39 had been destroyed in tank-to-tank action.

The first Commonwealth armoured units to arrive in Korea were the 8th King's Royal Irish Hussars and a Royal Tank Regiment squadron. These units were soon in action in support of 29 British Brigade, covering the withdrawal of the Royal Ulster Rifles at Chunhung Dong. The tank detachment, known as "Cooperforce," suffered 20 killed, including the commander as well as the loss of some of its tanks. The fighting was so fierce that some Centurions evacuating riflemen from the battlefield were awash with blood from their wounded passengers. The Hussars later saw action in a vain attempt to extricate the Glosters from their Imjin position in April 1951, and supporting 1KSLI in a successful counterattack on Hill 227 in November of that year.

Perhaps the first major Canadian connection with armour occurred at Kapyong, where 2PPCLI shared the distinction of a U.S. Presidential Citation for their role with Company "A" of the 72nd Heavy Tank Battalion of the U.S. army. In the words of the Citation, "Company 'A' … supported all units (PPCLI and the Australians) to the full extent of its capacity and in addition, kept the main roads open and assisted in evacuating the wounded."

Meanwhile, back in Canada, an armoured element was being prepared for Korea. Major "Jim" Quinn, an officer with a reputation for being "firm but fair," was tasked with forming what was originally entitled the "1/2 Royal Canadian Armoured Corps Squadron" in Camp Borden, Ont.. The squadron was named this to represent the two Canadian armoured regiments at the time. Major Quinn was lucky enough to be given *carte blanche* to select his own officers and senior NCOs. However, he was less fortunate in his allocation of weapons. Despite protests, the 1/2 Squadron was to receive the U.S. M-10 17-pounder, which was actually not a tank, but an open-turret self-propelled tank destroyer.

Both Quinn and Brigadier John Rockingham had to resist efforts by the British divisional commander to exert the U.K. influence on the unit. General Cassels would have liked to see the Strathcona's used as an additional squadron under command of the 8th King's Royal Irish Hussars, but Rocky was successful in keeping them in the 25 Canadian Infantry Brigade. (The order of battle for 1COMWEL Division listed LdSH(RC) as divisional troops, but apart from occasional fire support to other UN units, they remained more or less under Canadian control.)

More significant was the choice of tanks. Britain hoped they would adopt the Centurion, used by the British armoured units, in place of the M-10 SP anti-tank weapons. This was no doubt influenced not only by standardization, but the fact that the U.K. was desperate for dollars to pay off their World War II debts and could use the bucks. As it might have taken up to a year to obtain the Centurions, Quinn insisted on – and got – M4A Shermans, delivered immediately from U.S. stocks. It was a good choice. While the British tank had, arguably, the best tank gun of its time, the Sherman was far more able to deal with Korea's rugged terrain.

A week after the Shermans arrived, "C" Squadron was in action. On May 25th they accompanied R22eR on a general advance, sustaining their first casualty and later acquitting well on a nine-mile reconnaissance north of the 38th parallel, returning with a number of Chinese prisoners. The mixed nature of the UN forces was apparent when the Straths were called upon to support the Philippines battalion.

During the summer, many UN units carried out probes and what was called "reconnaissance in force." The Straths worked very well with the Canadian infantry battalions - with effective fire support from the tanks always forthcoming. Major Quinn and his successor, Captain V.W. Jewkes, developed and used infantry-tank liaison techniques and target indication procedures that later became the model for COMWEL Division. In particular, the rapport with LCol "Jadex" Dextraze of the Van Doos proved most effective, especially during the battle for Hill 227 in November 1951, where the Strathcona's tanks bolstered the infantry's heroic defence.

In October 1951 the squadron effectively supported 25 CIBG during MINDEN and COMMANDO – the last significant mobile operations on the Commonwealth front. During the advance, the Brigade War Diary reported: "'C' Squadron was in support and under the able direction of the (R22eR) company commander, literally fired the troops down the slope, across the valley, and on to the objective."

From October 1951, until the ceasefire in July 1953, the infantry dug in on the Wyoming Line and most tanks were moved into the forward positions and dug in as pillboxes. A small reserve of British Centurions remained as a counterattack force.

During the closing months of the war, "A" Squadron of the Strathcona's (which had relieved "C" and later "B" Squadrons) was used effectively in a somewhat sneaky scheme to neutralize Chinese pillboxes. The targets were plotted, the Shermans would move into forward valleys overnight and open fire on the enemy at first light, leaving before counter-artillery fire could be brought to bear.

Although the very nature of the war spotlighted the foot soldier, the Straths had their share of action. The Sherman proved to be an excellent weapon, which was able to get into spots inaccessible to most other vehicles and its multi-bank engine performed well under the adverse weather conditions. Even so, the regiment suffered losses in men and material. Five troopers died and tanks were destroyed or badly damaged by mines and shell fire.

There were lighter moments. MGen Phil Neatby later recalled one time when troops were awaiting inspection by Major Jewkes, who was a stickler for efficiency. The tanks were spotless an hour before the CO's arrival. However, during that fatal hour, an energetic Korean sparrow was able to build a nest in the muzzle of one of the 75-mm guns.

Jim Quinn, later recounted the story of SQMS Doug Everleigh, who contrived to draw rum rations for a non-existent tank delivery troop for a year.

Individual honours were bestowed on Major Jewkes (DSO) and his successor, "B" Squadron's Major Roxborough, who with his SSM, WO Armer, received the MBE. "A" Squadron's Major Ellis was awarded the Military Cross, and Military Medals went to trooper Roy Stevenson and Sgt. Allen – the latter for his work in supervising the recovery of a tank while under heavy artillery fire. The resourceful SQMS Everleigh and Trooper Wyatt received the BEM and 14 members were Mentioned in Despatches. Perhaps the most unusual award was the U.S. Distinguished Flying Cross, presented to Captain Bill Ward for 81 missions as an observer in the back seat of an AT-6 Harvard with 6147 Tactical Control Group.

The involvement of the Strathconas during the Korean War can be judged by the fact that the Regimental Committee on Battle Honours listed 10 engagements between May 1951 and July 1953 in which squadrons took part. Lord Strathcona's Horse proudly display the theatre honour "Korea 1951-1953" on their guidon – and well deserve it.[1]

~ ~ ~ ~ ~ ~ ~ ~ ~ ~

ALSO PRESENT WERE...
Of the five arms of the army, two have not yet been covered here in full.

Although Korea was an infantryman war, the successes of the Canadian infantry would probably not have been possible without the support provided by the Royal Canadian Horse Artillery.

In the offensive operations, enemy resistance was often reduced or overcome by preliminary and sustained fire from the RCHA's 25-pound howitzers, sometimes augmented by British and New Zealand gunners and corps heavy artillery.

In the defence there were numerous instances of artillery fire being called upon to break up enemy attacks by prompt and accurate fire on advancing enemy assembly areas, and even on occasion to cleanse our own positions when they were in danger of being overrun.

The importance of the forward observation officer and his team cannot be overstated. These gunners were in the forward position with the infantry and shared their risks and discomforts. Their task was to direct fire as needed. The number of gallantry decorations awarded to these artillerymen is indicative of their past.

Nor should we forget the hardworking gun crews, who had the arduous task of positioning the 25-pounder and maintaining a high rate of fire for sustained periods. The Canadians were sometimes called upon to provide fire support for their allies (a scroll of appreciation to 81 Field Regiment, later re-designated 3RCHA was presented by the 1st ROK Infantry Division in appreciation of their work).

That the infantry appreciated the artillery's past is indicated in a report one RCHA operations officer wrote following the November 1952 battle for Little Gibraltar: "The artillery won the battle due to a fire plan (the CO of 1RCHA) had up his sleeve ... the Chinese commander reported to his headquarters, 'I am boxed in by artillery fire – I can't get reinforcements forward.'"

The other arm serving in Korea was the Royal Canadian Signals. The signallers probably didn't get the recognition they deserved. However, all of the combat units had signallers attached and they shared the perils and discomforts of the line troops.

They maintained vital radio and telephone links between various levels of headquarters and forward units. Local weather conditions often provided a challenge to the radio operators, while phone lines had to be constantly maintained against possible breaks due to accidents, shellfire or occasional guerrilla activity.

The Royal Canadian Electrical and Mechanical Engineers performed another vital service as well. These craftsmen worked wonders in keeping the brigade's weapons and vehicles in good condition, making long hours and occasional improvisation a routine.

That the RCEME were not rear-echelon commanders was aptly demonstrated when one of their NCOs was decorated for his work in assisting in the recovery of a bogged-down tank, while under enemy fire.

Other corps provided smaller, but vital detachments. The Field Dental Detachment took care of dental problems, while the Canadian Postal Corps helped maintain morale by ensuring that mail from home, as well as other postal services such as money orders were promptly and efficiently carried out. The Canadian Intelligence Corps provided a field security section and worked with division intelligence staffs and the Air Photo Interpretation Section on the acquisition of information on the enemy.

Overall, the many and varied units and subunits of 25 Canadian Infantry Brigade proved to be a formidable team.

SAPPERS AT THE SHARP END

Military units are designated as either arms or services. In early days the arms were the actual fighting troops, while the services provided support. Today infantry units often provide administrative services in peacekeeping or emergency operations, while rear-echelon troops are getting more than their share of trigger-time. Boundaries between the sharp and blunt ends are no longer clearly defined.

One proud corps serves in both categories, although it is quite rightly designated as an arm (in fact it is the third senior of the five combat arms, taking precedence even over the infantry). The Royal Canadian Engineers justifiably bear their sole battle honour, *Ubique,* on their badges. (This term is Latin for the word "everywhere.")

Canadian sappers established an excellent reputation in both world wars. Their tunneling skills, in particular, were valued in France and Flanders. In 1944, Canadian engineers evacuated the Arnhem survivors across the Rhine under heavy fire. Their successors in Korea upheld the corps' high reputation.

Canada's contribution to the Commonwealth Division included an Engineer Field Squadron. When the first rotation, the 57 Fd Sqn RCE, arrived they found many unique challenges. The field troops were, in essence, Jacks-of-all-trades, whose activities ranged from road, airfield, and base facility preparation and maintenance, to combat-related functions such as mine-laying and clearance and preparation of defensive positions (many of these duties were also carried out by infantry pioneer platoons).

The engineers encountered many difficulties on arrival in Korea. The very nature of the terrain and the scarcity of adequate roads meant many supply routes had to be constructed from scratch. Much of the mountainous countryside limited use of heavy equipment and the Division engineers (which also included two British field squadrons) had to rely a great deal on an attached Korean Service Corps labour battalion.

Digging and hacking on the rocky slopes was a long and laborious chore, and the sappers spent many backbreaking hours each day with pick and shovel. Not only were extremes of temperature encountered, but also heavy rains and flash floods could often wipe out the results of days of toil.

One major obstacle was the Imjin River. Although the American engineers had constructed substantial bridges and a ferry across the Imjin, Commonwealth engineers were constantly upgrading the crossings and their approaches. The river could rise from knee-deep to over 10 metres in depth in a few hours. Floating debris, and occasional attempts by an enemy upstream to drift mines down the Imjin necessitated a constant state of alert (one Canadian tank was stationed permanently at Pintail bridge to open fire on these hazardous objects). On at least two occasions, Commonwealth units on reconnaissance in force were trapped for days on the Imjin's north bank as the raging river made use of pontoon bridges or ferries impossible.

Ted Barris, in his book *Deadlock in Korea*, recounts a feat of 57 Field Squadron (the Rochester General Construction Company). The Canadian sappers, with virtually no notice, built a 420-metre airstrip in a barley field in four hours. They later expanded it twelve-fold, and had it ready for General Matthew Ridgway's aerial entourage in 47 minutes.

Not all roadwork was carried out in the comparative safety of rear areas. Many Korea veterans recall the Mad Mile – a stretch of road that was in plain view of the Chinese, which ran beneath a tunnel of camouflage nets in an attempt to conceal any movement. Roads that had to be blasted from rock-hard frozen soil would disappear during the spring thaw.

Infantrymen (including myself) felt that the sappers had it cushy with the expertise and material available for their makeshift hootchies. In fact, this was seldom the case – not only was there little time for rest, but the field troops moved more frequently than the units they were supporting.

Nor were the engineers strangers to the sharp end. Their tasks included preparation and bolstering of defensive positions, obstacles and, conversely, the neutralization of enemy counterparts. Engineers were frequently called upon to accompany patrols, and to clear safe lanes through enemy minefields before allied advances. On a number of occasions, including the Imjin and Hook battles, sappers fought and occupied defensive positions as infantrymen.

One of the most hazardous engineer tasks dealt with minefields - friendly and enemy. At least one sapper was accidentally killed while laying anti-personnel mines. The mix of U.S. and British land mines necessitated a wide knowledge and use of caution in this function. Apart from the dangers of the mines themselves, these frequently had to be laid in front of our forward defensive localities at night or when fog screened the activity from the enemy.

Even more dangerous was the clearance of enemy mines. The North Koreans and Chinese used a wide variety of Russian, American, British, Japanese and homemade mines and booby traps. Many of these were simple, but effective, adaptations of hand-grenades and tripwires. Wooden casings on some mines reduced or nullified the use of mine detectors. I recall one night patrol when my section's function was to protect a sapper and his nondescript dog. The team then uncovered several mines in front of our position, some of them on our regular patrol routes.

It would be unfair to neglect the unsung efforts of the 64th Field Park Squadron, a British, Canadian and New Zealand unit that continually unloaded, sorted, reloaded and distributed vast quantities of material to the forward units. They also faced the unending task of maintaining the engineer equipment to cope with the trying conditions of Korea.

Eleven Engineers lost their lives in the Korean War. Their arduous and often perilous work was rewarded by a number of decorations, including a DSO for their first commanding officer, Colonel Don Rochester. To quote the words of Commonwealth Division historian, Brigadier C.N. Barclay: "The sappers of the Commonwealth Division did a fine job under difficult conditions, which often called for unusual methods and improvisation because of the extremes of climate and terrain."

CANADA'S SECRET ACK-ACK UNIT

Among all the high-performance aircraft on the Commonwealth Division front, you might occasionally see a canvas-covered light Auster monoplane from one of the two unique RAF units in Korea, 1903 AOP Flight and 1913 Light Liaison Flight. These were unique in that, while they were officially Royal Air Force units and were maintained by RAF craftsmen, their pilots were army personnel, which included some Canadians. One notable Canadian Air OP pilot was Capt. Peter Tees of the Royal Canadian Artillery who has the distinction of being the first army pilot since the First World War to receive the Distinguished Flying Cross.

Captain Peter Downward was a British liaison flight pilot. He well remembers one encounter with Canadian troops. His account is condensed from *British Forces in the Korean War*, edited by Ashley Cunningham-Boothe and the late Peter Farrar:

"On my flight to (Div HQ) I decided to do a bit of tactical low flying through the valleys in the rear area of the Division. I could identify the landmarks and the scurry of army vehicles. Ambulances were obvious — there had been a heavy attack on the Hook the night before. I entered a narrow valley around the back of Kamaksan with not much outlet on the starboard side and little more to port.

"As I was looking for the familiar landmark of the Imjin River, I felt a bump and looked to see if I had hit a bird. Nothing! I continued over the Imjin — keeping a sharp lookout for a platoon of 3-inch mortars that had given me a fright a couple of days before. After keeping clear of the trajectories of New Zealander 25-pounders, I returned to the Commonwealth airstrip at Div HQ.

"Soon after I had landed, the airman in charge of my aircraft asked me to come and look at my Auster. There was a whopping great hole in my starboard tail-plane. Investigative study indicated that the projectile must have come from above. It was quite obviously a missile, friendly or otherwise.

"After the repair had been made, the flight sergeant appeared with a grin on his face. 'I think we've found the answer to your flak damage, Sir!' he remarked. At the dispersal I saw a Canadian Brigade jeep, with a very worried-looking engineer captain.

"I greeted him with some inanity like 'nice to see you again' which immediately invoked the response, 'I'm not here on a social visit,' and muttered something about a board of inquiry.

"The captain explained that his troop had been working in the rear divisional area, close to the side of Kamaksan where they had recently excavated a quarry. They were doing one final blasting and all the proper precautions had been taken. Lookouts had been posted, the area was clear of local inhabitants, traffic was stopped and a loud-hailer warning was given. He pressed the plunger and up went another 50 tons of rock. 'But how the hell was I to know that one of your goddamned pilots was going to come swanning up the valley in his puddle-jumper just in the middle of my blasting?'

"Naturally, I expressed surprise — I suppose I could say that I was genuinely staggered at the thought of flying through a shower of turnip-sized rocks returning to earth from about three or four hundred feet. 'There was nothing I could do but pray,' he added. (I could see no signs of such supplication on the knees of his trousers.) I assured him that I would speak to the pilot concerned, that no serious damage was done, and there would be no question of a board of inquiry."

SERVITOR SERVIENTUM

When Newfoundlander Alex Tobin was removed from his fellow infantry trainees and transferred to the Royal Canadian Army Service Corps he was afraid that he would miss the Korean War action. When he returned to Canada over a year later, he had not only been shot at more than many infantrymen, but had been mentioned in dispatches for gallantry. Alex was one of the many members of the RCASC who quickly found that the work performed in Korea was very different from its peacetime operations.

The exploits of Canada's three infantry units – the PPCLI, RCR and R22eR – are all well documented. Less spectacular, but no less essential to the combat effort was another unit: 54 Canadian Transport Company.

From the start of the war and in just 11 days, the company grew from two to 319 other ranks (OR), and by the time they left Camp Borden for final training in Fort Lewis they numbered 11 officers and 378 ORs.

At Fort Lewis 54 Transport Company received its new vehicles – mothballed 2 1/2-ton GMC 6 X 6 trucks – the famous "Deuce-and-a-half." After intensive training in battlecraft, and the chores of preparing their vehicles for Korea, the Service Corps troops sailed from Seattle on April 19, 1951.

On May 4th the Canadians disembarked at Pusan. No doubt to the chagrin of the combat units, the first element of 25 Brigade to become operational was 54 Transport Company, whose task it was to transport the other troops to their areas. It was the proud boast of Laughton's Lancers (named for their commanding officer, Major Bob Laughton) that they were operational within two minutes of stepping off the gangplank.

Laughton's Lancers – together with the rest of 25 Brigade – reached their operational area near Seoul on May 17th. The Brigade advanced over 100 kilometres in the next fortnight, necessitating a number of moves for the RCASC Company. The round trip between the brigade area and the supply bases averaged about 100 miles over atrocious roads.

The company was responsible for transporting everything the Brigade needed – food, fuel, ammunition, defensive stores as well as Canadian and Korean personnel. They were often tasked with transporting Korean civilian refugees to relative safety behind the battle area.

Soon after, 25 Brigade joined 29 (British) Brigade and 28 (Commonwealth) Brigade to form the First Commonwealth Division. Service Corps functions for the Division were combined in the Commonwealth Divisional Column. While this facilitated central control of division resources, there were new challenges. Besides serving their fellow Canadians, 54 Company now supported British, Australian, New Zealand and Indian detachments, as well as the large numbers of Korean porters and attached U.S. and Korean troops. Eventually the company was given responsibility for lifting all the division's ammunition supply.

To further complicate matters, the Canadians received U.S. rations while the remainder of the Division used British "compo" rations, U.S. K-rations, or a combination of both. While the Canadians used the American GMC trucks and Dodge 3/4-ton ambulances, their British colleagues used other types of vehicles. Nor was the difference confined to the vehicles alone. The British-made vehicles were equipped with right-hand drive, and the Canadians often encountered a forgetful British or Aussie driver driving on his left-hand side of a narrow road.

The roads were hazardous even in clear weather conditions, which were rarely present. The main supply route that ran to Seoul and the railhead was gravel road, barely wide enough for two vehicles to pass. Although the U.S. engineers did their best, it was impossible to maintain it in tip-top condition. Supplies would be carried forward to supply and ammunition points close to the front lines. Here fuel, food, stores and ammunition would be offloaded and transferred to vehicles from the forward units. Many of the tracks – for road would be too extravagant a term to describe them – were tortuous narrow trails over mountainous terrain.

Besides weather hazards such as dust, rain, snow and ice, many of the roads were under enemy observation and sometimes artillery fire. Indeed, one famous stretch of road in the Division area was enclosed by a mile-long tunnel of camouflage netting. In other stretches, including the notorious Mad Mile, traffic had to be regulated by Provost Corps personnel, who would permit groups of vehicles to pass between sporadic periods of enemy shellfire. On dry days, a driver often had to decide between travelling fast and creating giveaway dust clouds, or driving slowly and remaining for a longer period in the danger area.

Sometimes the battle picture did not permit the leisurely transfer of necessities to other vehicles, and more than once members of 54 Transport Company and its successors had to drive into artillery positions and unload ammunition right beside the guns and mortars. On at least one occasion, one of the drivers became a casualty as a result of enemy mortar fire. The presence of these support troops in the sharp end is evidenced by a Russian-made field gun captured by Laughton's Lancers in May 1951, and currently on display in the Service Corps museum at CFB Borden.

Nor were the weather and enemy the only adversaries. The RCASC and RCEME technicians constantly worked round-the-clock to maintain the unit vehicles in running order. In fact, from the arrival of 54 Company in May 1951, through the tours of duty of 23 and 56 Transport Companies, and until the final departure of 3 Transport Company in November 1954 the Canadian transport companies reported a 100 per cent vehicle availability – a phenomenon which is unlikely to be achieved even by today's peacetime force! Bob Laughton recalled that once, as a favour, his attached workshop refurbished a pair of ambulances for the Indian Field Ambulance. The vehicles were returned in such good condition that the Indians refused to believe that they were the same wrecks that they had handed over.

There were other obstacles to overcome. Most of the Commonwealth military police were friendly and co-operative (even after one MP directing traffic was badly injured by a rock thrown from the twin rear wheels of a Canadian deuce-and-half). Some of the U.S. "snowballs" were more officious. One driver, who had left his vehicle to rescue a family from a burning hut, returned to his truck to find an MP writing out a charge report for "parking his vehicle on the MSR." Another driver recalled that one MP reported a vehicle for a dirty windshield in an extremely muddy area. (This is ironic as in many parts of the Division area shiny windshields had to be lowered and covered to avoid attracting enemy fire.)

Frank Cassidy, a Canadian who first served in Korea with the U.S. army and, on release, joined the RCASC and returned to Korea with 56 Transport Company, later recalled an unusual use of the vehicles: "Operation BIG SWITCH was a highly planned and organized troop lift, without troops," he said. "Why? Empty vehicles were used to pretend to bring new troops into the line, causing the Chinese to attack, when they would be met by seasoned troops who had never moved!"

Although the Herculean efforts of the transport companies deserve recognition, there were other RCASC members involved in vital tasks. The ambulances used by the Canadian Field Ambulances and Field Dressing Stations had RCASC drivers. Alex Tobin was one of these.

The FDS was usually close to the lines, and casualties had to be backloaded through areas in range of enemy mortar and artillery fire. Guerrillas sometimes ambushed ambulances, and orders were to drive at night without lights. "Although the order said no lights, the roads were so tricky that if I had to get my casualties back in a reasonable time I'd say 'to hell with it' and use my headlight," said Tobin. His unit would sometimes send out a 3/4 ton truck armed with a Bren, in the hope that guerrillas would attack it. "They didn't respect the Red Cross," he said. (From my own observation of wrecked, bullet-riddled ambulances in the battle area, I would agree that driving ambulances was not one of the safest occupations in Korea.)

Despite the claims of many other units, it can safely be stated that RCASC were first in the field as No. 2 Movement Control Group was operational in the theatre from October 7, 1950. They had the vital task of sorting out the people and material arriving from all directions, and ensuring that everyone and everything arrived as expediently as possible at their intended destinations.

The British and Australians were supported by Army Catering Corps cooks. In the Canadian Army, RCASC cooks carried out this function. These unsung heroes lived in the sharp end with their units, and when they were available they were able to perform wonders with the fresh rations and even with the C-rations when they were not. (I recall that whenever I visited a Canadian unit I always tried to arrive at mealtime).

RCASC clerks performed important functions in Brigade, Division and lines of communication headquarters and units.

The Canadian contribution was not without cost. Eleven RCASC members are buried in the United Nations cemetery in Korea. Nor were their efforts unrecognized. Seven RCASC members received decorations, while 25 were Mentioned in Despatches. Bob Laughton, of Lancer fame, received a well-deserved MBE.

Perhaps the most sincere compliment comes from Divisional Commander Major General Horatius Murray, who said, "Canadians seem to have a native genius for mechanics and to be born with the wheel of a truck in their hands." Certainly the members of the arms – armour, artillery, engineers, signals and infantry – upheld

Canada's military prestige in the "forgotten war," but they would have been helpless without valiant efforts of their Service Corps comrades-in-arms.

~ ~ ~ ~ ~ ~ ~ ~ ~ ~

MEDICS IN KOREA

Blood on the hills
There is blood on the hills of Korea
The blood of the brave and the true…

So begins a widely circulated poem known to most members of the Commonwealth forces in Korea. There was indeed blood – at times a great deal of it – spilt in many areas of Korea known only by nicknames (such as Hamburger Hill or The Hook) or by contour references (Hill 355, Hill 187). Many of the Canadians whose blood enriched the soil of the Korean peninsula did not return.

A surprisingly high number of Canadian casualties survived their wounds, and in many cases, returned to their units to continue the fight. Over 1,600 servicemen were wounded – in some cases more than once. Despite the primitive and unhygienic living conditions in the Korean battle area, the fatality rate of the injured back-loaded to hospitals was little over half of the Second World War figures.

A very significant factor was the speed in which a casualty could be given specialized surgical treatment. One innovation of the Korean War was the use of helicopters for casualty evacuation. It was in Korea that the chopper proved its worth. Instead of a long, dangerous, and uncomfortable trip over sub-standard roads, the wounded soldier could be taken directly to a field surgical hospital in a few minutes. The U.S. army helicopter pilots would bring their choppers right into the front line positions, and the medics quickly became skilled in providing emergency treatment en route. Despite the fact that the earlier S-52 models airlifted the wounded in stretcher pods outside the fuselage, the medics were able to perform life-saving work in the air, even providing blood transfusions.

George Forty, a former tank officer, himself a client of the service, recalled that "the casevac chopper, with its … external pods (containing stretchers) became a regular sight in the battle area. It was estimated that they could normally get a casualty on to an operating table within an hour of his being wounded."[2]

Unfortunately, not everyone could be evacuated by helicopter. Lack of suitable helipads in the rough terrain at the sharp end, enemy artillery and mortar fire, weather conditions and, sometimes, heavy casualty loads and limited numbers of aircraft were all factors. In many cases it was necessary for harassed medical officers or orderlies to establish triage systems to ensure that the air evacuation could be most effectively utilized. Abdominal and head wounds, and those requiring immediate surgery normally got priority. Even so, there were a few cracks in the system. One Korean farmer was treated at an advanced dressing station for minor injuries, and went to sleep on a stretcher outside. Unfortunately, he chose a bed at the Category A section of the triage area and awoke from his slumbers to find himself strapped to the side of a Sikorsky helicopter, hundreds of feet in the air. On landing at the MASH he reportedly broke all speed records in fleeing to his native hillside.

Even without the helicopters, the professional and efficient casualty-handling procedures undoubtedly saved many lives. Dan Bordeleau was one of a number of PPCLI soldiers wounded in the forward area by Chinese artillery. Despite the severity of his wounds, he was conscious enough to be amazed at the speed and efficiency that he was treated and back-loaded.

Corporal Dan Bordeleau's experience was typical of many. As soon as he was hit, unit stretcher-bearers treated him. (In some cases an Royal Canadian Army Medical Corps medical orderly would be located in a rifle company, but there were not always enough of these specialists to go around.) Field and shell dressings were applied to stop the bleeding. "Our troops are trained to use the victim's dressing – none of the heroic use of your own – which you might need yourself next," Bordeleau recalled.

The next – and perhaps the most uncomfortable – part of the back-loading process was the trip to the Regimental Aid Post (RAP) on a stretcher (I believe that the expression is now a "litter.") This took place over undulating ground, through narrow communication trenches and possibly as far as a mile or more. While the unit supplied stretcher-bearers (often a secondary role of the battalion musicians) most casualties were carried back by Korean Service Corps porters – the overworked, underpaid and unsung heroes who kept the troops in the line supplied with the necessities of life.

At the RAP, Corporal Bordeleau was examined by the unit medical officer, who diagnosed his injuries, changed his blood-soaked dressings, and dispatched him by ambulance to the Advanced Dressing Station (ADS) – a part of the Canadian Field Ambulance. In some cases, the Field Ambulance might set up Casualty Collection Points (CCP) close to the line. Les Pike, a RCAMC veteran of Korea, later recalled that these were so far forward that he and his colleagues often found themselves in the PPCLI or RCR lines.

Bordeleau recalled, too, that he was fortunate in that he travelled to the ADS in the relative comfort of a "real, box ambulance" rather than one of the Battalion's litter jeeps that may have been handy, but were decidedly uncomfortable and exposed to all weathers. 28 Commonwealth Brigade was served by an Indian Field Ambulance, which eventually became the longest-serving Commonwealth unit in Korea.

From the ADS, Corporal Bordeleau was transported directly to the Common-wealth Military Hospital in Seoul. One of Canada's significant contributions to the Commonwealth Division was a 200-bed Casualty Clearing Station (CCS) near the Tangkok railhead. Casualties were sent back from Tangkok by road or rail – one U.S. innovation was the conversion of civilian-type coaches for rail use, with provision for stretchers – a distinctly smoother ride.

After treatment in Seoul, Bordeleau was airlifted to Kure, Japan, to the Commonwealth Base Hospital – a permanent building with every available facility. Following a lengthy stay there he was considered sufficiently recovered to be given recuperative duties. The light duty in question was a spell at the Haramura Battle School in the hills, and the corporal was no doubt relieved to eventually return to his battalion!

I can almost hear the TV addicts crying, "What about the MASH? You haven't mentioned the MASH!" Like all of the formations in Korea, the Commonwealth Division was served by a Mobile Army Surgical Hospital. *M*A*S*H* fans, if they could be transported back in time, would be disappointed with our facility – Norway's contribution to the Korean War effort. There were no unprofessional shenanigans, none of the male members of the unit paraded in female dress and the dedicated surgeons and medical staff carried out their duties in a professional and efficient manner. The Norwegian flag in the Pusan military cemetery com-memorates two Norwegian MASH members who gave their lives in Korea.

The 60 to 70-bed MASH was the most forward location where major surgery could be regularly performed, and patients usually remained there until they could be removed to other hospitals. During its stay in Korea, the Norwegian MASH treated almost 100,000 military and civilian casualties, many of them Common-wealth troops.

Overall, the Royal Canadian Army Medical Corps, together with their fellow medics from other Commonwealth countries, the RCASC ambulance drivers, the casevac helicopter pilots and our Scandinavian allies constituted a complex but highly efficient medical system. Many times equipment was in short supply and improvisation was the order of the day – the extremes of climate were a problem, as was the ever-present dust from paddy-fields fertilized with human waste.

The value of the work of the RCAMC members in Korea is reflected in the fact that they were awarded 15 decorations, (including one of the only eight Distin-guished Conduct Medals awarded to Canadians in the entire war) as well as 14 Mentions in Despatches. However, the evacuation process began at the unit level, and it is perhaps fitting that the poem at the start of this story is attributed to an RCR stretcher-bearer, Pat O'Connor who was killed in the line of duty on May 30, 1951.

THE NOT-SO-GENTLE SEX

Ruth Tenzer Feldman later recalled the actions of the only U.S. army nurse stationed in Korea at the outbreak of war. Captain Viola McConnell worked without sleep for over 48 hours caring for almost 700 evacuees on a freight vessel designed for 18 passengers. She received the Bronze Star for her work.

She was the first of a succession of many nurses from United Nations participants. Canada was not lacking here as many Canadian nursing sisters and matrons served in Commonwealth military hospitals – from sharp end field dressing stations to the Base Hospital in Kure, Japan.

Jessie Urquhart-Chenevert served in the Medical Corps for a quarter-century, including tours in Korea and Japan, recalled: "We were flown to Seoul, and then … to 25 Canadian Field Dressing Station at Tokchon. A field dressing station is normally a mobile surgical unit, but the CO had scrounged buildings and equipment from Canadians and Americans to make it very immobile." (At the time of Nursing Sister Urquhart's arrival, the war had entered its static phase, which allowed for more permanent installations.)

"The Nissen and Quonset huts accommodated two surgical, one medical and burn wards, an officers' ward and various associated departments. The arrival of the party brought the total of nursing sisters to eight. At first the presence of the ladies was not altogether welcome by the medical assistants, who had been working on their own until then. However, the nurses soon proved their worth and the nurses and MAs soon were working effectively as a team."

Conditions were rudimentary – no running water, and earth-floors with pot-bellied stoves for warmth and water heating. Patients' beds were low folding cots, which entailed a great deal of uncomfortable bending or kneeling to tend the patients.

At first, Lieutenant Jessie Urquhart and her cohorts wore the blue uniform with brass buttons and a starched veil, like those worn in home stations. This quickly proved impractical for field conditions, and khaki drill and battledress were soonsubstituted.

She later expressed her pride in her role: "Certainly living and working conditions were austere, even primitive. The working day was long and the duties arduous, both physically and emotionally, but there was such satisfaction in knowing that you were helping the sick and wounded Canadian soldiers return to some semblance of good health. There was also the camaraderie of doctors, nurses and medical assistants to help make it all bearable. It is not a year I would want to repeat, but it was a memorable year and one that I would not have missed."

Their work did not go unrecognized. Captain (Matron) Betty Pense and Lieutenant (N/S) Josephine MacDonald were decorated with the Royal Red Cross for their services.

Although the role of army nurses in the forward areas and the Commonwealth hospitals in Seoul and Kure is fairly well known, almost 40 RCAF flight nurses also served in the Korean War. Historian Carl Mills reports that these nursing officers were attached to the USAF to assist in casualty evacuation.

AS OTHERS SEE US

I once received a letter from an Australian nursing sister who was inquiring about a Canadian soldier whom she had treated for serious burns in the Korean War. It turned out that the soldier, Corporal Henry Cancade of The RCR, belonged to the Korea Veterans Association and I was able to put him in touch with Captain (Retired) "Babs" Probyn-Smith, RAANC.

Following is a letter which I received from Sister Probyn-Smith, which I think is an indication of the fine work of all the Commonwealth nurses in Korea – Canadian, British and Australian alike.

"With the burns. Your terrible cries and screams as the horrific pain would break through the analgesic barrier. You tried to be so brave as the constant, seemingly never-ending, treatment relentlessly challenged that courage.

"Such was one of our many patients of that savage Korean War. A young soldier, Corporal Henry Cancade, Royal Canadian Regiment, who was grossly wounded by a hootchie fire in Korea. Although his friends managed to cover his head and groin area and pull him from danger, he suffered terrible burns. Medical evacuated him from Korea to our large Commonwealth military general hospital at Kure, Japan. He came to our Australian military surgical Ward 4, this boy with his massive body wounds and burns.

"The medical teams, we army sisters and nurses, military doctors, orderlies, pathologists, pharmacists, physiotherapists, radiologists, padres, and others of the hospital staff, all of those skilled and caring people, treated and cared for this boy, along with others from the convoy. Cancade was in bad shape – horrific burns from the neck down, covering his back, arms and right hand, both legs and his right foot. He had extensive skin damage, and some bone damage also. During his time with us he had much skin grafting and repair. He was with us for many months, and slowly improved. He was nursed on what was known as a stryker frame, a narrow board bed with removable padded base. The whole thing turned, with the patient well fastened in, every two hours for his care and treatment.

"Cancade was a brave young man, but sometimes he, like others so wounded, would cry, and sometimes, quite often in fact, we, his nurses, would softly cry for him.

"We would tease him, and he would laugh – except when we called him 'our little boy.' Like many of the wounded there, when the sedation had lost its effect, despite the pain, he liked us to talk of Australia, and we nurses and orderlies would do so. We would quietly tell our stories as we treated his wounds – as we did with others so hurt.

"One day, the chief military surgeon, a Canadian, during his early morning rounds, told our 'Canny' that he was to be medically evacuated home to Canada. The Chief was wearing a gorrilla mask, from a local shop – which he often would wear at appropriate times. It usually got a good reception. We girls thought it had a lot of pizzaz and that it did more for him than the face he usually wore.

"And, in a few weeks, our boy had gone home.

"Soon our ward was admitting the medical convoys of newly wounded and sick men from the battles of Korea. And the wards once more were filled with battle stretchers with their wounded on the floor between the occupied beds.

"From its harsh beginning to the very end of the Korean War, we Australian and Commonwealth military army nurses treated and cared for thousands of wounded and sick troops of the Commonwealth and other UN forces. And a few POWs, Chinese and North Korean, at our military hospitals in Korea and Japan.

"All this was many years ago. Some of 'we girls' would wonder about those wounded men we had nursed then. We especially wondered if perhaps our badly hurt Corporal Cancade survived. The early inquiries we made about him gave us no reply. Now, nearly half a century later, after attending the dedication of our national Korean War memorial at Canberra and meeting again with some of our medical teams of those times, we decided 'to have another go.'

"Our Melbourne, Victoria KVA, with its helpful Canadian treasurer Gerry Steacy (who now lives in Melbourne), sent a photograph of our 'Cancade boy' along with details (I had these items from our time with him at our Kure Hospital 1952), to the main Canadian KVA centres in Ottawa and along the Pacific coast, and all of the good people there checked it out.

"One night recently I answered the phone and a Canadian voice said, 'This is your 68-year old little boy.' Much delighted talk revealed that our young Henry had been hospitalized for years of treatment and his limbs and body, so greatly damaged, were gradually repaired and rebuilt, with much rehabilitation, etc., with excellent results. Surely, his surgeon must have been the original Dr. Frankenstein.

"And now, I wish to thank all of you from Canada, and Australia, you kind and helpful people who healed that wounded lad of ours and who let we, his nurses and orderlies of that war, know that he survived that horrific stage of his life. We are grateful to you all for your attention and great kindness in this matter.

"Hello to you Canadian nurses we knew, and sometimes worked with in Korea and Japan, at 'our war.' And a special greeting also to you Canadian military men of that war, who we worked with, and cared for when you came wounded and sick to our Aussie wards."

AIR AMBULANCES OF KOREA

Arthur Young designed a bubble-canopied helicopter with a simple two-blade propeller. Manufactured by Bell Aircraft Corporation as the Model 47, its design survived for three decades. The two-blade rotor made a characteristic "chop-chop-chop" sound that led to the nick-name chopper. Along with the Sikorsky S-51 and S-55, it did a yeoman's duty in Korea as an air ambulance.

At the outbreak of the Korean War in June 1950, the few helicopters available were mainly for use as scouts. Within a few weeks, however, their use as nearly unstoppable medevac vehicles was recognized and utilized. Modifications by ground personnel were ingenious, as usual, and the versatility of the chopper was demonstrated for a whole generation.

The Sikorsky S-51 was on the spot and suffered the indignity of having a window removed and straps added to hold a stretcher in place. When Bell Model 47s appeared, they carried side pods with Plexiglas screens to protect the patient. The opening sequence of the television show *M*A*S*H* featured Alan Alda's concerned countenance bent over just such a device.

The introduction of rapid medevac had an immediate impact on military medical philosophy. Since Phillip of Macedon added surgeons to his army, the brutal reality of the battlefield dictated that the most seriously wounded were the last attended to. Speed was of the essence for casualties, and a doctor could save three or four moderately wounded men in the time required to save one seriously wounded (who might die of shock anyway after his guts were sewed back in his belly). The mathematics of triage (separating wounded into light, serious and massive injuries), were turned upside down by the helicopter. Instead of several bone-jarring hours in a truck or jeep, even the most seriously wounded could be whisked to a MASH in an hour or less. Battlefield mortality dropped precipitately and continues a downward trend.

Of course, the system was predicated on normal weather, which was not a feature of the Korean campaign. Canadian Corporal Tom Mackay had his right leg shattered in a bunker accident, but had to endure 11 hours in an ambulance while rain poured down on the helicopter fleet.

THE ORDNANCE FUNCTION

The Royal Canadian Ordnance Corps played an unspectacular, but vital role in supporting 25 Brigade. Supplies and equipment including vital ammunition stocks were held and used in the brigade's ordinance field park and detachments at some of the other service units such as the RCEME workshops spare parts platoon. RCOC personnel were also attached to each unit.

One particular sub-unit achieved a modicum of fame in an unusual role reversal:

Lack of widespread skin diseases – common to troops in hot, damp climates (and Korea was a land of extreme temperature) was partly due to a group of unsung heroes – the Mobile Laundry and Bath Unit, provided by the Ordnance Corps.

The unit was established close to the line, usually at an engineer's water point. Troops were trucked from the line and were able to receive hot showers and obtain an issue of clean clothing. Facilities were not fancy, usually consisting of a number of shower heads, duckboards for the bathers, and perhaps a few benches. Lingering was not encouraged, as capacity was limited and there was usually a line of grubby soldiers waiting for their turn. The installation was not for the modest, as screening was, at best, negligible (although in winter attempts were made to bring the whole works into a marquee-type tent.)

Despite derisory remarks (bathers felt that the ordinance staff deliberately waited until everyone was covered with soap and then turned off the water) the MLBU served a very useful purpose. Its proximity to the sharp end was shown by the fact that the first Chinese prisoners taken by 25 Canadian Brigade had surrendered to the MLBU!

WHITE WEBBING AND WHIZZ-BANGS

So went the words of one of the popular ditties enjoyed by our troops in Korea, which described the misfortunes of an infantryman on R&R leave in Tokyo whose dress failed to meet the standards of a Canadian Provost Corps (C Pro C) NCO on patrol.

In fact, the members of the Commonwealth Division Provost Company and their fellow military gendarmerie spent a great deal of their time around the sharp end, performing duties which were often unpopular, always unglamorous and rarely appreciated.

When the first Canadians arrived in Korea, Sergeant Bill Larson accompanied 2PPCLI. He recalled that discipline was frequently rough and ready. In fact, one of the tasks of the first serious offenders was to build their own stockade, which eventually led to the establishment of a regimental slammer where many hard bargains were taught the error of their ways in order to perform well as infantry-men and junior NCOs in the battles that lay ahead. It is perhaps appropriate that the Patricias' CO, Col. Jim Stone, later became the army's provost marshal.

As more Canadians arrived in theatre, so did more Provost Corps members. While the behaviour of troops in Japan in transit, on training or on Rest and Recuperation leave in Tokyo was monitored with a watchful but indulgent eye, the traditional image of the meathead gleefully examining possible invalid passes or checking minor dress irregularities was dissipated. As in Korea, Canadians worked well as part of integrated Commonwealth units with members of the Royal Military Police and the Royal Australian Army Provost Corps.

Sometimes improvisation was introduced, for example, at the Canadian battle school. There were no C Pro C in camp and no guardroom facilities; offenders were secured to massive girders in a wrecked transmission tower.

In mainland Korea, the primary functions of the Commonwealth Division Provost Company were traffic control and security. Again most of the unit was British, with two Canadian and one Australian section. The company commander was invariably a Canadian – Major Bob Luker, being the first to hold the position. In addition, major units had their own C Pro C members, assisted where necessary by unit regimental police.

Traffic control was, in a way, reminiscent of the Italian campaign in the Second World War. The terrain was rugged, roads were poor and usually narrow, and, despite the Herculean work of the engineers, often impassable. In the hills, narrow tracks bounded by steep cliffs and precipitous drops often formed main supply routes and common axes for several units and formations, while road blockages caused by vehicles sliding off the track into glutinous paddy fields were common. The problems were compounded by a limited number of bridges and ferries across the Imjin River, which carried vehicles from the base areas and supply dumps to the forward positions.

Lionel Genest, who served with the Van Doos' provost detachment, recalled: "We had this stretch of the road called the 'Mad Mile' which was in direct view of the enemy and had to be concealed by camouflage nets. Jeeps, carriers and other vehicles would dash along this stretch to try and get through as quickly as possible. Our job was to try and get them to keep their speed down, as in dry weather the dust they kicked up would give them away. Because of tasks like this, we had to have unit RPs to help us as we were too thin on the ground."

Traffic control was always a problem. Pintail in particular, was a one-way pontoon bridge and traffic had to be controlled according to priority. Ambulances almost always had right of way. In the case of heavy fighting, the green light went to ammunition supply vehicles. To add to the MPs' problems at the bridges, the enemy would float mines and debris down the river, while certain classes of vehicles had to be rerouted to spare the structure. Colonel Andrew Ritchie, in *Watchdog*, a history of the Canadian Provost Corps, described another gruesome task which befell the military policemen.

The Imjin rose and fell rapidly due to rains and melting snow and ice, and the floating debris that arrived at the crossings often included dead bodies, some of them resulting from earlier fighting. The MPs' task was to recover and identify them. One story described the work of WO2 Chambers, who froze the cadaver, lifted a fingerprint and identified the victim as a missing Canadian soldier.

Generally, the Provost were too busy to deal with minor disciplinary problems, although an integrated special investigations unit dealt with a number of serious crimes, including two murder cases. From time to time, senior officers would "get a hair up their ass" and instructions would go out to improve saluting habits, avoid sloppy dress or remind troops to wear steel helmets and carry only their authorized weapons (to the chagrin of those who felt that possession of a captured – usually found – burp gun or other non-issue weapon gave them a "Combat Kelly" cachet). However, these minor transgressions were usually handled (if at all) at unit level.

Far more serious were the traffic infractions. The narrow tracks invited head-on collisions, as the British, Australian and New Zealanders were not always wholly accustomed to driving on the right-hand side and skids off the road into ditches, paddy fields or worse were frequent. A more serious result of excessive speed was the dust clouds that attracted hostile artillery fire. Colonel Ritchie later described the chagrin of the MPs when the units usually disregarded reports of these offences or, at most, imposed minor penalties on the culprits.

Some offenders had a good reason to dislike C Pro C members. Many Korea veterans have bitter memories of 25 Field Detention Barracks near Seoul. This facility hosted malefactors from all of the Division and, to say the least, it was no holiday. Detainees were on the hop from 0500-2100 daily, with no respite. Stories of beatings, harsh treatment, and even fatalities as a result of incarceration abounded. While these may or may not all be true, life in the line was so bad for the infantryman that if detention was to be deterrent, things had to be much worse in the slammer to avoid a flood of delinquents.

Other tasks that fell to the Provost Corps were security tasks (guerrillas could appear at any time, anywhere), escorts for VIPs, and the handling of captured or defecting enemy. That they shared the lot of their fellow Canadians in Korea is evidenced by the fact that three members of C Pro C lost their lives in the war.

To quote Charles I, in the 17th century: "The provost...is but one man and must correct many and therefore he cannot be beloved." Our Canadian Provost Corps members in Korea, together with their Commonwealth partners, may not always have been beloved, but every infantryman whose neck was saved by a timely supply of ammunition for his supporting artillery, or who was back-loaded safely by ambulance, owes them, at least, a modicum of appreciation.

THE SPIRITUAL SIDE

Unit padres were very much a part of the unit, and undoubtedly contributed a great deal to the high morale enjoyed by the Commonwealth troops (we must not forget the naval chaplains – *Athabaskan*'s chaplain, whose first name was appropriately Horatio, was one of the first RCN casualties when he was injured during a typhoon).

The army chaplains were a mix of Second World War veterans and hastily recruited clergymen who responded to an appeal from Colonel Sly Stone, the army's principal chaplain, to dioceses across Canada. The newcomers were far from callow youths – Padre Matt Roberts was 37 years old when he left his Newfoundland parish to serve in Korea. Walter Mann joined from his Whitehorse Catholic church at the same age.

Roberts later recalled that he was paid the princely sum of $234 a month, plus another $60 in marriage allowance. His introduction to military life was brief, consisting of an officer familiarization course at Camp Petawawa. One of the guest speakers was LCol. Peter Bingham, of the RCR, who told the potential chaplains what a commanding officer expected of his padre: "He should minister to all ranks, and not forget the CO, as often the chaplain is the only person in whom the commander can confide."

Colonel Stone reminded the new chaplains that they were, in effect, clergymen in uniform and if they neglected to make a spiritual contribution to the troops they would not be doing their job. However, in the battle area the task of the padres, both Roman Catholic and Protestant, involved far more than "Padre's Hour" and conversion of the heathen element. Before their arrival in Korea, chaplains were given extensive training in first aid so that they could render physical as well as spiritual assistance to the wounded.

Matt Roberts was fortunate in that the senior brigade chaplain, a Second World War Military Cross winner named Joe Cardy, chose to break in the new men gently. For the first few months Roberts was assigned to the field dressing station, the RCEME workshop and where perhaps his services were often needed, the detention barracks.

Padre Al Fowler, writing in *Dialogue,* the Chaplain Branch's newsletter, recalled that Major Cardy encountered Padre Roberts and invited him on a trip to the sharp end. The two chaplains were visiting a dug-in Sherman tank when the enemy (obviously no respecters of the cloth) opened fire with mortars. Both officers gained the cover of the tank, and Joe Cardy's main concern appeared to be the effect on Principal Chaplain Stone if he lost the newcomer on his first day in Korea.

Padre Roberts eventually joined 1RCR where he was able to curtail Colonel Bingham's welcoming briefing by reminding him that he had already been given the speech in Petawawa.

While many of his British counterparts were assigned all sorts of extra-regimental duties such as the officers' mess wine member, Colonel Bingham allowed

Roberts to devote his time to his proper duties. And indeed, they kept him busy. When the battalion was in the line, the padre made it a point to visit every company at least once a week, but usually much more frequently. During his tour he would talk to as many front line troops as possible – not necessarily on religious matters, but frequently to discuss family or personal problems. In many cases, a judicious word or two in the right ears, could partly or wholly resolve these issues simply by providing someone with whom the soldier could talk in confidence. Anxiety problems, which today are dealt with by batteries of psychologists and counselors, were often dealt with by the chaplains. "Tell your troubles to the padre!" was not necessarily an empty statement.

In his book *The Korea Experience,* Walter Mann recounts his life in the line as a Catholic chaplain. He remembers one enemy attack when, despite the concerns of the brigade commander, he went forward and spent the night assisting in the evacuation of many wounded, and granting absolution to the dead. He recalled, "We weren't supposed to say Mass in the front lines, but I wanted to do so for the boys … sometimes we had to hit the deck as they shelled very close to us."

Matt Roberts said he was fortunate in that he had only one fatal casualty to deal with during his tour with the RCR. In these cases, a brief prayer of committal would be offered in the battalion area, and a more formal short service held in the rear, after which the bodies were conveyed to the UN Military Cemetery in Pusan. (American dead were flown home for burial.)

In reserve, Padre's Hour formed part of the routine activity. Heeding Colonel Stone's admonition, Padre Roberts carried out his pastoral duties – so well that over a score of soldiers presented themselves for confirmation at Seoul's Anglican Cathedral, an excellent achievement as his flock numbered perhaps 600 souls. When the battalion was in rest, drum-head services would be conducted; usually well attended.

One of the less pleasant, but necessary, parts of the padre's work was the passing on of bad news from home. Matt Roberts conceded that his parish experience in Newfoundland helped here. At times adaptability and stretching the rules was necessary – one Protestant chaplain told me that he had been called to a dying Catholic soldier who had asked to hold the priest's crucifix. The padre had only his army issue clasp knife, which the fatally wounded infantryman kissed before expiring. The padre told me that he felt that his Maker would excuse this apparent blasphemy on his part.

The padres were fortunate in one respect. Because their duties entailed weekly visits to Brigade HQ and often trips to liaise with local missionaries, they were perhaps more mobile than most battalion officers. Indeed padre's driver was one of the most sought after jobs in unit transport sections.

The padre's life in Korea was no bed of roses. One British padre, Reverend

Stanley Davies, was captured with the Gloucestershire Regiment and spent years in captivity in North Korea. During this period he continued to minister to his flock, using a Chinese drinking mug for a chalice and a paten carved from scrap wood by a fellow officer. Padre Davies received a well-deserved MBE for his devotion to duty.

The Canadian chaplains also had it rough. Padre Johnson had his jeep blown from under him by a mine. Like Padre Roberts, Chaplain Alex Filshie with PPCLI was always on hand in the battalion CP whenever patrols were out, ready to offer help and comfort in case of casualties.

When the First Commonwealth Division was formed, a Canadian, Major J. Lupien, was appointed the First Senior Chaplain.

The services of Canadian chaplains did not go unrecognized, four of them, Captains Filshie, Fortin, Johnson and MacGregor received the MBE, while four more were Mentioned in Despatches.

After visiting Korea, Dr. Nicholson, moderator of the United Church wrote "our churches have carefully chosen men for the office of chaplain – men who have an easy approach … men who have mature experience of peoples' troubles, hopes and trials." The soldiers in their care would, I am sure, say "amen to that!"

NO PAY, NO UNIFORMS, NO GLORY: A SALUTE TO THE RICE-BURNERS

Often overlooked in the history books, the "Rice-Burners," performed an essential role. It is perhaps no exaggeration to state that without their efforts the defence of the Jamestown Line would have been difficult, if not impossible. Korean War veterans remember them with gratitude and affection. For some reason we saw few, if any, mules in Korea. On the other hand, we needed a great deal of material, for permanently occupied positions on the heights were far more than we used in our Hong Kong exercises. Moving into position with our basic arms, ammunition, rations and bedding was in itself a challenge. Obviously, we needed help to bring up from the jeep-heads the supplies, water, ammunition, equipment and defensive stores for life on the line (not forgetting, of course, the 24-quart-bottle cases of Asahi beer).

The answer lay in an organization of unsung heroes of a forgotten war. Just as Kipling's India had its Gunga Dins, the UN forces in Korea had the Korean Service Corps (KSC) and its predecessors.

Millions of Koreans served in the ROK army, which, by the war's end, developed from an ill-equipped and poorly trained body into a fighting machine second to none. Others served in a less spectacular, and poorly rewarded, fashion.

At first, units recruited civilian porters to carry supplies to forward positions.

Recruited is perhaps a euphemism. Able-bodied Koreans were simply rounded up and put to work. Niceties such as pay, uniforms and even rations were incidental. Many of the Rice-Burners (as opposed to "hay-burners") were entirely dependent on the generosity of their employers. Eventually, sporadic payments of a few cents a day were distributed.

Porters were expected to carry a minimum of about 25 kilos for 5 kilometres each day. While this may not seem a lot, most of those kilometres were usually through very hilly and rough country. This feat was achieved with the aid of what many Korea veterans consider to be the most important piece of equipment used in Korea, the A-frame.

An A-frame consisted of three poles lashed together to form a crude triangle with shoulder straps of roughly woven straw. A load, often far in excess of the standard 25-kg, was attached and carried on the porter's back. This primitive apparatus, together with the incredible stamina of the bearers, led rise to the boast "give a Korean an A-frame and he could move the world."

Heavy and awkward loads were not the only problems facing the Korean porters. As their ultimate destination was the sharp end, they shared the dangers of the line infantry, without the protection of steel helmets or defensive weapons. They were frequently called on to accompany reconnaissance in force or other combat operations. I can remember patrolling in front of my own position seeking a suspected enemy patrol in the area, accompanied by a very unwilling porter whose function was to demand the surrender of any enemy encountered. Many a Canadian, wounded in the line, was carried to the helicopter or jeep ambulance on a stretcher borne by Korean porters, frequently under fire.

In the early days, Korean porters developed strong affinities with their parent units. Some acquired cast-off or donated uniform items and proudly wore the unit shoulder-flashes and other insignia. They worked with designated porter guides from the Commonwealth units, who usually established an excellent rapport with the Koreans. Most Korea veterans will recall the sight of a train of perhaps 50 porters, heavily-laden with the necessities of front line life, steadily making their way over rough mountain tracks through atrocious weather, to our forward positions.

Gradually, other Korean nationals who worked for the units on an informal basis joined them. Abandoned or orphaned youngsters worked as houseboys, *mama-sans* served in rear-echelon units as laundresses and the more educated Koreans were in great demand as interpreters. Feeding and accommodation were provided in porter villages and units would often arrange for those helpers fortunate enough to be able to visit their families, to take along gifts of food, cigarettes and other luxuries. Some of the well-established porter villages were equipped with moonshine stills that would be the envy of Ozark mountaineers, producing a foul-tasting, but potent brew. Many Canadians, at one time or another sampled this oriental version of "Kickapoo Joy Juice," to their cost.

By 1951, the Korean Service Corps was established on a more military basis. Organized KSC units served under Republic of Korea army officers and NCOs. The 120th KSC Regiment was assigned to the Commonwealth Division. It had three battalions, each of up to 2000 men. One was assigned to the divisional engineers and worked on road repairs and other tasks – the rest were allotted to other units as carriers, vehicle loaders and for other fatigue duties.

Discipline was strict and summary. At least three veterans wrote of occasions where Korean workers were accused of minor thefts and executed on the spot by one of their officers. Ron Larby, in his *Armoured on the Left, Signals on the Right* wrote that an accused, who had apparently taken a few cigarettes, was first ordered to dig his own grave, and then dispatched with a pistol shot. Robert Hepenstall, in *Find the Dragon* quotes a Canadian NCO who felt that sometimes the loyalty of porters was suspect, and believed that North Korean sympathizers in the KSC ranks had removed mines by night which he and his comrades had previously laid during the day.

Nor were the porters unscathed by war's perils. At least five of their number died when 3RCR was heavily attacked in May 1953.

By the war's end, the KSC had a strength of over 100,000. I have seen memorials in Seoul to the famed "Capitol Division" and other distinguished Korean units and formations, but nothing to commemorate the unsung heroes of KSC and their predecessors. If any Korea veterans should find such a monument on their visits to the Land of the Morning Calm, I would be pleased to hear of it. Meanwhile, we remember with gratitude, respect and affection, the Rice-Burners.

Korean porters help to bring a wounded Canadian to a medical aid post. Nicknamed the "Rice-Burners," the locally employed Koreans were invaluable to the UN forces as auxiliaries. (DND)

ABOVE: *Plenty of suds. Canadian breweries were generous with donations of beer to troops in Korea. As a gesture of appreciation, Canadian engineers dedicated a bridge to John Labatt. The unit's "tac sign" normally displayed the figure "50" on a blue background – this was suitably embellished to resemble the 'Anniversary Ale' label. (DND)*

OPPOSITE PAGE: *Although the soldiers are shown wearing their helmets, Canadian soldiers in Korea normally preferred to wear their soft caps and tuques. The threat from shrapnel did not outweigh the discomfort factor. (DND)*

❧ LIFE ON THE LINE

THE INFANTRYMAN'S EXISTENCE IN KOREA was, in some ways, like that of his First World War predecessor. He lived a troglodyte life in an underground bunker (which he may have constructed himself) and would leave it to defend his position from an adjacent fire trench. However, here the similarities end.

While "Tommy Atkins" in 1915 France would be surrounded by muddy ground, with the enemy entrenched a few hundred yards off, the Korean soldier would be dug in on a hilltop with his Chinese or North Korean adversary a mile or so away.

The hootch where he slept was usually excavated into the side of a hill away from the enemy, and roofed with pickets, sandbags, and earth. If he was lucky, a poncho or tarpaulin in the overhead cover would help render his home waterproof. In time, refinements such as flooring and walls were made from discarded ration boxes, bunks of pickets, and signal wire (or in some cases "liberated" stretchers), and furnishings utilizing wooden beer cases would be added. He would usually share his home with one or more comrades.

If he were lucky, an improvised space heater using diesel fuel would provide some comfort in the bitter winters, while candles sometimes provided light. In this cramped area would also be his sleeping bag (not used in the line), his weapon, equipment, rations, and personal possessions.

Routine in the line was usually the same. A few minutes before first light he would be roused from his fitful sleep. Rising and dressing were little problem.

Although he had a sleeping bag, he would use it as a mattress and use blankets for warmth. Too many soldiers had been caught in their sleeping bags and killed in sudden enemy attacks, and the lesson had been learned. For the same reason, most forward troops slept at least partly dressed.

He would then move to his forward defensive position where, with his comrades, he would stand-to in case of an enemy dawn attack. As daylight came, he would stand-down. During this period he would no doubt be visited by his platoon commander or sergeant and given a Paludrine antimalarial tablet.

After sentries had been posted in the forward positions, the rest of the platoon would wash, shave, and clean up. In good weather this would be an easy task, but often this would be a matter of finding a way to dry out sodden blankets or break through the ice in washbowls.

Breakfast would be next. If a company headquarters was nearby, a fairly hot meal might be brought up in insulated containers. Usually the soldiers relied on C-rations prepared individually over sterno heaters. Sometimes the section would have a dixie of tea or coffee. The next activity was an inspection of the soldier, his weapon, and his hootch. After that, the day's work would begin.

Usually, this consisted of improving defences and living quarters. If there was fog on the forward slopes, improvements or additions to the barbed-wire obstacles might be carried out. Otherwise most work would take place on rear slopes or in other areas away from enemy observation. Much of the work was by pick and shovel – digging new bunkers, communication trenches, or garbage or latrine pits. Sometimes work would be carried out in fallback positions in the rear.

Meanwhile, the section would take turns as sentries and observers in forward weapon trenches, observing and reporting enemy activity. Midday and evening meals would be taken and, before last light, the platoon would again stand-to.

However, the day's work was not yet done. After dusk, the supplies and rations would arrive and be distributed. Orders would be received and passed on.

Sentries would be posted in pairs and relieved regularly. The night would be punctuated by random harassing fire at pre-set targets where the enemy might be working at night. Patrols might be sent out, including regular listening patrols a few hundred yards forward of our position. In addition, work on the forward slopes – such as wiring and laying mines – may be carried out under cover of darkness.

All in all, if a soldier was able to snatch three or four hours of sleep he would be lucky! Regardless of this, the front-line infantryman was relatively healthy and able to perform his function during the infrequent moments of sheer terror that punctuated his weeks of boredom.

~ ~ ~ ~ ~ ~ ~ ~ ~ ~

FOOD FOR THOUGHT

To aviation buffs a P-38 is the twin-boomed Lockheed Lightning fighter, while small-arms experts may identify it as an effective sidearm. Korea veterans may not recognize it by this nomenclature, but it is in fact a piece of equipment that they have probably used more than any other. This is the identification code name for the C-ration can opener, a little hinged metal doohickey most of us wore with our dogtags.

Feeding the multinational troops of the First Commonwealth Division was an achievement second only to the miraculous use of loaves and fishes over 1,900 years earlier.

The overall Commonwealth commander in the theatre was LGen Sir Horace Robertson, an Australian. Naturally, he hoped that the Commonwealth troops would use Aussie rations – Australia, like most Commonwealth countries, could use the dollars. In fact, after the limited British scale of issue, I found that Aussie food was excellent (including breakfasts of steak and eggs). However, Brigadier Rockingham dug in his heels, insisted that his troops were used to American food, and Canadians spent most of the Korean War on U.S. rations.

The overall supply problem for the Division was complicated by the fact that generally the British, Australian and New Zealand troops lived on U.S. C-rations in the line and a combination of Australian and locally purchased fresh rations and British "compo" rations in reserve. The Canadian Brigade enjoyed U.S. rations, while the Indian Field Ambulance had its own special food. This problem did not apply only to rations. Equipment, weapons and ammunition varied between the national units, necessitating, among other things, an additional 120 vehicles to pick up and deliver these from different supply points.

While C-rations undoubtedly had a high calorific value (I gained almost 80 pounds during the 18 months that they constituted most of my diet), they tended towards monotony. They arrived in cartons of six individual boxes, each of which contained one day's rations. (The large cartons were much sought after for lining bunker walls or for fuel.) Each individual ration contained meal units, which included such delicacies as ground meat and spaghetti, hamburger patties, chicken stew, beans (allegedly) with pork, and ham and lima beans. There was also a "B" unit, which included a jelly or chocolate disc, a small tin of jam and some crackers. A can of fruit was also included, as well as a goody package which contained matches, chewing gum, coffee, sugar, powdered milk, a disposable can-opener and – a real treasure to those so addicted – a package of 20 cigarettes. To complete one's dining pleasure, three plastic spoons were also included in the box. The food could be heated and eaten straight from the can, and the "B" unit cans made good drinking cups, so dishwashing in the line was reduced to a minimum.

C-rations could be eaten cold, heated over sterno cans or solid fuel "tommy-cookers" or, in bulk, immersed in dixies of boiling water until they were hot. My first experience of these was on the train from Pusan to the front, where the dining car proved to be a U.S. cook-sergeant dishing out a can apiece (there was no choice – you got what came up in the draw).

Out of the line Canadians were usually well fed. Where possible, fresh meat and vegetables were provided, and the cooks worked wonders on the M-39 cookers and anything else that they could improvise. Occasionally British "ten-in-one" rations would find their way into Canadian hands. These were designed to feed one man for ten days, ten men for one day or any combination in between. While many of their contents were unpalatable to Canadian tastes, they did contain several tasty items, such as oatmeal cookies and canned bacon. The ubiquitous bully beef was a British staple, and, of course, lots of tea (boiled with condensed milk).

Another treat was the U.S. 101-pack ration supplement. This contained all sorts of goodies including candies, more canned fruit, razor blades, lighter flints, candles, cigarettes and even chewing and pipe tobacco. The effect of chewing tobacco on unsuspecting novices to this addiction was awesome. Also included was Hershey chocolate bars (this gave rise to a derisive mocking of our U.S. allies "goddamn, the Fourth of July and *NO* Hershey bars"). Less popular were K-rations which were supposed to provide one meal. The omelettes were tasteless and almost impossible to heat over our sterno burners without becoming charred on the outside and cold in the centre. Fruit, other goodies and seven cigarettes came with these. On Koje-do, North Korean POWs were given time-expired K-rations (minus the cigarettes) to supplement their rice and vegetable rations. Some of us felt that, like Peter Worthington's gift of ham and lima beans to the Chinese, this may have constituted cruel and unusual punishment.

Occasionally, too, we would receive cans of British self-heating soup. This consisted of a can of tomato or oxtail soup with a chemical heating agent in the centre, which could come to boil in a very short time. It was ideal for wet and wintry nights in the slit trenches.

Thanks to organizations at home, food packages came along from time to time. (I remember one especially appetizing gift box from an Australian ladies' patriotic association.) When we were out on the line, we also visited the NAAFI road-houses for tea and buns, or the U.S. Red Cross mobile canteens which provided free coffee and donuts. Nor must we forget the staple beverage of North American troops. Its importance was evident on arrival in Pusan where, on the quayside, a large sign proudly proclaimed the presence of a Quartermaster Co., a Coca-Cola bottling unit.

Kimchi was a particularly potent form of Korean sauerkraut. Each family had its own jealously guarded recipe, but normal additions included garlic, hot peppers, other spices, and perhaps dried fish. It was an ideal food additive during the Korean winters and there is little doubt of its effectiveness as a blood purifier in summer. Its potency was unquestioned.

While some brave Canadians would obtain kimchi from the Korean porters to supplement their C-rations, all in all, our cooks and supply services did a pretty good job of keeping us well fed. I would be remiss if I did not also credit the porters of the Korean Service Corps who carried the C-rations, water and, of course, the Asahi beer quota to our forward positions. To our Service Corps and unit cooks and their British counterparts of the Army Catering Corps (ACC) a belated "thank you" from a grateful – and well-fed – Korea vet.

POTABLES ON THE PARALLEL

Over the centuries, soldiers and booze have been closely associated — sometimes unjustly. Certainly the ingenuity of Canadian soldiers over the last three wars in obtaining and concealing intoxicants of all kinds is almost legendary. (One popular story from Korea tells of a British medical officer who reported to his CO that he had discovered two cases of beriberi. The alleged response was to "give it to the Canadians, they'll drink anything.")

While some of the legends may be based on fact, in most cases the troops, particularly those in the sharp end have often been sorely maligned.

Perhaps the most sobering influence on our troops in Korea was lack of opportunity. While the troops in the "A" and "B" echelons and the supporting units were able to establish wet canteens, these were lacking in the forward company areas. In the first place, after digging weapon pits, communication trenches, mortar positions, living bunkers and latrines, very few infantrymen had the energy, the space, the time or the materials to construct a suitable drinking hole.

The nature of the job itself discouraged excessive drinking. A soldier on watch in his weapon slit would often find it difficult enough to stay awake for his two-hour stag without the soporific effects of over-indulgence. Although a number of unsubstantiated stories continue to make the rounds regarding heroic deeds performed under the influence of "Dutch Courage" a cool head and quick reactions were essential in battle.

The most deciding factor, however, was one of supply. Not only did the unit ration the quantity, but Korean porters had to carry every bottle to forward positions. Their numbers were limited, and other items such as ammunition, food, defensive stores, fuel and water were also back packed by these unsung heroes on primitive wooden A-frames. More operationally vital supplies often superseded the beer ration.

The prevalent brand of beer was Japanese Asahi lager distributed through the

British Navy, Army and Air Force Institutes – the NAAFI. This nectar was packed in cases of 24 quart bottles, each individually covered with straw. The wooden cases were greatly prized as makeshift furniture, fuel for wood-burning space heaters and toilet seats in field latrines. Asahi beer cost about 18 cents a bottle (even so, the impecunious British troops soon discovered that NAAFI would replace any broken bottles in exchange for bottlenecks with the caps still intact. They learned to remove caps without a mark, drink the beer, replace the caps, smash the bottles and return the necks for replacement.)

The bottles, too, had a certain value. By tying a piece of gasoline-soaked string around the body of the bottle, lighting it and, when it had burned out, tapping the head of bottle sharply, one would be left with a fairly serviceable drinking glass. Manufacture of these items was a fairly lucrative cottage industry among the few Korean residents remaining in the forward areas. Unsubstantiated legends also credit one Victoria Cross winner with retaking a Chinese-held position by throwing empty Asahi bottles at the enemy when he ran out of grenades.

Occasionally beer from home arrived. John Labatt's brewery, in particular, was generous in shipping samples of its product to Canadians in the field. In fact, one RCE unit expressed its appreciation by naming one of its bridges "Mr. John Labatt's Anniversary Bridge" to commemorate a specific brew. Other sources of the beverage were the UK brewers (through NAAFI) and, in Japan and some base areas, the Australian forces' brewery.

Perhaps the most potent legal beverage was the rum ration, which came in stone crocks marked "SRD." There were many versions of the meaning of "SRD," the most common being "Service Rum, Diluted." If SRD was diluted I would caution anyone against drinking spirit neat! It was normally issued in cold or wet weather, and each platoon would receive about a quart daily. Logistical problems precluded the use of regular mixes, although the U.S. Army Quartermaster Corps did in fact have a Coca-Cola bottling unit in Pusan. The recipient would usually drink his rum straight or add a mix of (chlorinated) water and lemonade powder, coffee or tea. In my platoon most of the members were teenagers, and despite the pleas of the old sweats, we would add the ration to a dixie of hot tea and issue a mug of the brew on conclusion of a sentry's watch, or on return from patrol.

In addition to the rum ration, senior NCOs and officers were allowed to purchase a bottle of whisky and a bottle of one other beverage (gin, rum, brandy etc.) each month. The cost was about a dollar a bottle. Although, theoretically, the rank and file were not allowed spirituous liquors, the ingenuity of the Canadian soldier came to the fore. Large loaves of bread in parcels from home were not intended to provide relief from C-ration crackers and hardtack, but often, hollowed out, concealed bottles of stimulating beverages.

While the NAAFI controlled most spirituous liquors, they frequently overestimated the demand for more exotic potions and were left with large stocks of Grand Marnier, Apricot Brandy, Creme-de-Menthe and similar fancy drinks. In exchange for a few bucks, the dollar-starved NAAFI staff might be prepared to let thirsty soldiers have a few bottles of these.

I remember on one occasion watching with admiration and horror as a Kiwi gunner "chug-a-lugged" a whole bottle of Benedictine. I once made the mistake of ordering a case of 96 bottles of Guinness for my platoon and found that the beer-drinking minority had become so addicted to Asahi that I could not unload any of it. The laxative effect of the stout alone (see use of Asahi beer box, above) necessitated mixing it and I was able to obtain a case of Moet & Chandon champagne at about 60 cents a bottle. This resulted in what would undoubtedly be a godsend to the detractors of the military today – a scruffy infantryman digging out pork and beans from a can and washing it down with messtins full of Black Velvet.

One aspect of our access to alcoholic beverages directly or indirectly affected most of the troops in the line. For some reason – I believe that it was pressure on the U.S. War Department by womens' temperance groups – our American allies were dry. This may have been to provide business for the Coca-Cola bottling unit mentioned above. In any case, they had the good stuff – space heaters, flashlights, batteries, .45 calibre pistols and other items that made life in the line more bearable. They also had lots of disposable income – a particularly attractive consideration to the British troops who were officially forbidden to possess the U.S. "scrip" which was a necessity for making PX purchases or using the U.S. clubs in Tokyo on R&R leave. Bootlegging operations reminiscent of the Capone-era were commonplace – you had only to visit a U.S. supply depot with a partly-concealed bottle of Scotch and the world was your oyster! The impecunious British found to their delight that the going rate for Asahi beer was the then unheard of $1.00 for a quart bottle.

Not all the beverages came from authorized sources. Former RCEME member Don Randall, writing in the *Uijongbu Club* newsletter, recalls that "those of who, against orders, tried the Korean home-made spirits kept in a crock in farmhouse kitchens will not even yet forget its fragrance, taste and kick. Surely some of you … have experienced unsteadiness and perhaps a fall into a moonlit rice paddy or worse after a night foray into the boondocks!"

In some cases the results were more severe. After celebrating St. Patrick's Day with a concoction of wood alcohol-based spirits, several members of 2PPCLI succumbed – four of them fatally. The Patricia's commanding officer, Lt.-Col. "Big Jim" Stone, reportedly had the battalion pass in front of the bodies in single file – a brutal but salutary object-lesson. Certainly the effect of locally produced liquors were not to be ignored and signs such as "Korean Whisky KILLS" were prominently displayed along roads in the Division area.

To quote Don Randall once again: "It is difficult ... for many of the Korea vets to think of their general experiences in the war in terms which are unrelated to alcohol ... In my unit, non-drinkers were rare and suspected of being possessed of other unsociable habits." Don recalls that, while in Japan, his group added another dimension to their imbibing experience by sending their houseboy to purchase supplies of saki. Notwithstanding these experiences and the undoubted excesses that occurred on R&R leave and in transit, alcohol abuse by the line troops was fairly rare. As Don Randall recalls, "we Canadians were trusted with alcohol to a greater extent than were American soldiers."

To quote John Dryden: "Drinking is the soldier's pleasure!" Thanks to NAAFI, the Canadian brewers and those intelligent supply authorities, that pleasure was not denied to our troops in Korea.

WAR OR NO WAR: IF YOU GOTTA GO, YOU GOTTA GO!

Disposal of waste – of all sorts – was a problem. There was no garbage pick-up in the line. Again, training paid off. The Army Handbook of Hygiene and Sanitation in the Field, which had provided so many sleep-inducing periods of instruction in Canada, became a much sought-after reference book. It was here that the Medical Corps sanitation NCOs, whose role was less glamorous than the field medics, proved their worth.

While rats, mice, insects and other disease-carriers could not be completely eliminated, their efforts were discouraged by careful burning and disposal of waste food and materials. (The Black Watch, mindful of the number of stray cats in their area, produced a classic order for the effective use of these animals in rodent control.)

However, the disposal of night soil provided the greatest challenge to our ingenuity. "Cat sanitation" (individual scrapings) was out of the question — space was limited in the forward positions. Similarly, the trench method was not practicable, as the positions would have to be occupied for months, or even years. The answers were the "Desert Rose" and "Thunderbox."

The "Desert Rose" — introduced in North Africa by the U.S. Eighth Army, consisted of a hole about 18 inches deep, in the bottom of which were placed pebbles (for drainage). A tube was then placed upright in the hole, and the remaining space filled with soil or sand. Shell or rocket containers made ideal tubes, and the hole (no pun intended) made an excellent urinal — the recycled Asahi beer being dispersed well below the ground surface.

Generally, these proved effective, although they had one small fault. Hootchies, were usually built below ground level for protection. Many ingenious hootchie builders had improvised space heaters from ammunition cases with chimneys of — you guessed it — shell or rocket container tubes. These extended about 18 inches above ground. Picture an individual snugly sitting by his heater, while up above, a colleague is desperately seeking a "desert rose" in the darkness — suddenly he finds a tube projecting from the earth... Enough said!

The "Thunderbox" owed much of its popularity to the aforementioned Asahi beer. This arrived in wooden boxes which each contained 24 quarts. To construct a latrine, the first thing was to dig a hole about four feet square and as deep as you could make it. Poles or pickets (steel fencing pickets were preferred) were placed crosswise over the hole, leaving a hole about two feet square in the centre.

Over the gap an Asahi crate was placed, with a hole about the size of a normal toilet seat in the centre. The Asahi crate was an ideal size for this. A Hessian screen and juice can (to keep toilet paper dry) completed the furnishings.

Periodically, the Sanitation NCO would visit the area and a mixture of one gallon of DDT diluted by 3 1/2 gallons of gas would be sloshed around inside the hole to keep down the insect life. This practice had bizarre repercussions for one soldier.

The individual, who shall be nameless although he was known to many of us, made his way to the latrine for a quiet five minutes "goof-off." He settled himself comfortably, opened his copy of the *Japan News* and casually dropped his cigarette end into the hole. Unfortunately, the petrol/DDT treatment had just been administered.

The resulting explosion caused "A" Echelon to rush to their defensive positions, expecting a guerrilla attack. Meanwhile, a battered storeman, shrieking with pain, rushed into the lines. After he returned from hospital, rumour had it that his rear resembled the Japanese "Rising Sun" flag, but no one could be sure as he was never seen at the mobile bath unit.

Regardless of the humorous aspects of some of their activities, there is little doubt that the RCOC staff at the Mobile Laundry and Bath Units and the RCAMC sanitation NCOs played a major role in ensuring that so many of our troops at the sharp end were fighting fit — and fit to fight.

A SECRET WEAPON

Throughout the war there were allegations by the Communists and their sympathisers that conventional weapons had been converted for unethical purposes (i.e., for bacteriological warfare). Thanks to the U.S. Korean War Veterans Association, I have learned of an amazing "secret weapon" reported in the 32nd Infantry Regiment's newsletter:

"An item that has not yet come up at any UN meetings but which, I predict, soon will is contained in a secret report of the Communist Intelligence People (which) reads in part:

"'Following no pattern and apparently placed with consideration of 360-degree radius of fire the UN forces … have located tubes of varying calibre. These are in areas occupied by troops. Apparently no ammunition has been received for use of these tubes yet, as none of our agents ever saw one fired.

"'That the Americans are worried that they might be removed is obvious by the fact that they are generally checked during the day by officers and enlisted men.

"'One of our observers … reported that it seemed to be a ritual for almost every member of a unit to go out and examine this weapon the first thing in the morning. Some of the men are so anxious to make sure the weapons haven't been tampered with that they rush out in various states of disarray…

"'We were able to remove one by stealth at night and attempted to determine the calibre of it. But before much could be determined it started to get daylight and our agents had to replace it before morning. Some of these tubes are capped, apparently to keep foreign material out of them. Others are not capped. In some areas an attempt has been made to conceal these weapons by placing a canvas screen about them.

"'It is our intention to risk stealing one of them and sending it to the Secret Weapons Section for close examination … as soon as feasible an official protest would be lodged claiming that these weapons violate the Geneva Convention. But first the Russians want to try and find out which covenant these tubes come under.'"

The writer of the report concludes: "I am at a loss to explain what these weapons are, but feel that the people at home should be informed of the nature of the instrument. It is foolish to attempt to safeguard this intelligence any longer as I predict that our returnees will soon divulge to their friends all details of this equipment." (The secret weapon was the Desert Rose.)

THE BIRDS AND THE BEASTS WERE THERE

Some animals did feature from time to time in our activities. One notable rumour reported in the COMWEL Division newsletter *Crown News*, was that our enemies had captured a number of large apes, which they had trained to throw grenades and fire close-quarters firearms. They would then be released behind UN lines as (the pun is irresistible) guerrillas. How they would learn to pull the pin before throwing the grenade was not explained, and I would expect a high attrition rate among these hairy warriors if the story were true.

Indigenous creatures included quite a few small (but tasty) deer in our Division area, which had been part of a game park in earlier days. At least two of these animals fell to the rifles of my unit sentries, who swore that they were firing on "suspicious movement in front of our positions." One of Brigadier Rockingham's aides recalls that the brigade commander frequently had a shotgun handy in case he met geese or other game birds whose time had come. Much more bulletproof were the ubiquitous water buffalo owned by Korean farmers. As they spent much of their time in paddy fields, fertilized by human and animal manure, they were universally known as "s--- buffaloes."

Perhaps the most common animals in the area were dogs and cats. Unlike our pampered pets of today, they earned their keep.

Sometimes these animals appeared in the role of unit mascots – a thinly disguised subterfuge that enabled the commanding officer or other influential personage to bring his pet along. At least one dog – Deuce Horn, a Great Dane – accompanied the Queen's Own Rifles to Korea as the battalion's official mascot. Apparently a number of our naval vessels had also acquired pets, including OS Sparky, the *Athabaskan's* dog. Canine lovers will be pleased to hear that *Cayuga's* cat was less heroic and jumped ship after her first taste of action.

I can recall one occasion when I was detailed for an escort patrol in front of our positions. I found that I was escorting a sapper and a very mixed-breed dog that were searching for unmarked mines. Any lofty ideas I had regarding my own status were quashed when it was made very clear that if we encountered any enemy, the priorities were to save the dog, the engineer and the escort in that order. However, having seen the effective way in which the dog detected and marked the mines, I didn't feel too inferior.

Any pets that adopted our troops usually did so in the rear areas. The forward positions were no place for a cat or dog. However, one of the first victims of the Chinese Communists was a cat that was very famous in its time.

In 1949, the frigate *HMS Amethyst* was trapped in the Yangtze River and came under fire from Red Army guns. During the three-month captivity, Simon, the ship's cat, was badly burned and later received a bullet wound. Despite his injury, the gallant feline continued his work in destroying the vermin that threatened the diminishing food supply. In the end, *Amethyst* made a dash for freedom, and Simon survived to be honoured with the Dickin Medal — the animal's VC. Sad to say, the black and white tomcat died in quarantine before he could receive the medal. Although dogs, carrier pigeons and other animals have been awarded this medal, Simon was the only cat to be so honoured.

The Black Watch of Canada also put the many stray cats in their battalion area to good use. In 1954, their status was regularized in unit orders. Sub-units were advised that only cats that earned their keep by destroying vermin would be tolerated. Successful killer cats were to be rewarded – others should not be fed. Periodical returns were required reporting the feline achievement. There was obviously no room for pampered pussies with the Highlanders. In a way, this policy may well have contributed to reducing the incidence of vermin-borne disease that affected so many Korea veterans. The rats, though prolific, could hardly be classed as pets or allies, although many were almost familiar co-residents of our bunkers.

Sundry other beasts appeared briefly on the Korean scene. The Welch Regiment left Britain with their mascot, a magnificent Barbary goat named "Taffy." Unfortunately, it appears that while the battalion left their troopship in Aden for a route march, it was too much for the unfortunate animal, which succumbed to heatstroke. A story in the *Globe and Mail* also reported of a pig that was raised by the Provost Corps in anticipation of a Christmas feast. When its keepers were suddenly rotated back to Canada, it was apparently disposed of by raffling it off to the Korean workers at Brigade HQ. Overall, the Korea War was a war of men and machines; nevertheless there was a place, albeit limited, for our four-legged friends.

SONGS TO THE BATTLE

From time immemorial, soldiers and songs have gone together.

Long before the days of the early military bands with shawms, serpents, hautboys, and other archaic instruments, troops marched into battle singing. It was reported that, even as long ago as Agincourt, the British archers defiantly chanted at the charging French. Certainly, in the Crusades, the knights and their entourages were encouraged by the Gregorian chants of monks (which must have been very difficult to march to if they intended to keep in step).

"Sing or Double" was a common command during the World Wars when long marches or bashes were an integral part of infantry training. What was sung was often incidental – despite noble efforts of the clergy and the proud regimental officers to sing songs extolling the virtues of the Lord or the regiment. For example, perhaps the most popular song of the British during the American Revolution was a song of marital misfortune called *The World Turned Upside Down*. The world did, indeed, turn upside down at Yorktown when Cornwallis' defeated troops surrendered their arms to that ditty.

While more totalitarian armies forced patriotic or martial songs (*We March Against England*, etc.) on their soldiers, the Commonwealth troops preferred more sentimental, obscene or apparently pacifist ditties. We had few equivalents of *Halls of Montezuma* or *Off We Go, Into the Wild Blue Yonder*. In earlier days we had *Goodbye Dolly Gray*, the ubiquitous *Tipperary* and a number of bawdy versions of hymns and popular songs (*Why Are We Waiting?*). The RCR march and the *Rick-a-dam-doo* were soon adapted as were the adventures of *Mademoiselle from Armentières*.

There was of course the universal *Lili Marlene* – surprisingly this most popular song of the Second World War was officially banned by the Nazi hierarchy as too "mushy." It was introduced on a German forces' radio station in Yugoslavia by a brave announcer whose taste in music probably jeopardized his career plans.

In Korea, there was little singing on the march. First of all, any marching that was done was usually in an extended file, and uphill. This meant that not only was there no need to keep in step, but few of us had much breath left for songs. The other usual sing-song locale – the Canteen – was limited because only when the unit was in rest could a gang get together to vocalize. Nevertheless, we did sometimes get a chance to beat out the odd song – for instance, when we were resting we would often pile on trucks to be conveyed to an area where we were digging fall-back positions. This gave us an opportunity to harmonize, especially if we were lucky enough to pass an unfortunate military policeman. He would then be treated to one of our more memorable songs which detailed the story of the misadventures of a soldier on R&R leave in Tokyo after months in the line, "where whizzbangs are flying and comforts are few, and brave men are dying for bastards like you."

We were usually well up on popular songs of the day. Portable radios – especially the excellent Zenith Transoceanic – were obtainable from the PX, and many of us listened in to the U.S. Forces Network. In view of the lyrics which are commonplace today, it is strange to recall that Rosemary Clooney's *Come on-a my House* was banned because the words were too suggestive.

Occasionally the USO, the British ENSA, or touring Canadian or Australian troupes treated us to a show. On one memorable occasion, Marilyn Monroe gave a performance in a tight-fitting dress with (reportedly) no undies. Although many Korea veterans remember the show, I have yet to find one who recalls just what song she was singing.

We adopted a few songs as our own. The First World War song *Fred Karno's Army* was updated to *Rocky's Army*, but perhaps the most well-known was our version of *Movin' On*.

Like many military adaptations, this appeared to be defeatist – "I hear the patter of running feet, it's the (fill in the blanks) in full retreat, I'm movin' on." If music be the soul of love, it didn't work for us in the Ginza beer hall in Tokyo when a group of Commonwealth troops broke into *Movin' On*, inserting the name of a U.S. formation in the blank spaces. As the drinking hole was crowded with the members of the division in question, the evening became very interesting.

New Zealanders had a song of their own that dealt with the parentage of South Korean President Syngman Rhee, who was not a favourite of ours. Fortunately, it would appear that when the Kiwis sang it in the presence of their ROK allies, their down under accents were not understood.

The UN troops were quick to adopt a number of Korean songs. At Korea veterans' gatherings, strong men grow misty-eyed as the strains of *Arirang* are played or sung. This is a Korean folk song that details the hardships of two lovers and which, for some reason, caught the fancy of Korea veterans. At the risk of being drummed out of the Korea Veterans Association, dare I say that I do not care for this song? To me it is a dreary tune. It is played so often that I am sure many veterans think that it is the South Korean national anthem. To compound my felony, I would add that the Korean song which I enjoyed the most was a subversive air supposedly entitled *The Big-Nosed American* which was presented by a massed choir of North Korean prisoners to greet us on our arrival at Koje-do. There were, however, a number of memorable songs presented to us by groups of South Korean children in our rest areas. One, I remember, was sung to the tune of *Auld Lang Syne*.

We also picked up several catchy Japanese songs – one I recall was translated (phonetically) as "Moosie Mae." There was also *Moon over Malaya/China Nights* which had a Japanese version (picked up on our Zenith radios or in Tokyo bars). I don't think anyone really knew the words, but it achieved immortality as "I ain't go no yo-yo."

Except for the ubiquitous *Airang*, for some reason Korea veterans in Canada do not emulate their Second World War predecessors by singing their wartime songs at reunions. It's a pity – *Movin' On*, *Oh Provost, Oh Provost* and *Rocky's Army* go well with a pint of brew and good friends. Still, "There's ice among the rice along the Yalu, and a Chinaman is sneaking up on you – just don't ask for me to come and stand beside you, 'cos I'm propping up the bar in Uijongbu!"

CLOTHES MAKETH THE MAN
Beware of all enterprises that require new clothes.
~ *Thoreau*

While the Canadian troops were more or less adequately prepared for their first Korean winter, the same cannot be said for other Commonwealth troops. The Australians, in particular, had arrived from occupation duty in Japan and were forced to rely on their American allies for such essentials as padded outer jackets and fur-lined head dress. The British were a little better off, although it was some time before stocks of their excellent winter gear arrived.

The Canadians were the best prepared. For a start, they were used to cold temperatures such as those found on the Korean Peninsula in winter (although at times even the most hardened Prairie native found the freezing gales from mainland Manchuria hard to endure.) Don Hibbs later recalled that during the winter the typical infantryman wore from the skin outwards a string vest, a normal undershirt, long-johns complete with 'back door' flap, flannel pyjamas (a gift from home), a shirt (flannel preferred), battle dress, a parka jacket, lined winter trousers and perhaps camouflaged denim, "windproof" anorak and trousers, and a woollen scarf.

Headdress varied. Ironically, on arrival in Korea many units back-loaded their steel helmets. Commanders felt that they were cumbersome, noisy and would, perhaps, encourage troops in forward areas to huddle in their weapon slits, protected by their headgear, when they should be up and observing. In my platoon, only two helmets were retained – these were used in a manner similar to an ancient pillory. As effective retribution for military misdemeanours was impractical in the line, a culprit would be forced to wear a steel helmet for a few days.

Berets were the official headgear. One beloved brigadier firmly insisted that all his officers would wear berets *only,* but frequently appeared wearing a Glengarry. A far more practical headdress was the balaclava helmet. Although some commanders discouraged its use in its usual form, as it might affect the ability to hear an enemy, when rolled up in the fashion of a navy watch cap it was comfortable, warm and convenient. British troops were issued with a "cap comforter," a two-layer hollow scarf that could also be rolled up to form a wool cap.

A Canadian alternative to the beret was the "cap winter peaked" which resembled a Second World War Japanese headdress. It had the advantage of fitting snugly under the hood of a parka. The Commonwealth Division sported a wide variety of headgear – the Aussie slouch hat, the New Zealand Stetson (worn by a few die-hards), and the turbans worn by the Indian Field Ambulance. Besides the Glengarries, Tam-O'Shanters and Balmorals worn by Scottish regiments, and the Royal Ulster Rifles' caubeens, most British battalions were issued with "hats, jungle" – a headdress closely resembling the "fedors" style headdress currently used in Afghanistan.

An Australian writer aroused the ire of the powers-that-be by alleging that their troops were ill prepared, but even their leaders agreed that the Aussies who were able to acquire Canadian shirts were on to a good thing. Indeed, these were sought after by many Commonwealth troops. British and Australian units at first wore "bush" jackets and pants, but these were later replaced by more rugged combat dress, which formed an integral part of a multi-layer all-seasons outfit topped, in winter, by an excellent garment which combined the virtues of a greatcoat, parka and jump smock.

Unfortunately, as often happens, these did not always find their way into the line. I had to settle for a Canadian parka, which was more flexible than the bulkier British issue, but not quite as warm. Fortunately, it had a strong zipper, as rumour had it that the plastic buttons on Canadian parkas could be used as instant soup tablets. I found that the buttons soon disappeared from the garment, while some members of my platoon gazed despondently at melted plastic discs in the bottom of canteen cups of hot water.

Battledress was soon replaced by combat clothing, although it was retained for wear on leave and in rest areas. Indeed you could usually tell a sharp end soldier because he tried to look sharp in his BD, while the rear-echelon fellows would hang around the NAAFI roadhouses or Tokyo leave centres clad in combat dress.

Footwear was, perhaps, one of the most serious problems. The regular boots provided little protection against the bitter cold, and frostbitten feet were common. (Indeed, the United States has recently recognized this as a pensionable disability for Korean War veterans.) U.S. boot pacs were effective to a degree (some readers may recall that a similar version of RBLT – rubber-bottom, leather tops – was in use in post-war years in the Canadian Army). The British came up with what was basically a regular boot with thickened soles and a mesh insole – these were called "Boots – CWW," but we called them "cold, wet and windy." Keeping feet warm and dry was a problem, and we could never understand how our Chinese enemies could survive the year round in cheap basketball shoes. (These were seldom changed and it was possible to detect the presence of an enemy several yards away by their odour.)

In the line it was often a case of anything goes – within limits. Scrounged U.S. or other allied gear, knitted gifts from home and purchases from the NAAFI, PX or civilian stores were often in evidence. I don't know how it got to me, but before I received my Canadian parka I braved the winter in my platoon position in a white naval duffle coat (which didn't stay white for long).

The Commonwealth Division, without a doubt, sported the widest variety of dress in the Eighth Army. To the wide variety of uniforms, weapons and accoutrements that were not in the scale of issue but were carried, ranged from Gurkha kukris (popular with the ex-Hong Kong set) to burp guns. The Brits had one last little fling towards individuality. En route home many troops availed themselves of the services of military tailors, and, on arrival in Britain, displayed to admiring friends and relatives exotic and unauthorized formation flashes with crossed rifles, maps of Korea and self-designed shoulder titles such as "Blankshire Regiment, Korea 1952-1953, Hill ***." The Military Police had a field day!

ALL WORK AND NO PLAY

Most Canadians in Korea had at least an opportunity to get away from it all for five days Rest and Recuperation leave in Tokyo. The lucky leave party would be able to recover their battledress at the unit rear echelon and cast aside their work-worn combat dress they wore in the line.

They would be trucked to a U.S. air base (usually Kimpo, near Seoul) from whence they'd be flown to Tokyo. On arrival they would be allocated a bed at the Commonwealth leave centre at Ebisu. However, few of them spent much time in the centre. The lures of the bright lights of the city centre Ginza, the bars and other forms of entertainment were usually irresistible. At Kimpo, groups of soldiers going on R&R and those returning often intermingled. The weary, exhausted, red-eyed groups were usually the returnees!

Later a Commonwealth rest centre was established near Inchon in Korea. Here, troops could spend a few days respite from the line and enjoy a rest in a bed with clean sheets, regular hot meals, a canteen and other facilities. Ladies from the Canadian Red Cross and British Women's Volunteer Service were on hand to help purchase gifts for home and other services.

When the soldiers were away from the line sporting events were organized (the "Imjin Gardens" hockey rink attracted spectators and participants from all the Commonwealth contingents). Movies were available periodically and some lucky soldiers were able to attend shows by army concert companies.

A welfare officer serving with the Eighth Army in the Second World War wrote what was needed to combat the sheer boredom of wartime soldiering overseas was "to see and talk to English women, who must be good looking, gay, and compassionate people but who, nevertheless, knew how to behave and would not get too friendly with the men."

The top brass heeded this advice. From Canada, Australia, and the United States came ladies from the Red Cross, while Britain recruited members of the Women's Volunteer Service.

The British War Office turned to this organization for help, and the first WVS volunteers arrived in Pusan in 1951. They joined Red Cross volunteers from the U.S., Canada and Australia. (My first ever North American donut came from a U.S. Red Cross lady in the Pusan rail station.)

They and the Canadian Red Cross workers were soon put to work. Recreational clubs – after a fashion – were organized, and they later established a more permanent recreation centre at the Commonwealth Division Rest Centre near Inchon. Besides dispensing cheer, coffee, and donuts, these doughty ladies often worked 12-hour days, with no days off, providing a touch of home to the war-weary troops. They did not confine their activities to the comparative comfort of the R&R Centre, but would travel by jeep to forward areas – taking orders for "say it with flowers" messages, passing out comforts, and, in many cases, helping out with personal problems at home.

It is estimated that 16,000 Commonwealth troops a month used the Inchon recreation centre during peak periods.

TOP: A U.S. mechanic studies the damage to a AT-6 Harvard by North Korean ground fire. (DND)

ABOVE: An L-19 Mosquito light observation plane above the 38th parallel. (DND)

OPPOSITE PAGE: The Korean War was the first clash of jet fighters. U.S. F-86 Sabres (shown) battled North Korean MiGs at the speed of sound. (DND)

❧ THE AIR WAR

AS A "GROUND-POUNDER," my personal insight into the air war in Korea consists largely of observing contrails high above my trench. I've therefore turned to an expert in this case, aviation author Carl Mills, to provide an overview of Canadian airmen and airwomen in the Korean War.

"At the time of the Korean War, the Royal Canadian Air Force (RCAF) was committed to providing F-86 fighter squadrons to the Cold War build-up in Europe. Except for the participation by 426 Transport Squadron, Canada chose to support this commitment rather than a large-scale contribution to the Korean air war. In spite of this, Canada provided a significant number of RCAF flight nurses, fighter pilots, and others, along with contributions from the Royal Canadian Navy (RCN), various regiments of the army, and civilians to aid in the air war.

"Canadian-built aircraft flown in the Korean War included the Canadair North Stars flown by 426 Squadron on the airlift portion, hundreds of L-20 de Havilland Beavers in service with the U.S. army, and 60 older-model Canadair F-86 Sabre aircraft. During Operation HAWK, 426 Squadron flew 599, round-trip flights between McChord Air Force Base in Tacoma, Wash., and Haneda airfield in Tokyo while working with the USAF on the airlift. Although Canadians did not fly the Beavers in Korea, DeHavilland sent a technical representative to service the aircraft. About 20 per cent of all combat missions by Canadian pilots were flown in Canadian-built Sabres and included some MiG kills.

"RCAF flight nurses attended classes and practical training courses at Gunter AFB, Alabama, for seven weeks. This was followed by a three-month tour of duty carrying out medical air evacuations from theatre in the South Pacific. All nursing graduates (USAF, U.SN and RCAF) flew with the 1453 Medical Air Evacuation Squadron and were stationed in Honolulu. They flew U.S. and Canadian wounded between Haneda Airfield, through Honolulu, to Travis AFB near San Francisco. The RCAF flight nurses program was continuous from November 1950 to March 1955, and involved some 40 nurses.

"The RCAF's 435 Squadron, stationed at RCAF Station Edmonton (and later Namao), was tasked with the delivery of the Canadian wounded from McChord. The squadron was equipped with DC-3 Dakotas specially equipped to carry 16 litter patients complete with oxygen. Occasionally, Ottawa's 412 Squadron (also equipped with the Dakotas) and 426 Squadron would participate in the evacuations from McChord. Flight nurses who served in the U.S. or South Pacific were stationed at various Canadian airfields and always accompanied RCAF medical evacuation flights in Canada.

"Twenty-two RCAF fighter pilots were sent to Korea for F-86 combat duties, serving from November 1950 until November 1953. They flew exclusively with either the USAF's 4th Fighter Interceptor Wing (FIW) at Kimpo or the 51st FIW at Suwon. RCAF pilots served for six months or on 50 combat missions, whichever came first. It usually took three to four months to fly 50 missions. On arrival at their assigned squadron, pilots were usually given an introductory flying program called 'Clobber College,' before going into combat.

"Missions consisted of flying 200 miles over enemy territory to the infamous MiG Alley (near the Chinese border), patrolling, contact and fighting with the Communist MiG-15s, and returning home. Although there were no Canadian fatalities, there were many close calls during combat. RCAF pilots accounted for nearly 900 combat missions with nine MiG kills, two probables, and 10 damaged. High scoring pilots included F/L Ernie Glover with three MiG kills and three damaged and S/L Doug Lindsay with two kills and three damaged. RCAF pilots received eight U.S. DFCs and 10 U.S. Air Medals. Glover was the last RCAF pilot to be awarded the Commonwealth DFC.

"One RCN pilot was assigned to the USN for combat duty in Korea. After a strenuous work up for combat duties, the squadron was assigned to the aircraft carrier USS *Oriskany*, one of up to four carriers in Task Force 77 in the Sea of Japan at that time. Because of his background, Lieutenant Joe MacBrien was appointed the squadron's weapons officer. His missions included combat air patrols over the fleet, photo escort missions, armed reconnaissance, and close air support. MacBrien flew 66 combat missions and was awarded the U.S. DFC for his courage and leadership in a difficult ground attack mission he led in February

1953.

"In 1952, the Canadian Army began sending a string of four Air Observation Post (AOP) pilots to Korea to fly in Auster VI aircraft with the 1903 AOP Flight, RAF. Captain Joe Liston was shot down and captured in August, on his 12th combat mission. He was a POW for one year and was released under Operation BIG SWITCH (the war-end exchange of POWs) in September 1953. His replacement, Captain Peter Tees, was an energetic combatant and achieved 211 combat missions during his 12-month tenure. He supported Canadian artillery units that were, in turn, supporting Canadian infantry units along the Jamestown Line. Two other AOP pilots followed Tees and achieved some combat flying, although they were substantially used in peacekeeping duties. Tees was the last Canadian to be awarded the Commonwealth DFC.

"When the Korean War broke out, Canadian Pacific Airlines (CPA) was flying once-per-week flights from Vancouver to Tokyo. It was a simple matter to convince the U.S. army and the Canadian government the airline was capable of participating in the Korean War airlift. CPA commenced four (later five) charter flights per week for the U.S. Army in August 1950. Unlike the service of 426 Squadron, CPA flew only passengers. These flights continued, using first North Star, then DC-4s and then DC-6B aircraft, until March 1955, providing over 700 charter flights. In July 1951, one DC-4 with a crew of seven (including two stewardesses), two Canadian sailors and 29 U.S. Army and USAF passengers, disappeared off the coast near Juneau, Alaska. In spite of an intensive two-month search, no trace of the aircraft was ever found.

"Several other Canadian airmen were involved in observation duties, technical and supply support, photo intelligence, exchanged flying duties with USAF transport squadrons, and top-secret combat missions, while a number crossed the border to join the USAF directly. In all, the Canadian airmen and airwomen did very well in Korea, flying over 2,000 combat missions and more than 1,500 round-trip airlift flights. They were awarded 57 Commonwealth and U.S. medals and commendations. This account would have been higher except for a strange rule imposed by the Canadian military that only allowed one U.S. medal per Canadian."[1]

~ ~ ~ ~ ~ ~ ~ ~ ~ ~ ~

THE SABRE JOCKEYS

John Coffey provided a specific insight into the "fast air" dogfights over Korea:

"Though the U.S. requested them, Canada's fighter squadrons did not put in an appearance in Korean skies. However, 22 RCAF fighter pilots did see action with American Squadrons.

"Flight Lieutenant J.A.O. Levesque, on exchange duty with the United States Air Force in November 1950 became the first Canadian pilot to see action. Andy MacKenzie, a former Spitfire pilot with eight and a half kills and a DFC in World War Two, he served with 51st Fighter Interceptor Wing in Korea and experienced four uneventful sorties. On his fifth in an F-86 Sabre, while attempting to catch up with his flight leader, he was mistaken for a North Korean aircraft and shot down by an American pilot. The Chinese captured him and he survived imprisonment, interrogation, solitary confinement, lack of food and mental torture, and he was held for a year and a half after the cessation of hostilities.

"Another veteran pilot was Flight Lieutenant Ernie Glover. He had flown Hurricanes for the RAF over France during the Second World War. In Korea, Glover successfully completed his tour, racking up three enemy fighter kills and damaged three others. After his return to Canada, Flight Lieutenant Glover received two Distinguished Flying Crosses - one Canadian and one American.

"The Korean War was the site of many firsts. The Lockheed F-80 Shooting Star triumphed in the first jet battle in history when on November 7, 1950, an F-80 shot down a MiG-15 as it crossed the Yalu River. In time, however, the MiG-15 aircraft proved to be more maneuverable, and against it the F-80 sustained a loss ratio in air combat of seven to six.

"The North American F-86 Sabre was a classic post-war first generation jet fighter. Derived directly from German research into subsonic flight, it was produced in larger quantities than any other aircraft since the end of the Second World War. The F-86 Sabre was the pride of the USAF during the Korean War, and the front line interceptor in most NATO and SEATO countries during the 1950s. The early versions, which received their air combat baptism in Korea, were armed with six M-3 .50 calibre machine guns, each with 267 rounds, mounted forward on either side of the nose. They could also carry eight five-inch rockets or two 1,000-pound bombs for ground support. The E and F models of the Sabre were the favourite with the pilots in Korea, capable of a maximum speed of 687 m.p.h. Though unable to climb as rapidly or to as high an altitude as the Soviet MiG-15, they were rugged and versatile, and quickly established their superior maneuverability, with a kill ratio of seven to three against the Soviet-built aircraft. By the war's end, Sabres had shot down a total of 814 enemy aircraft.

"The well-armed MiG-15 swept-wing single-seat fighter was the Sabre's greatest opponent over Korea, and served in large numbers both with the Red Air Force and with the air forces of the Russian satellites. It had a better rate of climb and ceiling than the Sabre, as well as a tighter turn and superior speed. Armed with a single 30-mm and two 20-mm cannons, the MiG-15 had a top speed of 746 m.p.h. The main drawback of this plane was that it was short ranged at 560 miles.

"The North Korean air force of initially 132 MiG-15s was knocked out of the war due to UN strikes on Korean airfields and transportation and the short ranged MiG-15 rebased in China could do little to support the North Korean army against UN air power.

"The UN forces were forbidden to travel north of the Yalu River, furthering the frustrations of UN pilots. On the ground as in the air, patrols and reconnaissance were undertaken over 'bastard-steep hills' to determine the intentions and dispositions of the enemy. These deadly games of hide-and-seek took place in all kinds of weather, and their essential purpose was to penetrate the fog of war and bring back information. As a defence, skilled troops on both sides practised effective camouflage in order to hide. The practice of Chinese troops and their uniform's dirt-colour made it difficult to identify targets. Through mist and rain, and in the air, through clouds, troops and pilots searched for an elusive enemy. Air support made the difference to the troops on the ground. From the early stages of the conflict, the UN fought to maintain air supremacy over the battlefields. UN heavy bombers struck as far north as the Yalu River and inflicted heavy casualties and damage on airfields, bridges, railways and tunnels. The fighters hammered the enemy's forward positions and forced them to move supplies and troops at night, while air reconnaissance aided the UN ground troops. The 22 RCAF fighter pilots and technical officers serving with the U.S. air force were credited with 20 enemy trains and trucks.

"While the Chinese and North Koreans could not match the UN in the air, they defended with a surprising amount of anti-aircraft artillery for the pilots whose job it was to fly through it. Anti-aircraft artillery was responsible for over 70 per cent of the planes lost. One can but marvel at the courage and dedication of the pilots who, while riding the cutting edge of an emerging technology, depended on the Mark 1 eyeball (not lasers and TV) for target identification, dodging killer flak to accomplish their missions."[2]

~ ~ ~ ~ ~ ~ ~ ~ ~ ~

THE OTHER AIRLIFT

To the average Canadian, the major post-war airlift was the allied effort to supply Berlin in the late 1940s. This was well documented in Leon Uris's best-seller *Armageddon* and the movie *The Big Lift*. In keeping with a policy of non-involvement at that time, there was no Canadian participation. A year later, despite the objections of several politicians, including the defence minister, the RCAF played a vital role in an even bigger and perhaps more hazardous airlift operation – this time in support of the United Nations war effort in Korea.

Political and military authorities moved quickly. A few days after the Korean

War broke out, 426 Thunderbird Transport Squadron was placed on notice to join its U.S. allies in the Pacific airlift. Less than two days after six North Stars arrived at McChord AFB, three of them were on their way westward with their cargoes of vital supplies. By the time the Korean War had ended, 426 Squadron would make 599 round trips and deliver 13,000 troops, several other VIPs, and 3,000 tons of material. On their return trips they would backload wounded, and convey bodies of fallen U.S. servicemen for burial in their homeland. These missions were conducted without the loss of any aircraft or personnel.

The North Star aircraft used was a military version of a successful civilian airliner produced by Canadair. It was basically a DC-4 airframe, with the Pratt & Whitney radial engines replaced by Rolls-Royce Merlins. According to Jim Shipton, a 426 Squadron navigator, this added about 50 knots to the airspeed. Oscar LeBlanc, a former aircrew member, later recalled that at times a North Star "would leave 30 minutes after its USAF C-54 (DC-4) counterpart, and would pass the DC-4 with one engine feathered in a show of one-upmanship."

Obviously the luxury of the Trans-Canada Air version was lacking in the military North Star. Most military passengers would agree that Air Force North Stars were probably one of the noisiest aircraft to fly in. LeBlanc said that for days after a flight his ears would be ringing. For the passengers, sitting wherever they could find a soft spot on the assorted cargo, conversation was almost impossible. There was no cabin heating system. Lack of a pressurization system necessitated flying at altitudes below 10,000 feet.

The usual route was a circular flight, leaving McChord via Anchorage, to the small island of Shemya at the end of the Aleutians and from there to Haneda airport in Tokyo. From Japan, the North Stars flew to Wake Island and on to Honolulu before the final long leg to San Francisco. Round trip time was 80-85 hours.

Cargo varied. One pilot, Paul Lemeux, said that the aircraft carried everything "from bullets to broomsticks." Passengers included American and Canadian troop reinforcements and several visitors, including Pierre Berton who later wrote a magazine article on the squadron. Jim Shipton's favourite VIP was broadcaster Kate Aiken, who presented each crew member with a "forty-ouncer" on arrival in Tokyo. Cargo was not confined to Canadian content as the U.S. Military Air Transportation Service controlled the operations (whose acronym MATS was cynically interpreted as "May Arrive Tomorrow Sometime").

While Thunderbird crews missed the short and sharp encounters with MiGs experienced by the RCAF pilots who were attached to USAF fighter squadrons in Korea, their life was hardly dull and teamwork was essential.

The pilots had to fly their four-engine aircraft through what one senior officer described as "some of the worst flying weather in the world." At times, the North

Stars would be airborne for close to their endurance limit of about 10 hours. The excessive noise provided little opportunity for relaxation even when another pilot was at the controls.

Nor was the navigator's task an easy one. Theoretically, radio navigation aids were in place. However, in the northern part of the 11,000-mile circuit it was not uncommon for Soviet stations to attempt to jam or distort signals. On at least two occasions, airlift planes were surprised to find clusters of lights below where there should have been empty sea. In *The Korea Experience*, Arthur Gauthier, an aircrew officer, stated that his aircraft was "coned" over the North Pacific by searchlights from a group of Russian naval vessels from Vladivostok that were "parading" in a show of force in support of the North Koreans. This information was welcomed by U.S. intelligence, which had lost the naval force.

George Knightley, another pilot, writing in *Korea Volunteer* said that on one trip they encountered a break in the undercast and found that rather than empty ocean they were flying over a large number of lights, which was either a fishing fleet or a town in the Soviet Kurile Islands, which should have been well to the north. Discretion suggested a quick turn southwards, and the aircraft eventually reached Shemya safely. Korean Air Flight 007 was less fortunate in a similar situation years later.

There was no free ride for the navigators. Besides the radio interference, comparatively low flight altitudes often meant that cloud cover hampered astro-navigation. Unpredictable winds made dead reckoning difficult and frequent fixes and checks were necessary. Sheyma and Wake islands were both insignificant spots on the chart. The former, a vital refuelling stop, was often inaccessible due to fog or other conditions, and the weary crews had to retrace their flight to Alaska. Jim Shipton had the highest admiration for the USAF ground control approach crews, who brought their charges in safely in what was, at times, literally zero visibility. It was not uncommon for a crew to be confined to the aircraft until someone could lead them through the fog to the mess hall.

At times, radio fixes were obtained from ocean vessels on station for that purpose. Paul Lemeux recalled that at one time his navigator was in a flap because he was passing over a vessel that identified itself as "Ocean Station Kilo" when his reckoning told him that he should have been over Station "Mike." After frantic checking and fruitless recalculation the navigator was relieved to receive a transmission from the ship apologizing and explaining that the radio operator had just been transferred from "Kilo" to "Mike" and had forgotten where he was!

The commissioned aircrew members were unanimous in their praise for the NCO flight engineers. Often, an extra engineer was carried. Not only was this vital crew member responsible for monitoring the performance of his four Merlins in flight, he had to carry out checks, refuelling and often conduct or supervise maintenance and repairs on the ground. As Shipton said, when the rest of the crew had landed and were on their way to their rest and a hot meal, the flight engineer would still be checking the aircraft and arranging – or in many cases carrying out – the refuelling. One former flight engineer recalled that when refuelling for the last trip (e.g., Honolulu to San Francisco), he would invariably insist on a maximum fuel load, regardless of his pilot's wishes, as once the point of no return had been passed unexpected headwinds could play havoc with fuel consumption. He said, on several occasions, the North Stars would be met and escorted to Travis AFB in California by B-17s equipped with droppable lifeboats – fortunately, these never had to be used. In addition to his official duties, many a flight engineer doubled as a cook, producing hot meals and drinks on an effective, if illegal, hot plate rigged in the cargo compartment.

The usual procedure was for a crew to fly their aircraft for one leg of the journey, when it would be taken over by a new crew for the next stage. The off duty crew would remain on the airfield until the next arrival (usually the following day) which they would then take to its next destination. While ensuring that crews had sufficient rest, there were two disadvantages. One was that squadron get-togethers were almost impossible as aircrews were scattered around the Pacific Rim. The other was that a crew did not have its own aircraft, which meant that pilots and flight engineers had to discover and cope with the idiosyncrasies of several different machines.

Rest stops varied. McChord was home to many airmen, some of who moved their families from Montreal. Tokyo and Honolulu made pleasant stopovers, especially when schedules allowed extra time there. Shemya was a desolate spot miles from nowhere, where in the words of Oscar LeBlanc, "we could experience four seasons in one day. ... We would walk into the mess hall in bright sunshine and come out to thick fog." Diversions were few. Fog, gale-force winds, and almost daily precipitation made the island a meteorologist's nightmare. As a grim reminder, a B-17 bomber that had skidded off the runway was still visible below the frigid waters offshore.

The excellent work and professionalism of the ground crews, often under exacting conditions, were major factors in 426 Squadron's fine record. Nor should we forget the work of the loadmasters in securing what was often awkward and difficult cargo.

Although, perhaps, many deserving squadron members were left out, the Thunderbirds did receive several awards for their work. The commanding officer, Wing Commander C.H. Mussels, whose DSO and DFC attested to his wartime experience, was awarded the OBE. Squadron Leader W.H. Lord received the MBE, while Air Force Crosses went to Wing Commander H.A. Morrison, Squadron Leader J.D. Dickson and Flight Lieutenants Edwards and Payne. Corporal

TOP: Quarters at Currie Barracks, Calgary, where many Special Forces recruits were trained. (PPCLI MUSEUM)

ABOVE: Brooke Claxton, minister of National Defence, visits troops of 2PPCLI on September 12, 1950 prior to their departure for Korea. Gen. Charles Foulkes, the chief-of-staff looks on. (DND PHOTO)

LEFT: A Canadian soldier in Korea furnished with a mixed bag of weapons and equipment. This soldier is carrying a WWII vintage Bren gun. (ILLUSTRATION BY KATHERINE TAYLOR)

ABOVE: Kapyong. Captain J.G. Mills, 2PPCLI, calls in artillery on his own "D" Company position, as the Chinese overrun his forward defences. More than a quarter of a million Chinese soldiers smashed into UN lines just before midnight, Sunday, April 22, 1951. (ILLUSTRATION BY KATHERINE TAYLOR)

LEFT: 2PPCLI moving into the line at Kapyong, April 1951. (DND PHOTO)

RIGHT: The .50-calibre Browning M2 machine gun was widely used in WWII and Korea. It entered Canadian service in 1942.

OPPOSITE TOP: *"Korea, Land of Morning Calm" by Edward Zuber. When the North invaded the South on June 25, 1950, the calm was broken in Korea. For the soldiers serving as part of the United Nations force, quiet moments were punctuated with violent attacks. (CANADIAN WAR MUSEUM)*

OPPOSITE BOTTOM: *Despite his wounds, Sergeant Neil McKerracher remains in his position at a front line observation post. (PUBLIC ARCHIVES OF CANADA)*

TOP: *"Holding at Kapyong," by Edward Zuber. Surrounded with their forward positions overrun, 2PPCLI holds Hill 677. C119 "Flying Boxcars" from a Japanese airbase drop supplies. The Patricias were later awarded a United States Presidential Citation for "outstanding heroism and exceptionally meritorious conduct." (CANADIAN WAR MUSEUM)*

ABOVE: *A Sten gun. Manufactured by Sheppard and Turpin – hence the name – this WWII vintage 9-mm submachine gun was widely used in Korea and had a bad reputation for jamming. Crude – it had only 47 parts – it was effective when it worked. First used by Canadian troops at Dieppe in 1942, it has a 32-round magazine mounted at right angles to the barrel and a range of 200 yards. The Sten was also known as the "Plumber's Delight."*

OPPOSITE TOP:
*"Incoming" by Edward
Zuber. Tanks were of little
use in mountainous
Korea, except in
defensive positions. (CWM)*

OPPOSITE BOTTOM:
*Korean children dressed
in Western clothing. The
war orphaned thousands
of children. (PPCLI MUSEUM)*

TOP: *With the stalemate
both sides dug in. These
Canadian snipers are on
the Hook, the key feature
of the Canadian defensive
position overlooking the
Sami-ch'on valley during
the winter of 1952-53.
("FIRST KILL, THE HOOK" BY
EDWARD ZUBER, CWM)*

RIGHT: *Canadian
breweries donated their
products to the troops in
Korea – much to their
delight. (BOB MAHAR)*

OPPOSITE TOP: *Sergeants John Richardson and R.A. Prentice of 1PPCLI engage a Chinese patrol while carrying a wounded comrade to safety.* (ILLUSTRATION BY SCOTT TAYLOR)

OPPOSITE BOTTOM: *Canadians were constantly amazed by the heavy loads Korean porters carried on their A-frames.* (PPCLI MUSEUM)

ABOVE: *The Royal 22e Regiment defends their position on the saddle of Hill 355 on the night of October 23, 1952.* ("CONTACT" BY EDWARD ZUBER, CANADIAN WAR MUSEUM)

RIGHT: *The Chinese were skilled at penetrating the UN lines at night to lay mines and booby traps. The soldiers pictured are using Russian-made box mines.*

OPPOSITE TOP: *Korea resembled the trench warfare of the First World War. Artist Ted Zuber, who served with the Royal Canadian Regiment, painted this scene recalling New Year's Eve, 1952.* ("NEW YEAR'S EVE" BY EDWARD ZUBER, CANADIAN WAR MUSEUM)

OPPOSITE BOTTOM: *Canadian soldiers developed a deep affinity towards hard-working Korean porters. They were fondly nicknamed "the Rice-Burners." (U.S. ARMY PHOTO)*

ABOVE: *A Canadian destroyer firing on shore targets near Hungnam on the east coast. In all, eight of the RCN's 11 destroyers served in Korea from the outbreak of war to the Armistice in July 1953.* ("DAYBREAK, GULF OF KOREA," BY EDWARD ZUBER, CANADIAN WAR MUSEUM)

RIGHT: *Ferdinand Waldo "Fred" Demara, an American, assumed the identity of Dr. Joseph Cyr of St. John, N.B., and served aboard HMCS* Cayuga *as a surgeon-lieutenant. His story was later told in the movie* The Great Imposter, *starring Tony Curtis. (DND PHOTO)*

OPPOSITE TOP: *The RCR holds the line in winter conditions that are as harsh as those in Canada. (*"WELCOME PARTY" *BY* EDWARD ZUBER, CANADIAN WAR MUSEUM*)*

OPPOSITE BOTTOM: *A Sherman tank of the Lord Strathcona's Horse negotiates some relatively flat terrain – a rarity in Korea. (*DND PHOTO*)*

ABOVE: *Fatigue. This is one of the most famous photographs of the Korean War. Several veterans later mistakenly claimed to be the tired young soldier pictured here. He is Private Heath Matthews, who served with the Second Battalion, Royal Canadian Regiment. (*PAC*)*

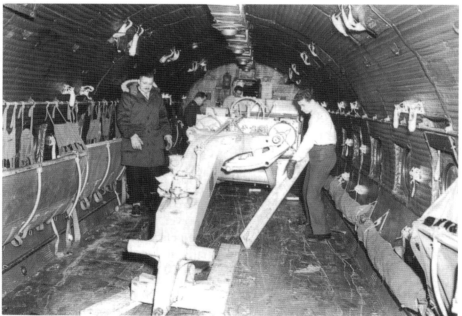

TOP: *An F-86 Sabre in Korea. Twenty-two Canadians saw action with American squadrons and were credited with 20 enemy fighters damaged or destroyed.* (DND PHOTO)

ABOVE: *The interior of a Canadian North Star transport aircraft. 426 Thunderbird Squadron shuttled passengers and freight between the state of Washington and Japan as part of the U.S. Military Transport Service.* (DND PHOTO)

ABOVE: Heading home. These Canadian soldiers are piped aboard a train for the long journey home and an indifferent welcome. (DND PHOTO)

RIGHT: A recuperating Van Doo and a buddy share a lighter moment at a military hospital in Japan. (DND PHOTO)

ABOVE: *As president of the Korean War Veterans Association, author Les Peate (centre) has championed the cause of his fellow veterans. Historian David Bercuson of the University of Calgary has described veterans of the Korean War as "the first breed of Canada's post-war military."*

RIGHT: *In memoriam. A PPCLI soldier kneels at the grave of a fallen comrade in the UN Cemetary, Busan, Korea. Overall, 516 Canadians were killed in the war.* (PUBLIC ARCHIVES OF CANADA)

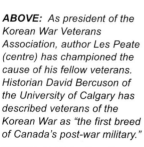

G.R. Reed received the comparatively rare award of the Air Force Medal, and several squadron members received the Queen's Commendation for valuable service in the air.

The RCAF, and Canadian Forces (Air) have since participated in many more airlifts under the UN flag. However, the unspectacular and often unsung participation in the Korean airlift should not be forgotten.

HAIRY TIMES OVER THE PACIFIC

I reviewed a history of RCAF 426 Squadron entitled *Thunderbirds for Peace*. I realized that many of the hazardous adventures of Canada's airmen in the Korean War occurred far from the front lines and MiG Alley. Author Larry Motiuk has allowed me to recount a few examples of the difficulties and dangers encountered during the Korean airlift.

One unusual problem arose in December 1950 at McChord AFB. All North Star engines had to be examined to determine the cause of an unusual defect. The 426 Squadron ground staff stripped, inspected, and reassembled 42 engines in five days. Apparently, when the engines were sent to Rolls-Royce in Montreal for overhaul, an overly conscientious worker not only cleaned the pistons, but in an excess of zeal, polished them. This caused some engines to have piston failures and the worker was fired. This was but one of the challenges faced by the squadron's ground staff whose almost superhuman efforts kept the North Stars flying under trying conditions.

Larry Motiuk wrote: "transport flying is … hours of boredom interspersed with seconds of stark terror." Flying officer Bob Edwards would agree with that, as a principal actor in two hair-raising experiences. In February 1951, he was captain of a North Star carrying 24 wounded U.S. soldiers to Wake Island en route to Hawaii. Edwards handed over to his co-pilot and moved to the crew rest area. Suddenly the aircraft encountered a massive storm cloud.

Chaos ensued after a lightning strike and pounding hail. In his rush to the controls, Edwards found himself pinned to the cabin ceiling. Due to the unexpectedness of the encounter, the litter patients had not been strapped in and in Motiuk's words they "lay scattered about the cabin floor along with coffee cups, blankets and loose equipment." To make matters worse, the flight nurse and medical assistant were hopelessly airsick, and the patients had to be attended to by the flight crew.

On arrival at Wake, the aircraft exhibited considerable damage. The radiator fins for the engines were bent and flattened by the hail. Normally the maintenance at Wake took two hours; in this case it took that long to open the radiator fins alone. Not surprisingly, two of the passengers refused to fly on to Honolulu, although one later changed his mind.

In April of that year, Flying Officer Edwards was a passenger in another North Star. As the aircraft made its approach to Ashiya, Japan, there was a cry of "Full Power!" from the pilot, followed by a tremendous crash. Air rushed into the cockpit together with a shower of leaves and branches. Fortunately, the North Star was still airborne and gaining altitude. After the squadron CO, WCdr C.H. Mussels had surveyed the damage he instructed Edwards to take over the controls since both the pilot and co-pilot were visibly shaken.

The collision had destroyed the radio compass loop antennae and damaged the pitot head, which was necessary to determine the airspeed, and the altimeter proved unreliable. In addition, one engine was out and the other was running at idle power. Few pilots had practised two-engine landings on North Stars with no indication of the airspeed. However, Edwards managed a somewhat hairy landing, and the astounded Americans in the operations centre produced six bottles of bourbon that were "rapidly consumed without ice or mix." For his courage and display of skill, F/O Edwards was awarded the Air Force Cross.

When I visited the Douglas MacArthur museum in Norfolk, Virginia I was surprised to see that among his many decorations was a U.S. Distinguished Flying Cross. When I remarked on this the custodian informed me that MacArthur had flown in his personal aircraft over the Inchon area shortly after the landing. My naïve inquiry as to whether, in that case, the crews of the C-119s who dropped 187 Airborne RCT north of that area also received medals, resulted in a frosty look. However, one Canadian transport aircraft did stray into the ground combat area.

WCdr Mussels was a passenger on a North Star with a vague sort of clearance to continue a flight northwards from Pusan. While the pilot and crew had misgivings about taking a strange four-engine aircraft to the combat zone, Mussels wanted to see where the fighting was. Suddenly two Texan spotter aircraft came on the air and, when Mussels tried to debate the issue, replied tersely "Get the hell out of here!" At this point the pilot reminded his CO that he was the captain of the aircraft, and turned back to Tokyo.

MOSQUITOS OVER THE IMJIN

Speak to a Second World War aviator about Mosquitos and you would probably generate stories of the versatile DeHavilland "wooden wonder." (One of the best of which is Dave McIntosh's *Terror in the Starboard Seat.*) Mention the Mosquito squadrons to a Korean War veteran, and in many cases you would receive only a blank look.

Exploits of the F-86 Sabres, F-84 Thunderjets and F-80 Shooting Stars, together with their naval counterparts the Panthers and Corsairs, and the Commonwealth's Mustangs and Meteors have been well-documented. Even Hollywood got into the act with such classics as *The Bridges at Toko-ri*. One lesser-known organization, vitally important to our front line infantry, was the Fifth Air Force's 6147 Tactical Control Group.

While the United Nations forces enjoyed air superiority, there was one significant limiting factor when it came to the provision of close air support to our ground forces. During the Second World War, many tactical air force targets consisted of vehicles and troop concentrations that were comparatively easy to spot from the air. In Korea the ground support aircraft were required to knock out well concealed gun positions and bunkers in mountainous terrain with few distinctive landmarks. In addition, with the exception of the Mustangs, which were soon replaced by jets, the higher speeds allowed little time for pilots to locate and identify their targets. (One unit of 27 Commonwealth Brigade suffered heavy casualties from an attack by friendly aircraft.)

The solution to the problem was the introduction of an unusual type of aircraft to the front lines. An innovative genius decided to take a number of AT-6 Texan trainers out of mothballs, and send them to Korea as spotter and ground liaison aircraft. Anyone who has heard the AT-6 (the Harvard in Canada) would recognize the distinctive drone of its Pratt & Whitney Wasp engine – hence its nickname – The Mosquito.

The AT-6 was ideal for its new role. Its maximum speed of 212 mph gave the pilot and observer much more time to search for targets – this compared with 580 m.p.h. for the F-80 and over 600 mph for the Sabre and Thunderjet. The rugged construction, designed to take the rough handling of student pilots, enabled it to withstand a great deal of ground fire. Finally, it was capable of carrying a supply of rockets used to mark targets, armour plate and two or more radios. The greenhouse cockpit provided a wide field of vision for a pilot and observer. As we will see later, the fact that the Harvard was originally built as a training aircraft proved vital to one Canadian officer.

The AT-6 pilots and support personnel became established as 6147 Tactical Air Control Group. They soon realized that close air support was a team effort, and USAF personnel underwent tours of duty with ground units, while the combat units from more than a dozen United Nations countries provided airborne observers. The teams were in contact with the ground units and with the controllers of the strike aircraft.

Generally, targets would be called for by the ground commander, through his air control team, or spotted by the pilot or observer in the AT-6. The spotter aircraft would call in a strike and if necessary fire smoke rockets to indicate the target's location. (This usually brought out the friendly infantry, who had a front-seat view of the ensuing air strike – bombs, rockets, cannon-fire or, the most spectacular of all, napalm.)

Perhaps the most daring strikes were conducted by the Mustangs of the South African Air Force. The Springboks would approach their targets by following the valleys, and then open fire from below the objectives, which were usually on hilltops or ridges. This approach proved costly – the SAAF's Second Fighter Squadron (the Flying Cheetahs) lost 42 pilots during their Korean tour.

Canadians had their share of 6147 Group's activity. Eight Canadian officers were decorated by the United States for gallantry in the air. Three of these, Captain J.R.P. Yelle and Lieutenant J.F. Plouffe of the R22eR, and Lieutenant A.J. Magee of the RCR, received the U.S. Distinguished Flying Cross. (As an aside, Captain Peter Tees, Royal Canadian Artillery, was the only Canadian Army officer to receive the Commonwealth DFC, awarded for his deeds as an Auster pilot with the British 1903 Air OP Flight.)

Lieutenant Plouffe's experience typified the hazards of the operation. The citation for his award reads as follows: "Captain Plouffe (who had apparently been promoted since his exploit) directed his pilot through intense enemy ground fire in a low reconnoitering pass to discover the location of six camouflaged enemy bunkers, four mortar positions and an artillery position behind a key hill. Disregarding his personal safety he directed the pilot in making these passes to mark individual targets with smoke rockets, for orbiting fighter aircraft. One of the fighters was hit by ground fire during the attack and Captain Plouffe's pilot escorted it to the nearest emergency strip.

"Upon returning to the area he continued to direct the fighters on to the targets, resulting in four bunkers, two mortar positions and one artillery position being destroyed.

"By his high personal courage, aggressiveness and devotion to duty Captain Plouffe brought great credit upon himself, the Commonwealth and the United States Air Force."

The citation did not tell the full story. Plouffe later recalled that his aircraft was hit and the fuel pump damaged. The pilot instructed his observer in the use of the manual pump, and Plouffe was told to "start pumping." As the aircraft made its way back to friendly territory, Plouffe recalled that "every time the propeller seemed to slow down, no matter how tired I was, I found the energy to pump harder!"

Despite the damaging effects of his efforts on the Chinese mortars, he was presumably readmitted to the mortar fraternity, serving at the School of Infantry as a senior instructor on that weapon. One can be sure that concealment of mortar base-plate positions from the air was a significant part of the course syllabus.

Another Van Doo officer who underwent a hair-raising experience in the back seat of a Harvard was Captain J.P.R. "Pat" Tremblay, a liaison officer at 25 Canadian Infantry Brigade headquarters.

Tremblay was flying as an observer in an AT-6 piloted by a USAF officer, Captain Wittom. As a qualified parachutist, he was no stranger to air to ground operations.

When they arrived over the forward areas Tremblay was able to identify several key features in the Commonwealth Division sector. He was able to locate the enemy trench systems, but could not spot any activity. As the pilot descended to make a more detailed search, the aircraft ran into a burst of light anti-aircraft fire. The Van Doo officer saw that some of the rounds had entered the pilot's cockpit.

Wittom was obviously seriously wounded – he was unable to speak coherently and was bleeding badly. Meanwhile the AT-6 was bouncing around in the air, with no one at the controls.

This is where the Harvard's previous role as a trainer plane paid off. Although some of the aircraft had been denuded of the rear-seat student's controls, Wittom's plane still had these in place. Recalling his basic knowledge of aviation, Tremblay (who had never before touched the controls of an airplane) knew that he could control the rise and fall of the machine by pushing the joystick forward or back. This enabled him to avoid crashing the plane into the terrain.

By trial and error, Pat Tremblay was able to gain some control over the aircraft and made his way back towards the UN lines. He was now faced with another problem – should he bail out or attempt to land the plane? Although his pilot was badly wounded, he was obviously still alive. There was no question of abandoning the aircraft.

After flying around for a while, Tremblay recognized familiar landmarks and eventually located the Kimpo airstrip, close to Seoul. Wittom had now regained consciousness, but due to his injuries was unable to operate the stick and rudder bar in the front seat. As the back-seat driver approached the strip and began a steep descent, the Air Force pilot realized that Tremblay did not know how to throttle back, and Wittom was able to slow the aircraft by activating the landing flaps. He was also able to drop the retractable undercarriage.

After a series of bounces and zig-zags, the AT-6 finally came to a stop with the assistance of a four inch wall. Despite flames licking around the aircraft engine, Tremblay lifted Whittom from the cockpit, which was no easy task, as the USAF pilot was over six feet tall.

Captain Whittom recovered from a number of shrapnel wounds in the spine. Although many of his comrades felt that Pat Tremblay deserved a Distinguished Flying Cross for his coolness and courage he did, in fact, receive a Military Cross for his efforts. Surprisingly, he did not receive an American award.

The Mosquito Group holds a reunion annually, and despite its decreasing numbers there is usually some Canadian participation. While the 6147th's role may have been overshadowed by the more spectacular fighter and bomber units, in one way it has achieved immortality. Comic book aficionados will recognize their hero, Steve Canyon, performing a stint at the controls of an AT-6 over the Korean front lines.

PLYWOOD AND FABRIC: THE STORY OF BED-CHECK CHARLIE

The primitive biplane, a melange of fabric, plywood and yards of bracing wire, powered by a rackety 100-horsepower engine, chugged through the darkness towards the enemy's rear areas. On arrival at the target, the pilot dropped two small bombs, which destroyed a fuel dump and thousands of tons of fuel. This sounds like the climax of *Dawn Patrol* and Errol Flynn's last flight, but in fact it describes a typical mission of one of the Korean War's unsung air heroes, "Bed-check Charlie." Thanks to Hollywood – and the stories of the exploits of Omer Levesque, Eric Smith, Andy MacKenzie and the other Canadians who were attached to USAF Sabre squadrons – aviation enthusiasts tend to regard the Korean air war as the milieu of jets or, at the very least, high performance propellor-driven aircraft. Nevertheless, a number of pre-World War antiques played their part in the conflict.

The adventures of several Canadians who flew as observers in the 1938-vintage AT-6 (Texan or Harvard) trainers that were removed from mothballs to serve effectively as target-spotters in the forward areas have already been related. Piper Cubs and their spin-offs, Taylorcraft Austers, served as air observation posts and on liaison duties. (These were even used on at least one occasion to drop ammunition and desperately needed rations to isolated units.)

Another early aircraft that saw extensive, if comparatively unrecognized service, was the 1937 Short Sunderland flying boat (the Flying Porcupine), which the RAF operated on maritime patrols from its base in Iwakuni, Japan. Nor can we forget the C-47 which circled overhead in the darkness, scaring the living daylights out of isolated listening patrols with a loud-speaker burst of propaganda in Korean, apparently right beside us.

Despite the loss of most of their combat aircraft to the U.S. Navy and 5th Air Force, the North Koreans did not give up completely. In a war that featured jets and high-performance propeller-driven aircraft such as the Sea Fury, Corsair and B-29, they turned to what was almost a museum piece, the Polikarpov Po-2. This antique machine first went into service in 1928, and was built for simplicity. For instance, the upper and lower wings of the biplane were interchangeable. The *Kukuruznik*, or "corn-cutter" as it was nicknamed, was powered by a 100 h.p. motor that gave it a maximum speed of 100 mph. The wood and fabric-covered Po-2 served in the Second World War as a trainer and in many other roles, coming into its own as a nuisance raider in support of Russia's guerrilla forces. One of its main advantages was an ability to operate from small grass airstrips near the front, which helped overcome its fairly limited range of 430 kilometers. Its ability to operate on low-grade regular gasoline was an asset to the North Koreans in light of the constant interdiction of supply lines by UN aircraft and naval vessels.

During the static phase of the Korean War (from late 1951), North Korean counterparts of Errol Flynn would climb into the open cockpits of their biplanes and head south. Sometimes an air gunner armed with a machine gun or, in at least one instance, a burp gun machine carbine, would accompany them. The intrepid duo would fly low and slow between the mountain crests, usually at dusk or in darkness, seeking targets of opportunity, dropping their bombs (or in some cases leaflets) and making their way home.

The M-11 engine sounded like a washing machine motor, which resulted in the UN nickname of "Maytag Charlie," although the habit of droning overhead after last light earned these raiders the more familiar sobriquet of "Bed-check Charlie." Their low altitude and wooden construction negated the effectiveness of allied radar, and their low speed, small size and maneuverability frustrated the efforts of the higher-powered UN aircraft. Despite this, several of the biplanes and other more modern "bed-checks," such as the YAK-18 trainer, fell to the guns of the U.S. fighters. Three of the latter were credited to the U.S. navy's only Korean War ace, Lt Guy Bordelon. Nor did the American fighters escape unscathed. Aviation historian Mike O'Connor, as reported in *Military History* (March 1998), stated that at least six high-performance aircraft, including three jets, met disaster at the hands of "Charlies." At least one of these, flown by an experienced jet jockey, stalled and crashed in a low-altitude attempt to out-manoeuvre a Po-2. On the plus side 13 "Charlies" were confirmed as destroyed in aerial combat.

During the last year of the war the Kukuruzniks were reinforced by another, slightly faster training aircraft, the Yakolev YAK-18. Developed in 1946, the YAK-18 monoplane boasted a closed cockpit and retractable undercarriage. Its bomb-aiming equipment consisted of the observer dropping the light missiles over the side. Like the Po-2, this aircraft could operate from primitive airstrips. Occasionally these aircraft were heard, but seldom seen, over Commonwealth Division lines. Although they had some success (*Military History* reported that, in the last month of the Korean War, a raid by a few YAK-18s destroyed 5.5 million gallons of fuel), their main achievement was their nuisance value. While some casualties were inflicted on the ground troops, perhaps "Charlie's" most significant effect was the loss of sleep by rear-echelon troops (a hardship which the sharp end sufferers who had heard the sounds of a washing-machine rinse cycle overhead heading south did not always appreciate).

ABOVE: *HMCS* Sioux (top) *was one of the original three ships dispatched to Korea waters in July 1950. (DND)*

OPPOSITE PAGE: *HMCS* Crusader *got off to a slow start, but soon became the undisputed "train-buster" champion. (DND)*

THE NAVY IS HERE!

While the brunt of the Korean War effort was, of necessity, borne by army units, the RCN was in no way a bystander to the action.

SUFFICE IT TO SAY the navy vessels were first in and among the last Canadian combat units to leave the theatre. On July 5, 1950 the first shift of three Canadian destroyers set sail from Esquimalt and, by month's end, had been placed under command of the Far East U.S. naval forces. Following a couple of weeks of escort duty, HMCS *Cayuga* joined a British frigate, HMS *Mounts Bay,* in bombarding an enemy strongpoint. On August 15, 1950 this vessel had the distinction of firing the first Canadian shots in the Korean War.

The Canadian naval forces served with distinction. The vessels were well suited to close inshore work, and soon established an enviable reputation for cloak-and-dagger operations in conjunction with South Korean marines and guerrillas.

I do not have space to describe the many achievements of the seven Canadian destroyers that, in turn, helped establish an exemplary reputation in the *Forgotten War.* Two achievements, however, are worthy of mention. HMCS *Nootka* has the distinction of being the only United Nations warship to capture an enemy vessel (a minelayer taken in October 1952). Most destroyers had a turn in the "train-busting club," bringing gunfire to bear on enemy railroad operations in the coastal areas. The Canadians excelled in this, and the undisputed Seventh Fleet champion train-buster was HMCS *Crusader*, which received the code-sign "Casey Jones" in recognition of the achievement.

In all, RCN vessels fired 120,000 rounds of ammunition during their Korean service. A total of 3621 officers and ratings served between 1950 and 1953, with many of them completing repeat tours. Nine members lost their lives, and 62 were decorated. I have recently discovered that all those who served under command of the U.S. Seventh Fleet are entitled to wear the official U.S. Navy Commendation Ribbon. It is well deserved.

~ ~ ~ ~ ~ ~ ~ ~ ~ ~

SHIP'S PERFORMANCE MERITS THE HIGHEST PRAISE

Canadian military enthusiasts are familiar with the well-deserved United States Distinguished Unit Citation awarded to the 2PPCLI for their stand at Kapyong in 1951. Less familiar is another unique award gained by a vessel of the Royal Canadian Navy that same year.

On December 21, 1951, it was announced that Syngman Rhee, the president of the Republic of Korea, had awarded a Presidential Unit Citation to HMCS *Athabaskan* - the only such award to any element of the Canadian Forces.

The citation reads:

"The president of the Republic of Korea takes profound pleasure in citing for exceptionally meritorious service and heroism Royal Canadian Naval Ship [sic] *Athabaskan*, for the award of the Presidential Unit Citation.

"This ship has formed part of the United Nations naval forces for over one year. It has taken part with great credit in all types of operations including support of the Inchon landing.

"In carrying out operations along enemy-occupied coast this was the first United Nations ship to organize and land raiding parties from its own crew to harry the enemy, to collect valuable information and to make contact with friendly personnel.

"The performance of this ship merits the highest praise."

In all, *Athabaskan* served three tours of duty in Korean waters. Accompanied by her consorts *Cayuga* and *Sioux*, the Tribal-class destroyer left Esquimalt on July 5, 1950 — only 10 days after the North Koreans had crossed the 38th Parallel - and arrived in Sasebo, Japan on the 30th of that month.

The crew did not have long to sample the exotic delights of that port. The next day they were on their way to join the colleagues from other Commonwealth navies on the west coast of the Korean peninsula.

To their chagrin, the distinction of firing Canada's first shots in anger in the Korean War fell to *Cayuga*.

Athabaskan's turn came the following day, on August 16th, when her guns destroyed a number of warehouses and artillery batteries in the port of Kunsan. Later the North Korean garrison of Popsong-po, further south, suffered heavy damages and casualties from *Athabaskan*'s fire.

On August 19th, *Athabaskan* moved close inshore to the strategically important island of Tokchok-to. The island lay near the entrance to Inchon harbour, and was garrisoned by North Koreans. In the early morning, *Athabaskan* and an accompanying Royal Navy cruiser opened fire on the island's infantry defenders, and supported the landing by a group of ROK marines. The North Koreans were all disposed of and a landing party was sent ashore from the Canadian vessel to assist any wounded civilians.

A few days later General MacArthur launched his famous landing in Inchon, and *Athabaskan* may well claim some of the credit for the success of this operation. In a way, these operations set the pattern for the role of the Royal Canadian Navy in the Korean War. They would provide covering fire to landing parties, which were usually ROK marines. A former *Athabaskan* described these as a "tough, mean lot of bastards." Their ruthlessness was probably justified as the South Koreans had suffered many atrocities under the Communists.

When possible, landing parties would be sent out from the Canadian vessels after the mission was accomplished. They would gather what information they could, and if there were civilian casualties, provide medical treatment and evacuation facilities. Their expertise, together with the readiness of the Canadians to take part in this type of combined operation, soon made them the acknowledged experts in this type of warfare. Later, the Canadian vessels were extensively employed in supporting friendly guerrillas on the islands off North Korea.

In his excellent story of the RCN in Korea, *Thunder in the Morning Calm*, Edward Meyers writes: "By night the destroyers shelled the Chinese-held islands, by day they hit targets further to the south. *Athabaskan* was probably the busiest ship in the fleet as she ran various errands, which included ferrying guerrillas to Taewha-do and carrying supplies to more outlying islets along the coast."

Nor were the Reds the only enemy. In late 1950, the fleet was heavily hit by a typhoon in which a seaman was washed overboard, to be saved only by what Meyers describes as a "combination of superb seamanship and almost unbelievably good luck." Other Commonwealth ships were less fortunate, sustaining heavy damage and several casualties.

There was little opportunity for ship-to-ship action. Enemy vessels encountered were usually junks and outgunned by *Athabaskan*'s armament (the Bofors crews were able to get in their licks in these actions). Land-based artillery posed a more serious threat. Although in most cases they were outranged by the ship's guns, it was sometimes necessary to move closer inshore within range of the enemy weapons.

Athabaskan's own awards were not confined to Korean Presidential Citations. Commissioned Gunner David Hurl was Mentioned in Despatches after disposing of a floating mine by attaching an explosive charge to the deadly weapon while tossing alongside it in a small boat. The captains on the ship's three tours, Commanders Welland, King and Reed were awarded a bar to the Distinguished Service Cross, a DSC and OBE respectively for their services. CPO Vander-Haegan and PO Shield received the British Empire Medal, while 12 members of the ship's company were Mentioned in Despatches.

In addition, *Athabaskan* became a member of the celebrated Train-busters club by destroying two enemy freight trains on the North Korean coastal railroad. Finally, this gallant vessel compensated for being beaten to the post by *Cayuga* when, on July 20, 1953, her guns fired the last shell by the Royal Canadian Navy in the Korean War.

~ ~ ~ ~ ~ ~ ~ ~ ~ ~

THE CASE OF THE SPURIOUS SAWBONES

In the fall of 1951, a lady glancing through her daily newspaper inadvertently unmasked one of the most unusual deceptions in Canadian naval history.

She was the mother of a doctor, Joseph Cyr, who was practising medicine in Grand Falls, New Brunswick. To her astonishment, she read an account of an emergency operation performed on the deck of a Canadian destroyer off the coast of Korea – apparently by her son. She contacted Doctor Cyr, who, after reassuring his mother he was indeed still in civilian practise, called the Royal Canadian Mounted Police. A bizarre story unfolded.

It began in early 1951, when an American named Ferdinand Waldo "Fred" Demara entered Canada and became a novitiate monk in Grand Falls. For more than a decade, Demara had held positions in a number of religious orders, as well as a psychologist, university lecturer, college department head, schoolteacher, and prison warden. Despite this impressive employment record, Demara had obtained and held these posts on the basis of forged, stolen or non-existent qualifications.

Demara became friendly with Doctor Cyr, and often visited the latter's office. Eventually the visits ceased.

In March of 1951, a Doctor Joseph Cyr appeared at the naval recruiting office in Saint John, N.B., and offered his professional services to the Royal Canadian Navy. He hinted that if the navy couldn't use him, the army or RCAF would be glad to accept him. At this stage of the Korean War and with Canada's new NATO commitments, qualified medical officers were desperately needed by all three services, and no time was lost in processing this valuable recruit.

His credentials were accepted without verification, and three days after his visit to the recruiting centre, he was commissioned into the RCN as a surgeon-lieutenant. The normal two-month enlistment process took about one day.

Had a thorough background investigation been conducted, the authorities would no doubt have discovered that "Doctor Joseph Cyr" was none other than the ubiquitous Fred Demara, whose medical experience was limited to a few weeks as an unskilled hospital orderly in the United States.

The bogus doctor was assigned to the naval hospital at HMCS *Stadacona* in the Halifax area. Retired naval Captain "Mack" Lynch, who was a department head at *Stadacona* at the time, later recalled that "Cyr" appeared to be a fairly competent medical officer, and a pleasant enough individual, although not a great mixer. Captain Lynch said that "Cyr" showed a great deal of interest in adapting aircrew selection psycho-physical test methods (which Lynch had taken in World War II) as a naval screening procedure.

"Cyr's" hospital patients apparently survived his ministrations by a combination of a generous use of penicillin, referral or consultation with other medical officers and, no doubt, a combination of physical fitness and sheer luck!

This idyllic existence ended on June 16, 1951, when "Cyr" joined HMCS *Cayuga* in Esquimalt, B.C. – leaving three days later for the destroyer's second tour of duty in Korean waters.

"Surgeon-Lieutenant Cyr" managed to cope effectively with the few minor injuries and ailments that occurred en route to the war zone. He was fortunate in that he had a capable sick berth attendant, PO Bob Hotchin, who handled most of the routine cases. The petty officer was surprised, and indeed gratified, by the way in which he was allowed to work with a minimum of direction and interference from his medical officer.

"Cyr's" biggest challenge came when he was forced to act as a dentist. His patient was none other than the *Cayuga's* commander, Captain James Plomer. In the rush to prepare his ship for her return to Korea, Captain Plomer had no time to obtain treatment for an infected tooth, which became a problem during the westward voyage.

The bogus doctor, highly perturbed, feverishly studied his manuals and racked his brain to recall any dental surgery that he had witnessed in the past. He eventually gained the courage to collect his dental gear, a large supply of anesthetic and make his way to the captain's cabin.

After administering a hefty dose of local anesthetic, "Cyr" successfully removed the offending tooth, and by all reports, Captain Plomer had no further trouble with it.

His confidence no doubt restored, the bogus doctor continued to handle routine shipboard injuries and minor ailments as *Cayuga* entered the war zone.

On arrival off the west coast of Korea, *Cayuga* and her crew became involved in operations that smacked more of the gunboat diplomacy of the 19th century than the traditional picture of naval warfare. Captain Don Saxon, who was a lieutenant-commander at the time, recalled that the Canadian vessels would take part in commando-type operations against enemy-occupied islands. Selected members of the ships' crews would accompany members of U.S. or Korean marines ashore and with their weapons and demolition charges generally create alarm and despondency in enemy circles. While our own casualties were light, the amount of hairiness involved was evidenced by a number of gallantry awards, including a Distinguished Service Cross for Saxon.

It was one of these commando raids led to Demara's unmasking.

Following a highly successful foray on the west coast of Korea, the only three seriously-wounded casualties – all South Korean guerrillas – were brought back to *Cayuga*. One apparently had a bullet embedded in his lung. The ship's medical officer operated on him on the spot, by all accounts successfully, although no one ever saw the bullet that was supposedly extracted. (Other reports indicate that "Cyr" also amputated a foot during these naval operations.) Whatever his qualifications, it would appear that the patients survived the attentions of the bogus doctor.

Unfortunately for the masquerade, news from Korea was scarce at that time. A pair of war correspondents snapped up the story of the open deck surgery – the account found its way into the Canadian papers, and into the hands of the real Doctor Cyr's mother.

The real doctor remembered that his medical credentials were missing, but attributed the fact to a recent move. He also recalled that "Brother John" (Demara) disappeared at the same time.

Eventually, in October 1952, Captain Plomer received a signal to the effect that his medical officer was an unqualified imposter. He found this hard to believe, as in the opinion of the ship's officers "Cyr" was a capable and popular doctor. Another message received the following day removed all doubts, and "Dr. Cyr" was sent to a British cruiser, HMS *Ceylon*, for transfer to Japan and subsequently to Canada.

Lieutenant Commander Saxon, with another officer, was detailed to search the doctor's cabin, and found letters and other documents that confirmed the imposture. Demara – there was no question of his identity by this time – had apparently taken an overdose of drugs that day. Whether or not this was a suicidal attempt is questionable, although Captain Plomer felt that it was.

On arrival in Canada, Demara appeared before a naval board of inquiry. There appears to be no record of disciplinary proceedings, and service records indicate that "Cyr" was given an honourable release and several hundred dollars in back pay. He left Canada (some reports indicate that he was deported) and returned to the religious field, eventually becoming a bona-fide clergyman under his own name.

John Melady, author of *Korea: Canada's Forgotten War*, recalled a telephone interview in which Demara "had good things to say about Canada, the Canadian Navy and the officers and men he knew on the *Cayuga*." Demara supposedly participated in a *Cayuga* reunion in Victoria in 1979. The Reverend Ferdinand Waldo Demara died in 1982.

One minor deception remained as a result of Demara's escapade. In 1961 Hollywood made a movie, *The Great Imposter*, starring Tony Curtis in the title role of Demara. "He was nothing like the real thing," chuckled Don Saxon. "Cyr, as we knew him, was a pretty chunky 200-pounder – nothing at all like Curtis. And Edmund O'Brien was just as much out of place in the role of Captain Plomer."

Commodore Plomer was listed in the film credits as a technical adviser but Saxon feels that his technical advice was not always heeded. Even I, as a "brown job" noted the incongruity of a Canadian naval board of inquiry consisting of group of officers properly clad in RCN uniform, but with every member sporting a black pencil moustache.

In one case, apparently, Commodore Plomer had his way. He was able to ensure that the correct hull number was used for his ship. This generated a deception that Demara would surely have enjoyed.

Cayuga (hull number 218) was on the east coast – the film crew was working out of Esquimalt, B.C. As George Guertin, a naval veteran of the Korean War recalled, "In 1961 I was out west on HMCS *Athabaskan*. We got an unusual order to 'paint ship.' A bunch of us had to close up the 9 on our side number to make our '219' read '218.' We were told that it had something to do with a movie. When we saw *The Great Imposter*, we realized that there were really two imposters – Demara and *Athabaskan*!"

~ ~ ~ ~ ~ ~ ~ ~ ~ ~

SUB-SURFACE MATTERS...

There was very little naval surface action during the Korean War. Indeed, there was only one recorded incident of anything resembling a ship-to-ship encounter. On July 2, 1950, a brave but foolhardy North Korean naval lieutenant, Kim Kun Ok, led a force of four Russian-built aluminum-hulled torpedo boats against a British-U.S. force of two cruisers and a frigate off Korea's east coast. The uneven battled ended with the loss of three of Kim's vessels, which were unable to get into torpedo range. The allied warships remained unscathed, later destroying most of the supply trawlers that the MTBs had been escorting.

Each Canadian destroyer serving off Korea carried a torpedo anti-submarine officer. The lack of enemy submarine activity had an unexpected spin-off effect in some cases. On *Cayuga*, the TAS officer, Lieutenant Don Saxon, learned that his skills were not in great demand, and was told he "was the officer who could be best spared for the guerrilla support acitivites" and was assigned as a landing party officer. His new role provided him with an exciting war and subsequent award of the Distinguished Service Cross.

Surprisingly, much warship time was devoted to screening the major vessels, especially the U.S. and British aircraft carriers, from anticipated submarine attack. Rumours persisted that the U.S.S.R. had provided a pair of submarines to North Korea. Soviet submarines, too, were known to be operating from the Pacific port of Dairen. In 1950, the U.S. and British naval commands stated "a submerged submarine construed a threat of aggression, and should be driven off by any means available in self defence."

Britain's HMS *Cockade* supposedly depth-charged and sank an unidentified submarine, although surprisingly no record exists in the ship's log regarding the ASDIC contact or the firing of depth-charges.

Members of *Cockade*'s crew recall the operation vividly, and at least two of them remember picking up debris. The plot thickens: Two crew members recall ship's officers discussing what they thought was "S-46" – which was identified many years later as a submarine of the Soviet Union's Pacific Fleet that had been reported lost "in the early 1950s." The mystery lies in the "S" designation, as there is no letter "S" in the Cyrillic alphabet. It may well be that both sides decided that nothing would be gained by publicizing the incident, and it was quietly hushed up to avoid escalating the conflict. Officially, however, there were no submarines – although reports of shadowing of UN naval forces by Soviet vessels were not uncommon.

This did not mean that the threat of submarines was ignored. *Athabaskan*'s Ed Dalton later recalled that when the Chinese entered the war in late 1950, there were fears that their submarines would take part. Dalton, a sonar operator, said that one rock off the coast of Korea returned a "ping" just like a submarine and was constantly being depth-charged.

Perhaps the most deadly weapon used by the North Korean navy was the mine. These were encountered several times by Canadian warships. Ed Dalton remembers one occasion when a mine was sighted. The ship was unable to move close enough inshore to sink the mine by gunfire (the usual and safest method) and he accompanied Commissioned Gunner Hurl, PO Tom Shields and two fellow ABs in a dinghy while Mr. Hurl attached charges to detonate the mine. Dalton had to hold the lifting rings on the mine to make sure that it would not hit the boat and explode. For some reason, the team had to wear steel helmets during the operation – a useless and dangerous accoutrement. PO Shields received the British Empire Medal for his work, Mr. Hurl was Mentioned in Despatches and "the three ABs got an extra tot of rum."

The mines encountered by the Canadians turned out to be Russian-designed "contact" mines. North Korean fishing vessels often randomly laid these. Mr. Hurl's crew, in steel helmets, was probably fortunate in that they did not encounter the (then) top-secret Russian influence mine. Don Loney, a member of the Ottawa Rough Riders' winning Grey Cup team in 1951, volunteered for the underwater training unit in Halifax. While attending a course in Maryland, he was introduced to one of these, recovered in Korea. In his story in *Dippers Digest* (the Canadian Naval Divers Association newsletter), he recalled that he had no knife – essential for underwater mine clearing. He purchased one from a military surplus store, and used it to tap the mine. His U.S. instructors casually asked if the knife was "non-magnetic" as anything with a magnetic influence would have detonated the thing. Fortunately for all concerned, he had luckily (and unknowingly) bought a non-magnetic implement, and so lived on to coach the *Stadacona* Sailors football team.

While the North Korean mines had a nuisance value, they also took their toll. Four U.S. minesweepers and a trawler were sunk, as well as at least one Japanese vessel, operating under an "E" flag as Japan was still, technically, an enemy country. In addition, mines damaged five U.S. destroyers.

The underwater menace was ever-present. The fact that, during the Korean War a total of 1,535 reported mines were destroyed is an indication that this threat was not to be taken lightly. How many uncharted mines still pose a threat off Korea's coast is anyone's guess.

TRAIN BUSTING

Apart from the fact that many of us lived a mole-like existence in holes in the ground around the 38th parallel, tunnels played quite an important role in the Korean War.

Our navy quickly learned the significance of railway tunnels in their efforts to gain admittance to what was perhaps one of the most exclusive clubs in the Far East.

With a paucity of seaborne targets for the guns of the destroyers off the North Korean coast, the vessels played an important part in disrupting the enemy's rail communications. As a morale-boosting initiative, the U.S. Navy formed what they called a "Train-Busters Club." To qualify for membership, a vessel's guns had to destroy an enemy train, including the locomotive. Subsequent points were added for other trains demolished – for these the killing of the locomotive was optional.

Despite the fact that her tour in the productive area was far shorter than other, mainly U.S. vessels, HMCS *Crusader* became the undisputed champion of the club. However, at first even the *Crusader's* 4.7-inch guns were foiled.

The coastal railroad was plentifully endowed with tunnels. In order to protect their precious and dwindling stock of railway engines, the North Koreans' practice was to uncouple the locomotive and hightail it into the next tunnel as soon as the train came under fire, leaving the wagons and their contents to their fate. As the locomotive's destruction was a necessary first blood for Club membership every effort was made to knock out the engine before it gained cover. *Crusader's* prey escaped on the first attempt but there was no mistake the following night – the Canadian vessel's final total was four trains. *Haida* and *Athabaskan* soon joined crusader in this elite fraternity.

LEFT: *Canadian troops get a chuckle out of the propaganda signs they recovered during a patrol in no man's land.* (DND)

OPPOSITE PAGE: *UN prisoners in custody of the Chinese.* (DND)

🐚 PRISONERS & PROPAGANDA

Unwilling guests of the Communists.

IT WAS SUGGESTED THAT I produce an article for *Esprit de Corps* magazine on the experiences of Canadians in captivity during the Korean War. This proved a little more difficult than I expected. First of all, the number of Canadians held by the enemy was comparatively small, and, secondly, most of those taken were captured when the war had been in progress for some time, and many of the horror stories occurred during the earlier days. Although I have picked the brains of three Canadian captives, much of the material has been gleaned from the recollections of British prisoners, especially those of 29 Brigade who fell into enemy hands following the Imjin battles.

That is not to say that Canadians had an easy life, or were forgotten. Indeed, Lance Corporal Paul Dugal of the Van Doos, who was captured in June 1952, was awarded the British Empire Medal for his fortitude and assistance in identifying other Canadian captives whose whereabouts had been unknown. This was despite the fact that during much of the time he suffered terribly from untreated injuries. The story of Squadron Leader Andy MacKenzie, who was held for almost 18 months after the ceasefire in an attempt to exact a spurious confession of violation of Chinese airspace, has already been told.

Conditions in the North Korean and Chinese POW camps bore little resemblance to the Stalags of the Second World War. There was little need for machine gun towers, double-wire fences or other measures to keep the prisoners closely confined. The sheer isolation, together with the near-impossibility of a Caucasian to remain undetected for long, were formidable deterrents to escape. Nevertheless, a few determined allied prisoners did make the attempt, but were usually quickly recaptured and punished.

Many of the 29 Brigade prisoners had no illusions. Some of them had served in the Far East in WWII where a number of them had been prisoners of the Japanese. They knew that Koreans, serving under the Japanese flag, were among the most sadistic of their captors. In many cases, their fears were justified. Three George Crosses were awarded for heroism during captivity – two of these were posthumous awards. The Chinese, on the whole, appeared more correct than the North Koreans in their treatment of the POWs.

One propaganda message from the Chinese People's Volunteer Forces left in front of the Commonwealth Division lines read: "In the April battle 701 officers and men of the British 29th Brigade were captured … we sent them to the safe rear for learning … they play ball and amuse themselves after studying every day."

They were the lucky ones. Many UN captives never even made it to captivity. While at times the Chinese treated wounded prisoners and even directed them back to friendly lines, in other instances captives were simply executed en masse. The North Koreans perpetrated most of these atrocities in the earlier months of the war.

Indeed, following the repatriation of a few severely injured prisoners in 1951, word of the methods used in attempts to obtain information for prisoners became known and the training film *Resisting Enemy Interrogation* was produced. "Not to be shown to recruits," the film described some of the methods the North Koreans used at that time on prisoners of war.

The theme of the film was the necessity for prisoners to retain their cohesive integrity. One Communist ploy was to cultivate loners and create dissent within groups. While this worked to some extent on American prisoners, many of whom were demoralized by the shock of capture early in the war, it proved less effective on Commonwealth captives. As an example, the death rate in captivity for American prisoners was over 35 per cent, while less than 50 of the 1,188 Commonwealth prisoners died in enemy hands. This difference may be attributed to the mutual support and, perhaps, the training and discipline of the Australian, British and Canadian troops.

Padre Stanley Davies, of the Gloucesters, recalled that their captors felt they were "more to be pitied than blamed" as "tools of reactionary warmongers" and "hirelings of the barbarous Rhee puppet-government," but that they would be given the chance to "learn the truth through study."

For many United Nations personnel captured in Korea, the initial impression was one of confusion. Despite the stylized propaganda photographs both sides circulated, the groups of captives neatly posing with their hands up and covered by their captors were the exception.

Captain Joe Liston was flying an Auster aircraft, spotting for artillery. In one respect he was fortunate: Earlier the Air OP pilots flew without parachutes, but following the death of an Australian pilot who was unable to bail out, the rule was rescinded. Liston's aircraft was hit, but he was able to bail out. He noticed that numerous enemy troops were waiting for him, but most of his captors appeared friendly, even offering him cigarettes.

Canadian prisoners were relatively few and most of these were captured during the final 12 months of the war. On the night of May 2, 1953, the last major Canadian battle was fought. Len Badowich was one of the seven members of 3RCR captured on Hill 187. He was ordered to warn the Canadians to get under cover as Ed Hollyer, his platoon commander, was calling down fire on their own position. "That's when I ran into the Chinese and I was captured," he recalled. With his comrades, he was taken to a farm in the Chinese rear, given blankets, and allowed to sleep.

Like most prisoners he was interrogated and questioned, but these were quite simple. This did not mean that gentle and not-so-gentle coercion was not practised. The aim, however, was more to score propaganda points and to break the will to resist among POWs. Co-operation was rewarded and resistance was punished. Thus, for example, when Squadron Leader Andy MacKenzie was captured and held in captivity for almost a year and a half after the ceasefire, he was subjected to mental pressure including isolation and haranguing. The Chinese were not seeking information on his aircraft, or allied air tactics. They were looking for a written confession that, when he was shot down, he was violating Chinese airspace.

John Melady, in *Korea: Canada's Forgotten War,* recounted the experience of George Griffiths, captured on Hill 355 in October 1952. Griffiths was shuttled through a Chinese trench-and-tunnel system that ran on for miles, until he was interrogated by a Chinese soldier who drew a Canadian and U.S. flag on the table. When he indicated his nationality, the Chinese all stabbed the U.S. flag with their bayonets, to Griffith's relief. "I sure picked the right flag!" he said.

After assembly and preliminary interrogation, the Commonwealth prisoners began the long march northwards. Conditions varied, apparently depending on the current policy towards POWs and, in some cases, the individual officers in charge of the escorts.

The columns often marched by night to avoid detection from the air (pine boughs notwithstanding). A U.S. air attack frustrated an escape attempt by George

Griffiths and a companion, which fortunately caused no casualties, but resulted in a tightening-up of guard surveillance. In any case, the chances of a Caucasian remaining at large in enemy territory with little or no food or protection from the severe climate were slight. There are few, if any, recorded cases of successful escapes by Commonwealth personnel from North Korea.

The journey to the final destination was made almost exclusively on foot. Jim Gunn, in 3RCR, later recalled a short lift by truck, but said it was mostly one long march. One frustrating aspect was that (like many route marches under more pleasant conditions) it was a case of hurry-stop-hurry rather than a steady pace. Daily rests were usually made in Korean villages. The inhabitants (if any) were rudely moved out of their homes, which were allocated to prisoners and their guards.

As the prisoners moved further to the rear, interrogations became less frequent and political indoctrination began. As a taste of things to come, the Commonwealth troops would be lectured on the Chinese "lenient" policy and the "atrocities committed by Syngman Rhee and his American imperialist allies." They were to endure more of this when they finally arrived at their final destinations.

One newsman was shot and captured by the North Koreans in 1950. Suspected of being a British spy, he was held for almost three years and tortured for 17 months, including being tied to a chair, naked, sitting in his own excrement. He survived to take his place in the Canadian Senate as Senator Philippe Gigantes.

The Chinese guards were often required to protect their charges from the North Koreans, who frequently tried to take prisoners hostage.

George Griffiths was constantly interrogated, more to obtain propaganda material than for military information. For almost a year of captivity he was subjected to daily Communist indoctrination, euphemistically termed "social studies." While prisoners were allowed to write home, letters would be censored and would not be delivered until they satisfied their captors. Although other prisoners later reported that they were issued with blue cotton uniforms and quilted outerwear in the winter, Griffiths said he was not allowed a change of clothes. It was only in June 1953 (eight months after his capture) that he was provided with fresh clothing and minor luxuries such as toothpaste, and received medical attention for wounds he incurred during his capture.

On arrival on the Yalu, the captives found that their new home bore little resemblance to Second World War prison camps. While prisoners' huts were crowded – the inmates had been organized into 10-man sections, each of which shared a small room – at least they usually provided more shelter than the caves and barns where they were quartered en route. Occasionally, some of the villagers remained. One British POW hurrying out of his hut for roll call accidentally bumped into a Korean woman in the roadway; he was sentenced to a fortnight in the penal camp for attempted rape.

Other camps were hastily constructed Korean pattern houses. Jim Gunn recalled that the camp where he was confined backed on to a quarry or mine of some sort. A single strand of wire marked the perimeter. Although a number of allied prisoners managed to evade their captors in the early stages of captivity, few, if any, got away from the Yalu camps.

A typical day would begin with reveille over the loudspeakers, usually at daybreak. This might consist of Russian or Chinese military marches or Paul Robeson's rendition of *The Internationale*. After falling in, the groups would disperse for the first of the day's "information sessions." Breakfast – a portion of sorghum or millet – would follow, and then perhaps more lectures. Fatigue parties might be organized, usually to collect wood for fuel and more "political education" and, perhaps, a meagre ration of meatless soup.

The American prisoners were surprised to find that the British troops kept active, exercising by walking around the compound or organizing sporting activities. At times they would confound their captors by odd acts of defiance, such as pretending to be helicopters and "flying" around the compound, or riding imaginary motorcycles and exercising invisible dogs. While many Americans viewed these antics with disfavour as "rocking the boat," it is only fair to note that a number of U.S. prisoners refused to accept their condition quietly and were greatly admired by the British for their stubborn resistance.

Ted Beckersley remembered that almost daily one or more American captives had passed away, and their bodies were carried past the British compound to what they called "Boot Hill." During the doleful parade, the loudspeakers would play the *Blue Danube* – a waltz that he would be unable to tolerate for years after his release.

Work parties were usually engaged in "self-help" tasks such as gathering wood. As wood became scarce, the Chinese, probably to preserve what little there was for the North Korean inhabitants, brought in fire logs from China across the frozen Yalu.

Food was monotonous – sorghum or millet three times daily. This was later augmented with rice, which was easier to digest. Len Badowich later recalled that one of his companions in captivity enjoyed being one of the last to be served with rice, as the stuff in the bottom of the pot had become crisp and was supposedly tastier. Dysentery and beriberi were commonplace. Many Americans refused to eat the mush, and eventually passed away. The British, however, would force any reluctant recipients to eat the food, if only to keep alive. Later in 1952, and especially as the prospect of repatriation neared, the rations were augmented with tea, sugar, flour, potatoes and even pork, chicken and eggs.

Nevertheless, following the armistice when the Canadian POWs returned to the UN lines in August 1953, they fell upon the luxuries of milk, fresh bread and ice cream with a great deal of enthusiasm.

~ ~ ~ ~ ~ ~ ~ ~ ~ ~

KILLED OR CAPTIVE?

During the night of October 12, 1952, in the shadow of Kowang-San (the notorious Hill 355), "B" Company of 1RCR conducted a company-strength fighting patrol against Chinese troops occupying the point 227 feature.

In the words of the patrol debriefing report: "The patrol reached approximately (MR 163194) at 2335 hours and at this point encountered an enemy ambush. This ambush was apparently well planned and coordinated. It consisted of a reinforced enemy platoon sited on ground which was advantageous to the enemy. The ambush was in the form of a U, or three sided box and well armed with burp guns, at least one LMG (light machine gun) and grenades. In addition, the enemy called a mortar DF into the centre of this U. The two scouts were immediately wounded and no more was seen of them."

The lead platoon continued to receive heavy fire from the Chinese, including a machine gun situated on Hill 227, and were almost surrounded by the enemy. About half of them were now wounded. An attempt by another platoon to outflank the enemy was unsuccessful, and after the company commander had called for artillery close support the two lead elements withdrew, closely followed by the enemy who harassed them with small arms fire and grenades. This effectively prevented attempts to recover the two wounded scouts.

The two point soldiers, Lance Corporal John Fairman and Private Joseph Kilpatrick, were reported "Missing in Action" the next day and over a year later, when no word had been received of their fate, were presumed dead and listed as "Killed in Action."

Captain John Clark, who commanded one of the platoons on that patrol, still has his doubts regarding their death. "I knew both of these men, and I'm sure that they wouldn't get taken without a fight," he insisted. "Fairman was a strong member of the battalion hockey team and Kilpatrick was pretty tough, too." Yet when Clark volunteered to lead a small group back to the scene, a thorough search of the area failed to produce any trace of the missing men. "There were no signs of a struggle – no bloodstains or anything," he said.

Captain Clark suspects that the two Canadians may have been captured and passed to the Chinese or even to the Soviet Union for questioning, brainwashing or in an attempt to obtain confessions for propaganda purposes. A number of facts support this theory. The "B" Company war diary indicates that a deserter surrendered to the neighbouring PPCLI and reported that two prisoners had been taken on the night of October 12th.

In fact, a Chinese political officer did give himself up to the Patricias, but both the preliminary and detailed interrogation reports make no mention of UN prisoners being taken.

What was received from the PPCLI area was a radio intercept of a Chinese radio transmission emanating from their front that read, "We are going to meet them pretty soon. You call them to get their grenades ready for meeting the enemy's rush. If the situation is not so good for us, kill the two prisoners first." As no attack was carried out on the Chinese positions, there is no reason to believe that this would have been carried out.

The British Air Ministry (whose team intercepted the message) passed this information to the Canadian authorities, which felt that the evidence was insufficient to change the status of these soldiers to "Missing, believed POW."

One interesting item of information came from the PPCLI's Chinese defector. He reported that his unit had been instructed to capture 10 POWs during the month of October, supposedly to "better comprehend the UN situation."

"Spiriting away" of UN prisoners was not without precedent. A year earlier, Corporal Dick Toole of 2PPCLI disappeared in an early-morning fight with the enemy. Again, no trace was found, and Toole was also reported "Killed in Action." Unofficial reports, including a *Toronto Star* story, indicate that Toole may have been among a group of prisoners moved to Siberia.

Recently declassified documents from U.S. archives in Washington report the transfer of "several hundred" UN POWs from China to the Soviet Union at the railroad station at Manchouli, on the U.S.S.R.-Manchurian border. Although these were described as American it is quite possible that the group may have included members of other UN contingents.

In the breakup of the Soviet Union, many records were deliberately destroyed, although some documents are still held. As recently as 1998, Moscow refused to turn over a secret KGB document that related to captured Americans being passed to the Soviet Union "for intelligence-gathering purposes."

Where are these prisoners now? How many of them are still alive? In the words of former Russian President Boris Yeltsin: "Our archives have shown this (the transfers) to be true. Some of them were transferred to the territory of the former U.S.S.R. and were kept in labour camps. We don't have complete data and can only surmise that some of them may still be alive."

It is perhaps worthy of note that Fairman and Kilpatrick were both members of "B" Company 1RCR and had served at the Koje-do POW compound earlier that year. These troops were a prime target for enemy interrogators, who hoped to extract admissions of brutality towards Chinese and North Korean prisoners. With the changed climate in the former Soviet Union, it is hoped that any records on

POWs held or encountered by their members might be made available.

Altogether there are 16 Canadians reported killed who have no known grave. Most of these can be accounted for, in many cases as victims of heavy shelling. Two members of 1PPCLI were lost under similar circumstances shortly after the RCR members disappeared, but reliable reports indicate that they were almost certainly fatally wounded at the time. Meanwhile, despite the official reports, the fate of LCpl. John Fairman and Pte. Joseph Kilpatrick (and perhaps Cpl. Dick Toole) remains uncertain to a number of Korea War veterans.

~ ~ ~ ~ ~ ~ ~ ~ ~ ~

THE PROPAGANDA WAR

Much enemy propaganda consisted of allegations of bacteriological warfare employed by the United States. Captured aircrew were constantly badgered in attempts to provide evidence of the use of airborne germs and viruses. Containers allegedly used for contaminated feathers were displayed to neutral and Communist media.

One condition imposed by the rebel prisoners of Koje-do was an admission of ill treatment of Communist POWs. On the other hand, the Chinese went to great pains to publicize the lenient treatment supposedly given to allied prisoners.

Attempts by the Chinese to destroy the UN allies' will to fight and to alienate other UN forces from the U.S. were virtually unsuccessful. Both sides used "safe-conduct passes" – fired from artillery shells, airdropped or, in the case of the Chinese, left close to our forward positions.

Troops in the front lines were often entertained by enemy loudspeakers, which alternated popular music with tales of how "Mr. Moneybags is enjoying his vacation with your girlfriend in Florida while you are suffering out here!"

In Korea I heard a story about members of my unit who had been captured, treated and released by the Chinese forces. For obvious reasons, these stories were hushed up by the powers-that-be, and it was not until I read William Johnson's excellent work *A War of Patrols* that I learned the facts.

The following is an extract from the PPCLI War Diary as quoted in Johnson's book:

"Shortly after first light (on November 20) an English voice was heard shouting for help outside 'C' Company's wire. A small patrol sent to investigate found a wounded British soldier lying on the ground beside a roughly lettered sign saying 'come pick up your buddy' stuck in the ground. Beside the soldier was a large, neatly tied bundle of propaganda. The patrol carried the soldier back to the company, and as they were leaving, several bursts of burp gunfire were heard across the valley. The soldier was brought to the RAP and questioned by the IO.

He turned out to be Private P. Smith of 2 Platoon, 'A' Company, King's Shrop-shire Light Infantry, and was suffering from a fractured hip and several flesh wounds. Smith had been captured by the enemy on the night of 17/18 November during the Chinese attack on the KSLI on our right. His slit trench was blown in by shell fire and he and four others hid in a bunker. A Chinaman with a burp gun entered the bunker, captured the five and took them to the base of the hill on the way back to enemy lines. The party was caught in our artillery and mortar DF, the Chinaman lost a leg and all five KSLI soldiers were wounded. Smith lay for over an hour, was twice again wounded by our fire, and lost touch with the other four soldiers.

"A Chinese stretcher party picked him up and after a three-hour carry, he was laid in a bunker with a wounded Chinaman. There he remained until last light. He was accorded good though limited medical treatment, as verified by the MO who states that the dressing on his wounds were well put on. He received enough to eat, was given cigarettes and visited by a number of Chinese soldiers who all seemed very friendly. He was interrogated for several hours, apparently by a Chi-nese officer through a Chinese interpreter.

"The interrogation appears to have been skilful in that it succeeded in getting Smith involved in a long political discussion and argument. It appeared to Smith that the enemy were well in the picture on our order of battle. Last night he was told that adequate medical attention was not available and asked if he would like to return to his own lines. He was told that a corporal of his unit had been released the night before. (This was later verified by the KSLI.) Early this morning he was carried by relays of stretcher-bearers for several hours, was deposited with the bundle of propaganda and told he was outside Canadian lines. He was to wait for first light and yell for help. The Chinamen said they would watch him and fire a burp gun when he was picked up.

"The Chinese were quite successful in creating the desired impression on the soldier and Smith talked freely of his good treatment. While we have reason to believe that the Chinese do accord prisoners good treatment (in contrast with the North Koreans), it was obvious that they had bent over backwards in Smith's case. Smith was duly warned of the significance of this enemy propaganda and a report was made to Brigade Headquarters and the CO, KSLI. "The bundle of propaganda, though in great demand as souvenirs, was despatched to intelligence at Brigade."

I had heard several versions of this incident, including the fact that due to shortages of adequate medical supplies crepe paper bandages were commonly used by the Chinese medics as dressings.

~ ~ ~ ~ ~ ~ ~ ~ ~ ~

ALLIED USE OF BACTERIOLOGICAL WEAPONS

A contentious issue raised was the use of bacteriological warfare by the allies. Canada's Doctor James Endicott denied reports that China intervened in the war, and stated that he had evidence of use of germ warfare by the U.S. (Although he later admitted that some of his statements were untrue, much of the damage had already been done. This future moderator of the United Church would have done well to heed the Ninth Commandment, which deals with bearing false witness.) A proposal to place Dr. Endicott on trial for treason was dropped, supposedly to avoid the possibility of imposition of the death penalty.

The North Koreans and Chinese alleged that infected feathers, dead animals, and insects were inflicted on North Korea through the use of bombs, shells, and small arms. They cited a number of cases, some of which bordered on the ridiculous (in one example a couple ate clams, became ill, and blamed it on an American aircraft that had flown overhead in their vicinity some days ago). As proof, bomb-casings designed to hold leaflets were displayed and Dr. Endicott stated that they could be adapted to carry feathers, etc. (It presumably never occurred to the propagandists that they could also have been used for their original purpose: to hold leaflets.)

Also, the confessions obtained from U.S. airmen were widely publicized. Although I was able to quote two instances of methods used on Canadian pilots in attempts to produce false statements. Much was made of the fact that nuclear, bacteriological and chemical warfare experiments took place in Canada and the U.S. This *was* true. However, at that time, we were engaged in the Cold War and these efforts were not necessarily directed at North Korea. And mysterious diseases were not confined to the enemy — some Canadians suffered from the deadly Manchurian Bug, but no one blamed the Chinese for it. While an "independent investigation" was carried out by a Communist front organization, the Chinese refused to allow the World Health Organization or the International Red Cross to look into the matter.

~ ~ ~ ~ ~ ~ ~ ~ ~ ~

THE GOOD, THE BAD, THE UGLY

Any veteran of wartime or peacekeeping operations would surely agree that hostilities can bring out the best and the worst of us. Reports of cruelty, selfishness and disregard of human rights unfortunately complement tales of heroism, compassion and self-sacrifice. The Korean War was no exception. While few of us consider ourselves knights in shining armour, our general conception is that we were, on the whole, good guys. Happily, this impression is mostly justified. However, as in any segment of society, there are a few blots on the record.

Perhaps a typical example of the good guy attitude towards the innocent victims of an inhumane war is the story of Willie Royal. Willie's story exemplifies that of many Korean waifs, abandoned or orphaned, and adopted by uniformed strangers from far-off lands.

In 1951 members of 2RCR found a small boy crouching in a rice paddy. He was alone, scared and hungry. The troops took him in, provided him with bedding and a meal, which he wolfed down as if he hadn't eaten for days (he probably hadn't). The lad, about six years old, was christened "Willie Royal" and more or less adopted by the battalion. The troops hid him from their officers at first, but soon Willie's presence became an open secret and, in his cut-down Canadian battledress, he became a familiar figure in the chow lines.

Willie was passed from the Second to the First Battalion as the troops rotated. In the meantime, he had acquired an English vocabulary (embellished by less orthodox military expressions – he was almost caught at a provost checkpoint when he hollered "Meatheads" from his concealed position in an RCR vehicle).

When the First Battalion went home, the Protestant Padre, Captain Matt Roberts, arranged for Willie to be placed in a Seoul orphanage (supported by a generous financial contribution from a whip-round of the departing battalion). Thirty-five years later, Willie Royal (a.k.a. Noh Nong-Joo), a successful public servant, visited Canada's Korea veterans as a guest of his RCR friends.

~ ~ ~ ~ ~ ~ ~ ~ ~ ~ ~

While there was certainly no large-scale racial extermination plan during the Korean War, estimates of up to a million executions by both sides have been reported.

Prior to the start of the war, communism was rife in South Korea. The American-organized Korea Constabulary was responsible for keeping order after the Japanese left, but major units of this force were full of militant left-wingers. During a vicious guerrilla war in the south of the country, thousands of right-wingers — especially policemen, soldiers and their families — were executed by the Communist occupants of mountain areas. When Syngman Rhee's shaky government finally restored order, another round of judicial slaughter took place with the erstwhile executioners facing the firing squads in their turn.

Certainly, there were atrocities on both sides. While our allies were not lily-white in this respect, they were not alone. According to Max Hastings in *The Korean War*, "The process of discovering the meaning of Communist liberation was extended through the four months that Kim Il-Sung's army occupied [their area of South Korea]. … [T]he behaviour of the North Koreans, their ghastly brutalities and wholesale murders of their enemies, decisively persuaded most inhabitants ... that whatever the shortcomings of Syngman Rhee, nothing could be as appalling as communist tyranny."

In the city of Taejon alone, UN troops discovered 5,000 bodies. Overall, between June and September 1950 Kim Il-Sung's soldiers slaughtered an estimated 26,000 South Korean civilians.

Nor were atrocities confined to civilians. On August 17, 1950, U.S. troops recapturing a Communist position were horrified to find 26 of their comrades, hands bound with signal cable, riddled with burp gun bullets. Photographs of the victims were published in *Life* magazine, and horrified the complacent Americans at home.

Ironically, the only allegations of attempted genocide were directed at the United States — the Chinese and North Koreans tried consistently to obtain confessions of the use of germ warfare from captured airmen.

Less creditable was another encounter with the Korean populace a little earlier. Court martial appeal board records tell the story of three infantrymen in a rest area in a not unusual search for liquor and/or feminine company. The trio formed a disastrously erroneous impression in a small settlement behind the lines.

Hearing sounds of merriment and female voices in a nearby house, they assumed that they had stumbled upon a "pleasure house." Unfortunately, this was not the case, and instead South Korean officers and their wives occupied the house. After being politely but firmly evicted, the Canadians expressed their frustration by tossing a grenade through the window, killing at least one of the Koreans. They were subsequently convicted of manslaughter.

Massacres of civilians were commonplace. For the North Koreans there was the Taegu example. On the other side of the coin, on at least one occasion, a Commonwealth Division officer dissuaded South Korean police from executing a group of men, women and children, by threatening to open fire on his "allies" if they persisted in their action. The crime of the South Korean peasants? They had failed to leave their meagre farms during the advance and retreat phases of the early months of the war. This, in the eyes of the Constabulary, made them *ipso facto* Communist sympathizers.

Recently, however, what is probably the most shocking story of atrocity and military cover-up has surfaced.

Before condemning the soldiers it is perhaps important to place the situation of that time into perspective. It was the last week in July of 1950, just over a month after the North Koreans had swept through the weak South Korean defences, and the 7th U.S. Cavalry had just arrived in Korea in an attempt to bolster their allies' resistance. The situation was, to say the very least, a giant mix-up. Rumours abounded – many of them substantiated – that North Korean soldiers and Communist guerrillas would don the almost universal white peasant garments and mix with the massive flow of refugees. Perhaps most significantly, there were no physical differences in the appearance and dress of North and South Koreans, who were in fact one people arbitrarily divided by a line on a map.

As the outnumbered troops retreated southwards, the Division's war diary reflected, "No one desired to shoot innocent people, but many of the innocent-looking refugees … turned out to be North Korean soldiers. There were so many refugees that it was impossible to screen and search them all." Divisional HQ stated, "No refugees [were] to cross the front line – Fire on everyone trying to cross lines. Use discretion in the case of women and children."

This was the situation on July 26, when hundreds of refugees were ordered from the road and herded into a railway underpass at No Gun Ri. The chaos began when USAF P-51s strafed a nearby group of refugees, killing perhaps a hundred Koreans. The Air Force originally claimed that this was an error and had mistaken the group for a military target some miles away. However, other pilots reported that they deliberately attacked "people in white" as suspected guerrillas.

Later, the army troops opened fire on the refugees sheltering in the railway underpass. There are conflicting statements about this event. Most of the officers who allegedly gave the order to open up with machine guns are now dead – the battalion commander involved denies any knowledge of the shooting and avers that he "didn't give such an order."

Many GIs refused the order to fire on the Koreans, while one of the few survivors suggested that the "shots" coming from the underpass were in fact ricochets from American rounds. Some U.S. witnesses claim that among the bodies were North Korean soldiers, their uniforms concealed under white peasant clothing – others disputed this.

By the time the shooting was over, between 200 and 300 Korean women, children and men (most of them old) lay dead.

Army documents had no record of the battle, or indeed of any mention of the hamlet of No Gun Ri. However, after years of research, a group of ex-GIs came forward with their story.

The final tragedy occurred at the Naktong River crossings at Waegwan and Tuksong-dong. As Major General Hobart Gay watched from the east bank, his First Cavalry withdrew across the remaining bridges as the advancing North Koreans were massing a few miles to the west.

General Gay had a tough decision to make. Refugees were still swarming across both bridges. Combat engineers had prepared demolition charges, but the efforts of the cavalrymen to stem the flow of civilians proved ineffective. Finally, with hundreds of Koreans still crossing the bridges, the fatal order was given.

According to one witness, General Gay stood up in his jeep and cried "Blow the son of a bitch!" and hundreds of refugees, together with spans of steel and other debris, plunged into the Naktong. The exact count of civilian casualties, just as in No Gun Ri, will probably never be known.

Perhaps one of the hardest decisions that a commander must make is to balance humanitarian principles against military needs. In this age of total war, there are no spectators. General Gay died in 1983; who can know just how much his decision may have rested on his conscience over the last three decades of his life.

General Sherman said it all – "[War's] glory is all moonshine … war is hell."

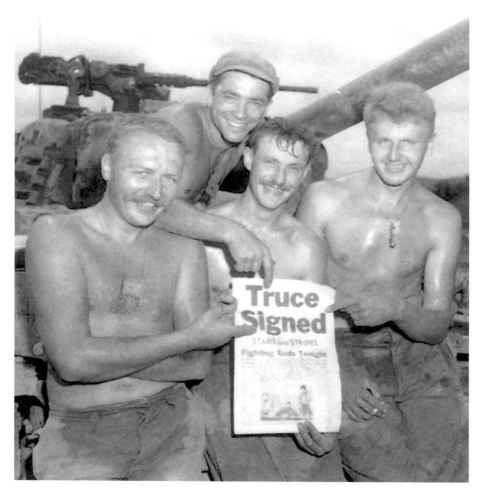

ABOVE: *A staged photo-op of Canadian front-line soldiers celebrating the ceasefire. (DND)*

OPPOSITE PAGE: *North Korean and Allied generals negotiate the truce at Panmunjom. (DND)*

❧ THE AFTERMATH

The peace that wasn't.

AT 10:00 P.M. ON JULY 27, 1953, the guns fell silent.

Since early 1951, negotiations had been underway to achieve a cessation of hostilities, July 1st of that year UN, North Korean and Chinese delegates met in a tea house in Kaesong (a village on the 38th parallel) to discuss terms. Items included fixing a demilitarized zone, arrangements for a ceasefire, appointing an armistice supervising commission and preparing for repatriation of prisoners of wars.

The talks ceased for a number of reasons, including Communist allegations of breaches of the neutrality of the area.

On October 25th of that year, talks were resumed at nearby Panmunjom (the area was marked by a giant searchlight, whose vertical beam provided an excellent navigation aid for night patrols). It was quickly agreed that the ceasefire line would be the positions currently held at the end of the war.

In April 1953, a number of wounded POWs were exchanged (Operation LITTLE SWITCH), while final arrangements were made in June (the agreements were jeopardized when South Korean President Rhee arranged the escape of 25,000 North Korean prisoners who did not wish to be repatriated).

After the ceasefire the Commonwealth troops were amazed by what appeared to be millions of Chinese who emerged from their positions opposite the lines. The erstwhile enemy set up platforms where male and female Chinese entertained with songs and dance (not forgetting the inevitable peace and harmony slogans).

Canadians had little time to relax. They had 72 hours to destroy or remove all their arms, ammunition and defensive material five kilometres south – thus creating the demilitarized zone (DMZ) which was to figure prominently in past war affairs.

It was not yet time to end the story of Canada's Korean involvements. The troops in the line had taken up their new positions, but would be relieved soon afterwards by a fourth rotation, consisting of the Queen's Own Rifles, Black Watch of Canada and the Canadian Guards, together with their supporting arms.

Although hostilities had ceased, it was necessary for the defenders to remain in a state of constant alert. Indeed, the toll of Canadians who died in Korea continued to grow. The final major unit, 2nd Battalion Queen's Own Rifles, left for home in April 1955, and the last Canadian, a Medical Corps officer, returned in 1967.

Despite the ceasefire, there was still no time nor opportunity for the South Korean and United Nations forces to relax. A comprehensive defensive system was established south of the DMZ, intended to delay or halt a North Korean advance on Seoul. The United States continues to maintain a strong military presence in South Korea.

The government of "Beloved Leader" Kim Jong-Il (son of Kim Il-Sung) continues its sabre-rattling stance and has been found guilty of several covert and overt acts.

In one case, a group of U.S. troops removing a tree on the UN side of the demarcation line near Panmunjom was set upon by North Korean troops and suffered fatal casualties. (The subsequent attempt to clear the tree – Operation PAUL BUNYAN – was supported by the full weight of the U.S. army, navy, marines, and air force elements and was achieved without further incident.)

As well, spies and saboteurs frequently turn up in South Korea. One of the most bizarre incidents was the discovery of a wrecked submarine supposedly constructed of plastic on the east coast of South Korea. Its occupants – a group of North Korean special forces troops – were eventually rounded up.

Far more sinister, perhaps, are the tunnels constructed by the North Koreans after the war ended. Following the armistice, military movement was prohibited in the DMZ (although recent events indicate that the North Koreans are infringing this agreement).

In 1974 an alert Korean NCO patrolling the southern side of the DMZ located what turned out to be a ventilation shaft, which in turn revealed a tunnel wide enough to allow a whole regiment of troops to pass into South Korea in a single hour. To add to South Korea's concern, this tunnel's exit was only 65 kilometers from the capital of Seoul. Kim Il-Sung's North Korean government dismissed the reports of the tunnel as "a mere political trick fabricated by the UN forces." Nevertheless, items of equipment in the tunnel were identified as being of Soviet or North Korean origin.

A few months later a defector blew the whistle on another, larger, tunnel which was located further east. This was designed to have five separate exits south of the DMZ, and had its start just north of a North Korean army guard post close to the zone. It was large enough to permit passage of vehicles, artillery and up to 30,000 troops an hour.

Three years later, following the use of more sophisticated seismographs, a third tunnel was discovered close to the Truce Centre at Panmunjom. This too was capable of handling heavy weapons, vehicles, and a division of troops in an hour. If completed, this tunnel would have its exit a mere 45 kilometres from Seoul. Tunnel No. 3 is something of a tourist attraction, and visitors are permitted to pass down an adit from the UN base camp area into the tunnel itself, to find a heavy steel mesh barrier with ROK military police on the one side and North Korean counterparts on the other. My wife descended into the tunnel a few years ago, making us perhaps one of the few couples who have both been eyeball-to-eyeball with North Korean soldiers. Perhaps more alarmingly, the North Korean defector, one Kim Pusung, had personally participated in the tunnel building and reported that he had observed a total of nine tunnels. So far, despite the use of modern technology, none of the others have been detected. According to a report in a UK newsletter by Korea veteran Mick White, Korean and UN authorities left no stone unturned (no pun intended) in an effort to find the tunnels. The famed Israeli psychic, Uri Geller, was even called in to assist, and was reportedly offered $10 million to "divine" the location of other tunnels. His ESP failed to pay off, and his helicopter pilot was, perhaps understandably, apprehensive about flying continually over the DMZ boundary.

To quote the Republic of Korea Defence Department, "Even as it was engaged in the South-North talks with the Republic of Korea in the early 1970s giving rise to hopes of peace and reunification of all Koreans, North Korea was frantically digging underground military tunnels southward along the demilitarized zone. It was acting a wolf in sheep's clothing!"

It perhaps pays to be wary of North Korean soldiers carrying shovels. They may simply be practising field sanitation – or could they be working on Kim Jong-Il's version of the Trojan Horse?

Meanwhile, North Korea continues to pose a threat to peace in the Far East. With a population still on the verge of starvation while the leaders engage in extravagant expenditures on the military, and a reported nuclear capability, the

Pyongyang regime continues to be carefully watched by its apprehensive neighbours.

As a result, the threat still remains. Hopefully, our grandchildren will not have to follow in our footsteps in a second Korean War.

Besides the obvious military threat, which was recently aggravated by moves of army and air force units towards the DMZ, a continual propaganda campaign is carried on. Surprisingly, apart from the obvious diatribes against South Korea and the United States, the major emphasis appears to be the glorification of Kim Jong-Il and his father, the late Kim Il-Sung. One particularly fascinating store relates "Beloved Leader's" sporting prowess. Although he had only recently taken up golf, he achieved an 18-hole score of 38 strokes (including five holes-in-one). One must assume that either leader Kim also walks on water, or that the Pyongyang Golf Club is, in fact, a putting green or miniature golf facility.

~ ~ ~ ~ ~ ~ ~ ~ ~ ~

A MATTER OF HONOUR

A regiment's most prized possessions are their colours. These revered silken rectangles carry the unit's traditions and, in the form of emblazoned battle honours, the regimental history.

In 1956, representatives of Commonwealth participants in the Korean War determined which engagements of that war might merit the award of battle honours for participating units. The group identified a total of 31 actions. The first of these applied mainly to British and Australian forces, as the Canadians (2PPCLI) had not yet arrived in the line.

The remainder consisted of Hungnam (November-December 1950); Uijongbu, Seoul and Chungchung-Dong (January 1951); Cheum-Ni, Hill 327 and Hill 419 (February 1951); Maehwa-San (March 1951); Kapyong-Chen, Imjin and Kapyong (April 1951); Chail-Li (May 1951); Kowang-San (October 1951); and the defensive actions of Maryang-San and two battles for Hill 227 in November 1951; Hill 355 (October 1952); the two battles for the Hook in November 1952 and May 1953; Pochon-Ni (May 1953); and finally the Sami-ch'on in July of 1953, during the closing days of the war.

The next step was to invite submissions from the infantry and armoured regiments who took part in the hostilities. In addition to submissions for individual actions, the theatre honour "Korea" with the appropriate dates could be requested.

What appears to be something of a dog-in-the-manger attitude had already crept in. The Canadian battle honours committee felt that "the Canadian Army would be satisfied with the award of only one honour, i.e. campaign honour

'Korea' (sic). [I]t was felt that to award a multiplicity of honours for such relatively minor operations as those of the Commonwealth Forces in Korea might have a cheapening effect on the award and display of honours."

The letter (from Canada to the Commonwealth committee) went on to say that if Britain were to award honours for separate engagements, Canada was prepared to follow suit. (The Brits did, Canada didn't!)

It would seem that the Second World War veterans were afraid that Korean War honours might detract from their own hard-won achievements. That this view was not universal will be evidenced later.

The regiments submitted their applications. Each applied for, and received, the theatre honour "Korea." The Strathcona's submitted Kowang-San for emblazonment, as well as Chail-li, Maryang-San, Hill 227 I and II, Hill 355, The Hook (1952 and 1953), Pochon-Ni and the Sami-ch'on. The RCR submitted Kowang-San for emblazonment, Chail-li, Hill 355 and Pochon-Ni. From PPCLI came Kapyong (to be emblazoned) and Hill 419, Kowang-San, Hill 227, The Hook and Meahwa-San. Despite their heavy share of the fighting, the Van Doos were content to submit only Hill 227 for emblazonment.

The DND pundits went to work and with the exception of Kapyong, rejected them all. As the United States had already awarded a Presidential Citation for Kapyong it was a virtual must. (This was a gesture that was not appreciated by Canada's politicians, who had not been consulted, resulting in a delay of several years before 2PPCLI were finally allowed to wear the insignia they so richly deserved.)

Some rejections were well founded. One claim actually resulted from a unit member finding a piece of shell casing in his bedding after a battle fought by the Australians. Others arose from unfortunate errors. The turning-down of the RCR claim for Kowang-San is one example. Kowang-San and Hill 355 are the same feature. However, "Kowang-San" was designated for the offensive action in Operation COMMANDO, while the action, which is still commemorated annually by the regiment, is the defence of the feature in October 1952. Sadly, the submission for the major action listed as Kowang-San, was assessed accordingly and disapproved.

The Royal 22nd Regiment also got a raw deal. Their well-justified claim for Hill 227 was rejected on the grounds that only "D" Company was directly engaged in the battle. This does not agree with the war diary nor with the official Commonwealth Division history. One significant factor is that the GOC Quebec Command strongly supported this submission. The other Commonwealth countries were more generous. For example, Operation COMMANDO was a two-part operation with both parts being equally important and hazardous. 25 Canadian Brigade was successful in Phase I, after which 28 Commonwealth Brigade took over. Each British and Australian infantry and armoured unit received the Kowang-San battle honour, but the Canadian committee rejected their troops' part.

The Royal Australian Regiment received 11 battle honours for their part in the Korean War. The Middlesex Regiment earned seven and the King's Royal Irish Hussars five. The King's Shropshire Light Infantry were awarded three honours during their 16-month tour in Korea. Although the former units were there during the advancing and retreating stages of the war, most Canadians served during the defensive stage; the resulting imbalance is evident.

This time it cannot be blamed on the British and Australians, as it was our own Canadian committee who rejected the claims.

~ ~ ~ ~ ~ ~ ~ ~ ~ ~

VALIANT VAN DOOS

In November 1951, the Van Doos were holding the feature Hill 227 on the western flank of the vital height Hill 355 in the Kowang-San area. For two days the battalion, and in particular "D" Company, were under heavy attack by Chinese forces. So vital was the position that (to quote the GOC's letter) ... "its recapture would have required a major attack and might even have forced the withdrawal of the whole line back to the Imjin River at a distance of about five miles."

The Adjutant-General, MGen Smith, upholding the denial, described this operation as "relatively minor" and that the participation did not justify an award "because only "D" Company was heavily engaged throughout this engagement and the remainder of the unit was committed piecemeal to help restore the situation."

The GOC Quebec Command, on the other hand, noted that the battalion mortars fired 10,000 rounds in the battle, that "A" Company was twice attacked, that "B" Company provided supporting fire throughout the operation, and that Battalion HQ and other support elements played an important part. After-action reports also credit the remaining rifle company for bringing up ammunition and supplies to the beleaguered "D" Company, under heavy fire.

The GOC Quebec Command who wrote the letter was Major-General J.M. "Rocky" Rockingham, who should certainly know the score since he was the Canadian brigade commander during the action. Rocky had participated in several actions in northwest Europe resulting in the award of honours to his units, so his opinion should be valid and unbiased. In his letter, he said, "I cannot think of an operation which is more deserving of a battle award than the R22eR's courageous and determined defence of the flank of Hill 355."

Even the Historical Section appeared to contradict itself. Rejecting a claim for the honour by the Lord Strathcona's, their report said, "No. 3 Troop moved forward to support 2R22eR, whose "D" Coy was heavily engaged throughout and qualifies that unit for the honour." Yet their comments on the Van Doos' claim state that "D" Coy of R22eR was heavily engaged throughout, and the remainder of the unit was committed piecemeal to help restore the situation. "D" Coy command was awarded a DSO. Casualties 49, including 15 killed. Recommendation: No. Incidentally, while the number of casualties is not necessarily an indication of the intensity of a battle, it is significant the Van Doos lost twice as many dead as the Patricias at Kapyong.

~ ~ ~ ~ ~ ~ ~ ~ ~ ~

"FOR VALOUR" AND "FOR GALLANTRY"

Next time you are gathering together with a group of veterans and are placing beer bets, you might ask how many Victoria Cross winners served in Korea. The answer will be probably four — the number of VCs awarded in the Korean War. In fact there were at least eight!

What is perhaps less known is the fact that three soldiers in Korea were awarded the equally prestigious George Cross. These are the stories of the Korean War VC and GC recipients.

The first VC of the war was awarded posthumously to Major Kenneth Muir of the Argyll and Sutherland Highlanders. On September 23, 1950, the Highlanders had seized the feature Hill 282. Major Muir and the battalion second-in-command accompanied a party of stretcher-bearers and organized the evacuation of the "B" and "C" Company casualties. Heavy enemy mortar and shellfire was followed by increasing North Korean infiltration.

As enemy pressure increased, Major Muir took command of the two companies and continued to encourage his men, all the time under heavy fire.

Shortly after noon, a misplaced air strike resulted in heavy casualties from napalm and machine gun fire. The defending force was now reduced to about 30 effective members. Major Muir realized that the enemy had been slow to take advantage of the friendly fire error and, with his small force, recaptured the hill crest. As ammunition ran out he took over a two-inch mortar and continued to engage the enemy at close range until he was mortally wounded by two bursts of automatic weapon fire. His last words were: "The Gooks will never drive the Argylls off this hill!"

Two VCs and one George Cross were awarded to soldiers serving with the Gloucestershire Regiment in the Imjin River battle in April 1951.

The first Cross was awarded to Lieutenant-Colonel James Carne, the Gloucester's Commanding Officer. Between April 22nd and 25th the battalion was heavily engaged by overwhelmingly superior enemy forces. During the entire period Colonel Carne's coolness and air of confidence inspired his troops. Showing complete disregard for his own safety, he moved among his battalion under heavy mortar and machine gun fire, and twice, armed with a rifle and grenades, led assaults against the enemy. He realized that his unit had been outflanked, but continued to hold his position to avoid a major breakthrough, which would have endangered the whole UN Corps.

Finally, when relief was impossible, on orders from higher authority he organized small parties to break out. While leading one of these he was captured by Chinese troops. Although his actions as a POW were not included in the VC citation, Carne continued to set an example to his troops and resist enemy pressure while in captivity.

The other VC was a posthumous award, to Lieutenant Philip Curtis, a former member of the Duke of Cornwall's Light Infantry recalled for service in 29 Brigade, and attached to the Gloucesters. On April 23rd his platoon was ordered to dislodge the enemy from the "Castle Hill" feature. During the assault the platoon was held up by heavy fire, and a close-quarter engagement ensued. Lieutenant Curtis rushed the main enemy position, being severely wounded by a grenade. Breaking free of his men, who urged him to remain in safety, he again charged the enemy, but was killed by a burst of fire just short of his objective.

His determined action discouraged the enemy from further attempts to seize the initiative, and thanks to this officer's sacrifice, his company was able to withdraw safely. Lieutenant Curtis was survived by a young daughter.

Lieutenant Terence Waters was a member of the West Yorkshire Regiment attached to the Gloucestershire Regiment. He was a comparatively inexperienced officer, recently commissioned from Standhurst and was captured after the Imjin battle.

Although seriously wounded in the head and arm, he encouraged and cared for his comrades to the best of his ability during the long march to Pyongyang, and the subsequent captivity in the notorious prison camp, "the Caves." Food was scanty and there was no medical attention. Men died daily from these privations.

A North Korean political officer attempted to entice the prisoners into providing propaganda for the Communists by promising them food and medical treatment. In an effort to save the lives of his men, he ordered them to pretend to accede to these blandishments, but steadfastly refused to do so himself. Despite concerted efforts on the North Koreans' part to enlist this officer to their cause, he refused to give in. As a result of his determined resistance, he died in captivity.

The remaining crosses were awarded to private soldiers. Unfortunately I have been unable to obtain the citation for Private "Slim" Madden, of the 3rd Battalion, the Royal Australian Regiment, who was taken prisoner at Kapyong. His conduct, while wounded, under unbearable living conditions and repeated torture by his captors, and his steadfast refusal to give in to his captors, resulted in his death in captivity. Private H.W. Madden was posthumously awarded the George Cross.

Fusilier Derek Kinne was captured on the last day of the Imjin battle while serving with the Royal Northumberland Fusiliers in 29 Brigade. Within 24 hours of capture he attempted to escape from the Chinese but was retaken a few days later. During his captivity, he continued to be a thorn in the side of his captors. For his refusal to co-operate he was severely beaten and subjected to various tortures, including being forced to stand tip-toe with a noose around his neck for periods of 24 hours.

He again escaped, was recaptured and punished, and after accusations of sabotage of compulsory political study, he was confined to a small box cell where he was made to sit at attention for a week and continually beaten and abused by guards. At one point as he was being beaten by the butt of a burp gun, the weapon went off, killing the guard commander. For this Kinne was beaten senseless, stripped and thrown into a rat-infested hole for over a month. He was sentenced by a Chinese military court to a year's solitary confinement and when he complained, the sentence was increased to 18 months.

In June of 1953 he was again sentenced to solitary confinement for daring to wear a homemade rosette to celebrate Coronation Day. Although threatened with non-repatriation for his stubborn demand to speak to Red Cross representatives, this gallant soldier was finally released on August 10, 1953. Fusilier Derek Godfrey Kinne G.C. now lives in Arizona.

Many Canadian Korea veterans have met the fourth Victoria Cross recipient. Private Bill Speakman was serving with the Black Watch in Germany and volunteered to join the King's Own Scottish Borderers to serve in Korea. On November 4, 1951 he was a member of the KOSB's Baker Company headquarters.

During the day the Borderers were subjected to increasingly heavy artillery and mortar fire and in late afternoon the enemy in their hundreds advanced on the Scots. Fierce hand-to-hand fighting took place and the section on the left of "B" Company's position was being overrun, having taken heavy casualties. On his own initiative, Speakman assembled a party of six men and, armed with a large number of grenades, went to drive the enemy from the position. He led a number of charges, and successfully drove continuing waves of enemy from the hill crest.

After 10 separate assaults, Private Speakman was severely wounded in the leg, but continued to lead charge after charge until directly ordered by a superior officer to pause for treatment. After a field dressing was applied, he returned to the fight and continued to hold off the enemy until the company was eventually withdrawn after four hours of bitter fighting.

Following several months in hospital, Bill Speakman returned for a further spell of duty in Korea before returning home, where he became the first service-man to be decorated by his new ruler, Queen Elizabeth II. After a spell with the special air service in Malaya, he retired from the army but, over 50 years after his exploits in Korea, Speakman was in uniform again - this time as a Chelsea Pensioner.

At least four more Victoria Cross holders served in the Korean War. Two of them won their awards during the Second World War. Both were submariners. Lieutenant (later Rear-Admiral) Basil Place, commanding midget submarine X-7 carried out a daring attack on the battleship *Tirpitz*. He later served on flying duties aboard HMS *Glory* during the Korean War. Lieutenant Peter Roberts won his award for his daring removal of two unexploded bombs from his submarine's gun casing, following a successful sinking of an enemy vessel in the Mediterranean.

Two former members of the Royal Australian Regiment received the Victoria Cross for bravery while serving with the Australian Army Training Team in Vietnam. Warrant Officer II Rayene Simpson won his award for the rescue of a fellow warrant officer on May 6, 1969, followed by a single-handed action against heavy odds to cover the evacuation of a number of casualties. Later that month Warrant Officer II Keith Payne exhibited outstanding leadership and courage in saving the lives of many of his soldiers after an attack by an enemy in superior strength.

Two other heroic Commonwealth soldiers deserve mention. One was Canadian Corporal Ernest Poole. During Operation COMMANDO, Corporal Poole was the RCAMC NCO in charge of "B" Company, 1RCR stretcher-bearers. During the advance, a number of casualties were incurred, many of the wounded lying among thick underbrush on the steep ascent to the company objective. Regardless of his own safety, he continued his search under heavy fire, and saved the lives of at least five men. When urged by officers to consider his own safety he declined, saying "It's my job." Corporal Poole was recommended for the VC and the award was approved through Canadian channels, but at higher levels (British and Australian) the award of a DCM was approved instead.

The DCM is second only to the Victoria Cross as a decoration for other ranks. Corporal (later Sergeant) William Rowlinson of the Third Battalian, Royal Australian Regiment, held the unique distinction of receiving this award *twice* during the Korean War. The DCM and bar were gazetted within six weeks of each other.

Three George Cross holders also served later in Korea. William Goad of the Royal Navy and Albert Guerisse (alias Patrick O'Leary), who served with the Belgian Battalion in Korea, won their George Crosses during the Second World

War, while Royal Navy member Alfred Lowe received his award in 1948.

~ ~ ~ ~ ~ ~ ~ ~ ~ ~

ALL ABOUT GONGS

Between the Old Guard column, my two-hatted functions as president of the Korea Veterans Association of Canada, and being the Korean War editor of *Esprit de Corps*, I think that I can safely say that most complaints or queries that I receive concern medals. They refer not only to the official left-breast medals, but a host of other demi-official or downright unofficial adornments.

First of all, the Commonwealth Korean War Medal. Of the Korean War medals, this takes priority under a special grandfather clause that details the wearing of Commonwealth medals awarded prior to June 1972.

Any Commonwealth orders, decorations or medals awarded since that date are worn after Canadian medals, with very few exceptions. Qualification for this medal is 28 days afloat in Korean waters, one sortie over Korea for aircrew, or 24 hours on the strength of an army unit in Korea between July 2, 1950 and July 27, 1953.

Originally paired with the Korean War Medal was the United Nations Service Medal – Korea. Initiated in December 1950, this was awarded for one day or more of service in the Korean theatre, which included Japan and Okinawa as well as Korea itself. The qualifying period is longer than that of the War Medal, service from June 27, 1950 to July 27, 1954 is eligible for this award. It is awarded with the clasp "Korea." At that time, the United Nations authorities could not foresee the multitude of future UN operations, and considered that a single medal with one or two clasps would cover them all.

The third of the Canadian medals is the Canadian Volunteer Service Medal for Korea. Unlike the others, this is handled by the Government House Chancellery, rather than DND or Veterans Affairs. Established in 1991, the qualifying criteria are more or less the same as the UN medal. Originally, Canadian Korean War veterans were awarded a lapel pin (still available from Veterans Affairs), but many felt more recognition was needed.

Veterans who served in Korea for 30 days after July 27, 1953 are eligible for the Canadian Peacekeeping Service Medal.

One contentious issue is the ROK War Service Medal (often referred to as the Syngman Rhee Medal). This was awarded to all UN participants who served in Korea between June 25, 1950 and July 27, 1953. The British government refused to approve its wear, and other Commonwealth nations followed suit.

In a recent breakthrough at the request of South Korea, U.S. Korean War veterans are now permitted to wear this medal on the left breast as an "approved foreign award."

One semi-official award (right breast) medal is the Korean War Medal, sometimes called the "Ambassador of Peace." This is awarded by the ROK Veterans Association to Canadian veterans who participate in re-visit programmes.

SHINING MOMENTS

Eight Canadians received the U.S. Bronze Star, two with the "V" device (for valour). One Canadian recipient of the Medal and "V" device was Lieutenant Commander J.G.H. Bovey, commanding officer of HMCS *Crusader*. The citation for his award reads:

"On April 15, 1953, HMCS *Crusader*, under the outstanding leadership of Lieutenant Commander Bovey, was positioned and controlled so as to inflict great damage to the enemy while interdicting the North Korean East Coast rail supply route. A record to date was established in the number of enemy trains stopped and the amount of damage inflicted by any one unit of the interdiction forces in a single day. Stopping one northbound train in the morning, the accurate guns of the *Crusader* destroyed three cars, damaged five cars and caused secondary explosions. Later on the same day the *Crusader* continued her outstanding performance and destructive gunfire effect by stopping two southbound trains and causing considerable damage. In addition to the constant threat of enemy shore battery fire, the additional hazard of mines was brought to mind rather sharply when the *Crusader* sank a Mark 26-type mine between train-stopping actions."

The one RCAF recipient was Squadron Leader J.T. Reed.

Canadian Army recipients included LCol. Edward Amy, DSO, MC (General Staff Officer 1 at COMWEL Division HQ), Major Charles Huggard (1PPCLI), Major Richard Medland, DSO (2RCR, Liaison Officer 1 COMWEL Div), Bdr. Gavin Reid (1RCHA), Capt. Robert Staples (RCA, Liaison Officer) and Major Edward Williams (1PPCLI). Of these, Major Williams was the sole recipient of the "V" device. His citation reads:

"Major Edward J. Williams, Infantry, Royal Canadian Army (sic) a member of the 1st Battalion, Princess Patricia's Canadian Light Infantry, 25th Canadian Infantry Brigade, distinguished himself by heroism in action against the enemy in Korea on October 23, 1951. Company 'A', commanded by Major Williams, was charged with the mission of capturing an enemy held hill which obstructed the advance of friendly forces. Despite the intensive defensive fire of the numerically superior foe, under his skilful guidance the company advanced steadily toward the objective. Disregarding his personal safety, he moved to a forward position where he could observe the hostile machine gun fire. Through his sound judgement and proficient grasp of the tactical situation, he realized that the machine gun emplacements constituted the keystone of the enemy defence. He summoned supporting friendly artillery and mortar fire and then, in face of withering hostile fire, directed the final assault on the objective.

"Inspired by his fighting spirit, the unit successfully stormed the hill, driving the foe from their position. The courage, determination of purpose, and the devotion to duty displayed by Major Williams during this action reflect great credit on himself and the military service."

ABOUT MEMORIALS

Since the Korean War ceasefire, veterans returning to the "Land of the Morning Calm" regularly paid homage at two memorials – the Canadian Korean War Memorial in the Kapyong area, and the Commonwealth memorial nearby. One memorial that has usually been overlooked is a more modest monument that commemorates an action involving the 2PPCLI, 16 New Zealand Field Regiment and elements of the United States marines. The Patricias also have a memorial in the Kapyong area.

In 1999 Vince Courtenay entered the scene. A former member of PPCLI, Vince had been working in Korea for a number of years as a freelance writer. Vince Courtenay and Colonel Bowness, the Canadian defence attaché in Seoul, enlisted the enthusiastic support of Canada's ambassador to the Republic of Korea, H.E. Arthur Perron, and Chip's assistant, WO Gerry Tummillo. The group developed a strategic plan for the Monument to Canadian Fallen, to be placed in the United Nations cemetery at Busan (formerly Pusan). They were supported in Canada by a number of Korean veterans, including Henry Martinak of Windsor, who played a major role in fundraising. It was agreed that the monument would be financed by private subscription.

The results exceeded expectations. Donations from individuals, Legions and other veteran group branches, and major contributions from donors such as the United Auto Workers and the City of Windsor more than covered the cost.

Meanwhile, Vince took a personal and continuing interest in the progress of the memorial. Master Artist Yoo Young-mun was given the task of creating the memorial, but Courtenay was continually on hand to ensure that details of dress and other items were authentic. At times, to "get it right," Vince even took a hand in casting some of the details himself.

The final memorial consisted of a life-size statue of a Canadian soldier with two Korean children. This was a reminder of the compassionate care that our service personnel had given to the many Korean orphans and refugee children in their operational area. While the statue is well detailed, the shoulder title contains no regimental or corps indication; it represents all Canadian servicemen. The youngsters represent the young Korean children who, 50 years later, are now controlling South Korea's social and economic life.

No weapons are carried – the memorial symbolizes the end of hostilities. The children carry bunches of maple leaves and roses of Sharon – the floral emblems of Canada and South Korea. There are 21 maple leaves, representing the 16 missing Canadians who have no known grave, and five Royal Canadian Navy members who gave their lives in the war.

In April 2001, the time came for groundbreaking at the site in the UN cemetery. Although at the time our prime minister was heading a government delegation to Korea, no federal representatives attended. However, HRH Prince Andrew was present, accompanying a British veterans' group, and he gladly accepted an invitation to join Kapyong veteran "Smiley" Douglas, MM in turning the first sod. (The Prince sent an official letter of tribute to the Canadians who fell, which was read at the unveiling of the completed monument in November 2001.)

Following the excellent fundraising drive, sufficient surplus was left to create an echo copy of the memorial, completed the following year and shipped to Canada by air freight.

It was re-assembled by sculptor Mr. Yoo, and appropriately placed on temporary public display in Windsor, Ontario. Finally on September 28, 2003, 50 years after the armistice was signed, it found a permanent home in Ottawa. With assistance and support from Veterans Affairs Canada and Heritage Canada, the Monument to Canadian Fallen was formally dedicated on the escarpment which bounds Confederation Park – a few hundred yards from the National War Memorial, the Tomb of the Unknown Soldier and the Aboriginal Monument.

The Republic of Korea donated a massive granite base obtained from the terrain that our soldiers helped defend half a century ago. This was arranged through the good graces of the Korean Ambassador to Canada, H.E. Chang-Ki-Ho. The statue is now situated directly facing the graves of the fallen Canadians who lie buried in Busan – 7,100 miles distant. The names of the 516 Canadians who gave their lives in the Korean War are inscribed on the base of the statue.

This is the second major national memorial to the Korean War. The National Wall of Remembrance, which includes plaques for each of the 516 Canadian Fallen, is situated in the Meadowvale Cemetery, Brampton, Ontario.

~ ~ ~ ~ ~ ~ ~ ~ ~ ~

TIME MARCHES ON

Fifty years after the first Canadians arrived in Korea, it is time to look back on the intervening years.

For those who survived, our lives were generally changed. Many of us established bonds of comradeship that still exist today, while others fell into bad habits as a result of their experiences. We hadn't yet heard of the expression post traumatic stress disorder and many of us suffered from a lack of compassion which is now extended to our peacekeeping successors, who have their own vivid memories to cope with.

Most of us got on with our lives. Our ranks include successful businessmen, members of parliament and provincial representatives, and (especially among the ranks of PPCLI) prominent writers. Ted Zuber, Peter Worthington and Frank McGuire are just a few of the Korean War alumni in the field of arts and literature. Many remained in the service, some of them, such as Ramsey Withers and J.A. Dextraze, achieved the ultimate appointment as chief of the defence staff.

Most of us led satisfying, if unspectacular, lives. We have had our share (albeit small) of societal failures. A few years ago one of the Korea Veterans Association units followed up on a news story of a Korean War veteran who lived in a cardboard carton under a railroad bridge. It turned out that he didn't want any help, and preferred that lifestyle.

The KVA of Canada began in a small way in 1974. At one time membership peaked at around 5,000. Now, owing to increasing attrition due to ill health and sadly, increasing appearances in obituary columns, our numbers have fallen to below 3,000. We youngsters went out to war. Some were idealistic, others sought adventure but, for most of us, we were regular soldiers (or, in the case of British and American veterans, draftees) and simply went where our political masters sent us. For 516 Canadians, there was no future, and when at remembrance services we repeat the phrase "they shall grow not old," we remember them "straight of limb, keen of eye, steady and aglow," just as we last knew them in the prime of life.

With the ever-present possibility of a sudden end to our young lives caused by enemy action, we gave very little heed to our standards of living a half-century later.

We considered ourselves invincible – except for a few of our number who contracted haemorrhagic fever (the Manchurian Bug), malaria or, in the case of a few who had celebrated their R&R leave not wisely but well, what was euphemistically described as a "social disease" – so future health concerns were far from our minds.

We took our living conditions for granted. Our hootchies, excavated in many cases in soil that had been fertilized for centuries with human waste, were infested with insects in summer and often rats and mice in winter. Many were not waterproof, and mud, water or ice on the earth floors was frequently present. In winter, temperatures often fell below –30 degrees Celsius, and whatever heat was provided came from homemade wood burning stoves contrived from ammunition boxes, or effective but dangerous drip-feed space-heaters using diesel fuel or, in the case of the fool-hardy, gasoline. (Severe burn casualties from these were common.)

In summer we suffered extreme heat and humidity. When it rained, we underwent a virtual monsoon. Not only were floods common, but in at least one case, several fatalities occurred when heavy rains washed away a minefield marker. For days, our inadequate waterproof covering (the standard six by three foot groundsheets) meant that we wore soggy summer olive drab that dried on our bodies. On the other hand, in the winter, frostbite was an ever-present danger, although after the lessons of the first winter, fairly adequate winter clothing was provided. In the forward weapon pits, charcoal and homemade burners were provided; not to keep the sentries warm, but to keep the oil on the working parts of our automatic weapons from freezing.

Sanitation was primitive. Urinals, which were often neglected at night because they couldn't be found, took the form of "desert roses," shell containers or other tubing partly buried in the ground. For "number two" we dug pits that were covered with Asahi beer crates with an appropriate hole on top. When they were filled, these pits were covered in and new ones were dug. As space was usually limited in the forward platoon and section areas, by the time a locality had been occupied for up to two years there was very little, if any, unsoiled ground. If we were lucky, every two or three weeks we might pay a visit to the mobile bath unit and get a shower. This was not always possible, and often in dry weather the dusty road would leave us just as grubby when we returned.

The powers-that-be were well aware of these problems. One of the ways in which we were protected from the rats and insects in our hootchies and weapon pits was by the liberal application of DDT – in those days the be-all and end-all when it came to disinfection. This substance was sprayed by hygiene personnel, administered by "bug bomb" individual aerosol cans, and mixed with gasoline and dumped in toilets. Powdered versions of the chemical were routinely sprinkled in our clothing and, in the case of the many refugees in our forward areas, into the hair and bodies as well. It also was used in individual sprays in tents, bunkers and trenches, as well as from vehicle-mounted spray guns and even by air.

Surprisingly, in many cases, the problem was the cure (or the preventative measure) rather than the disease itself. *The Handbook of Army Health* identifies insects and small animals, often rats, as the main carriers of these ailments; countermeasures included elimination of breeding places, use of insecticides and repellents, and preventative medication. Two of the more commonly used repellents were DMP (a cream) and DDT. In some cases, insects became resistant to DDT, and Gammexane (also known as BHC) was used. All of these have since been identified as having possible harmful effects.

Even the routinely administered Paludrine could cause side effects, including stomach upset, ulcers, hair loss, and other reactions (although it was approved in civvy street as an over-the-counter drug). And there are reports of other hazards. An array of germ warfare weapons was allegedly used against North Korea in the form of infected feathers, insects and rodents. This has been disputed by U.S. officials.

Nor were our sailors immune. Due to ignorance of the effects of minuscule asbestos flakes on human lungs, Canadian destroyers' gun turrets were lined with this material (a practice abandoned by the Royal Navy), with the result that when the guns were fired more mineral particles floated around.

All of this we took in our stride – after all, we were young and invincible!

Reality hit about 30 years later.

Wearing my Korea Veterans Association hat, I began to receive increasing numbers of complaints regarding medical conditions among Korea vets. One of my first steps was to contact allied veterans' groups in Australia and the United Kingdom, whose living standards corresponded to our own. Their findings were much the same as ours. A preliminary survey conducted by KVA Canada in 1994 indicated that in a random sample of 400 Korea veterans, 59 per cent suffered from arthritis. While this is undoubtedly a disease partly resulting from aging, this seemed to be much higher than the general average for our age group. The constant grind up and down the Korean hills was no doubt a factor; as long ago as 1951 the redoubtable Tommy Prince, MM, was evacuated with this disability.

Other, more serious medical disorders were reported. Forty per cent of the respondents reported nervous conditions – this was long before post traumatic stress disorder was recognized as a pensionable condition. Heart problems were reported by 59 per cent of the respondents, and about 25 per cent noted allergies, respiratory ailments, skin afflictions and, surprisingly, malaria. (The latter was compounded by the fact that the preventative medication Paludrine itself had a number of detrimental side effects.)

One example of the effects of the noxious chemicals to which our troops were exposed is the case of Jim Cotter. Cotter, who served with the RCHA, was subjected to DDT, and possibly other harmful elements. His health deteriorated to such an extent that virtually all of his organs were affected in one way or another. After 40 years of frustration, including incessant research and submissions by the veteran and his son, as well as support from a number of veterans groups and the media, he is finally receiving an adequate disability pension. One problem was that chemical sensitivity was not recognized as a contributing factor to his ailments in Canada, and he was forced to use his life savings and borrow extensively to attend a centre in Texas where his condition, and its causes, was confirmed.

Meanwhile, reports of ailments continue to arrive with some frequency from

Korean War veterans. From Australia came a list of 42 dangerous chemicals that troops in Korea may have contacted as well as 17 endemic diseases to which Australians (and Canadians) were exposed. Our British co-ordinator, Ashley Cunningham-Boothe, died prematurely after years of suffering from the effects of his Korean War service. Like Jim Cotter, Ashley suffered from a multitude of ailments.

I could continue to catalogue the chemicals comprising what Ashley Cunningham-Boothe calls a "cocktail of contamination," ranging from disinfectants through heating tablets (which could be lethal in closed hootchies) to the tear gas which 1RCR encountered on Koje-do. According to one report I received, even some of the preservatives in our C-rations were harmful. As far as endemic diseases are concerned, I will quote one Australian source: "If the Australian Army wanted to choose a country in the early 1950s that would expose their troops to the greatest ... health risks, Korea would have headed the list." For "Australian" we may as well read "Canadian."

What can be done? First, on the basis of the increasing awareness of environmental conditions and chemical use, which is arising from more recent operations, the claims of Korean War veterans should be re-assessed. Veterans Affairs has since agreed to examine surveys on the health and early demise of Korea vets vis-à-vis their comparable age group. This has already resulted in the attribution of some cancer cases to service in Korea.

~ ~ ~ ~ ~ ~ ~ ~ ~ ~

BACK TO THE FRONT

Every five years the Department of Veterans Affairs conducts a pilgrimage to Korea to remember the 516 Canadians who gave their lives in the Korean War. In 1998, I was privileged to take part in this event. Pilgrimages take place in several areas around the world where the Canadian Forces have played a significant role. They include several European battlefields, as well as Hong Kong, Korea and the United Kingdom. They are usually held on multiples of fifth anniversaries of significant events. (The Korea pilgrimages commemorate the ceasefire in 1953.) Veterans representing those units that participated in the Korean War, as well as delegates from major veterans' organizations, took part.

I can assure you this was not a junket – like most participants, I was physically and emotionally drained long before our return to Canada; and there were no free-loaders. Everyone – not only the veterans, but the armed forces members, youth representatives and especially the VAC staff – was kept busy from well before our departure until long after the old sweats had left for home. The tour began with an assembly of the Eastern Canada participants in Toronto, where our

VAC escorts briefed us.

We were able to meet the Honourable Fred Mifflin, then minister of Veterans Affairs, and his wife. From the very start, this couple impressed us with their very real interest in each individual participant. Their very active, time-consuming and often emotional role in our group's activities was very evident. Then the remembrance ceremonies began.

The following day we took part in a commemorative service at the Korea Veterans Wall of Remembrance in Brampton with the service conducted by the pilgrimage's chaplain, Major Lloyd Clifton. Then it was on to Vancouver. Here we met the rest of the participants, including "Smoky" Smith VC, whose indefatigable activity level belied his 84 years. We remembered our friends, first at Vancouver's unique Canadian Memorial Church and later at Mountain View cemetery.

Time out in the form of a harbour cruise was available for the veterans. At Esquimalt a memorial ceremony was conducted at the Veterans Cemetery – a resting place of many veterans and servicemen from over a century ago, until today. The British Columbia office of Veterans Affairs thoughtfully provided umbrellas to combat what easterners allege is typical B.C. weather (these were retained as prized mementos of our trip). Then back to Vancouver for our flight to Japan.

Free beverages flowed, including excellent Scotch and what was, in many cases, the first sample of Asahi beer that our veterans had tasted since the early 1950s. After an overnight in Yokohama, we visited the Commonwealth War Graves cemetery. After paying our respects to those of our comrades who had died in Japan – many of them after medical evacuation from the Korean battlefield – we laid wreaths in the Hong Kong plot.

Later we attended a reception hosted by the Canadian ambassador in Tokyo that evening. We had passed the halfway mark of our tour, and it was on to our final – and most significant destination – Korea.

The morning after our arrival we rose early to visit the ROK National Cemetery in Seoul. This is an impressive and wide-spread memorial garden in honour of the South Korean servicemen as well as other honoured dead (such as police and fire officers who died in the line of duty). At the entrance is a magnificent memorial fountain with statues commemorating the war dead, while just inside is an impressive monument where Minister Mifflin laid a wreath and ceremoniously fed an incense burner that honoured the more than one million ROK servicemen who died between 1950-53. Our group was honoured by a four-service Korean guard of honour, whose turnout and deportment could not be faulted, even by CWO Zacharak, our RSM.

The next event was unscheduled, but was perhaps one of the most emotional of the entire pilgrimage. After a bus trip to Panmunjom (the old, rutted main supply route – the MSR – having been replaced by a speedy four-lane highway) five of our members were invited to take part in a very significant ceremony. Some weeks ago, the remains of five UN soldiers were unearthed north of Pyongyang, in North Korea. The North Korean government handed the caskets over to UN authorities in Panmunjom – the site of the truce talks and the subsequent discussions regarding the control of the demilitarized zone. It was a solemn occasion. Five aluminium caskets were carried by goose-stepping North Korean troops to the dividing line, where they were taken up by combined ROK and U.S. bearers, all immaculate in their dress uniforms. A guard of honour drawn from American, Belgian and Canadian veterans was drawn up at the end of the row of coffins. After a short prayer, the caskets were removed for Hawaii, where attempts would be made to identify the victims.

Following the service, the Canadian party was able to visit the meeting room between the two centres. The room was divided by a microphone wire that runs down the centre of the table, and is the actual boundary between North and South Korea. Many veterans were able to cross into North Korea for the first time. Unfortunately, the DMZ is strictly out of bounds to civilians, so any aspirations to visit Hill 355 and our other old stomping grounds were quashed.

After returning to Seoul, our next day was comparatively free. Most of our group took the opportunity to visit Korea's magnificent National War Museum. There are still good bargains in the Iteawon shopping area in Seoul, and some of us were even able to find the odd watering hole (only to find that the ubiquitous Asahi beer was supplanted by an equally refreshing Korean beer named OB).

On Sunday, October 11th, we visited Kapyong, where ceremonies were conducted at the Commowealth Memorial and later to the Canadian Memorials at Naechon. A number of PPCLI veterans had the honour of laying a wreath at their Regimental Memorial there. One moving experience occurred en route. As our buses were leaving Seoul a taxi passed us, the passenger trying to flag us down. When we stopped, an elderly Korean came on to the bus and, through our interpreter, explained that he had been a KATCOM with the PPCLI. Our new friend joined us at the Naechon where he joined his Patricia buddies in the ceremony at the PPCLI Memorial.

The last leg of our odyssey took us by rail to Pusan. For those of us who had sampled the delights of rail travel in 1951, it was an eye-opener. The trip, which took a full day in the fifties, was accomplished in four hours, with the luxury of comfortable seats. The scenery, which in our time was sheer desolation, was now a continual succession of modern and prosperous centres. In Pusan we held our last, and perhaps most significant memorial ceremony of the trip. Even the weather co-operated. After torrential rainstorms, the sun shone through briefly – just long enough to enable us to pay homage to our own comrades in the United Nations cemetery. This was a very moving experience. Here we were meeting, once again, those friends who had given their lives in the cause of freedom almost half a century ago. I think that I can safely say that not one of our party was unmoved by the experience - from the minister himself, through the veterans and our VAC helpers, the military contingent and perhaps, most of all, our youth representatives.

On their grave markers in the immaculately maintained cemetery, I read the ages of some of my fallen buddies. At the time of their death we were all young, but to view, from the ripe old age of 69, a series of "Age 18" and "Age 19" inscriptions was almost too much for me. For a while, after the ceremony, we walked quietly through the rows of our comrades' graves, and remembered. Our youth representatives unobtrusively joined us with single roses, which they offered us to pay a last tribute to the fallen. Then it was back to the hotel for a farewell dinner and once again we enjoyed Japan Air's hospitality. A further night in Vancouver, more jet lag, and finally home - physically and emotionally drained, but with an experience that we wouldn't have missed for the world.

During their return visit to Korea in 1998, author Les Peate and the delegation of Korea War veterans visited the Canadian plot at the UN cemetary in Busan. (PHOTO BY LES PEATE)

ABOVE: *An international delegation lays a wreath beneath the Canadian plot at the UN cemetary in Busan (formerly Pusan), Korea. (DND)*

OPPOSITE PAGE: *Illustrating the diversity in uniform and headgear five members of the commonwealth division pose for a propaganda photo. (DND)*

🐚 ALLIED IN THE FIGHT

IN ALL, 22 DIFFERENT NATIONS participated in the Korean War. One of them served incognito. The exploits of the major UN participant, the United States, have been well documented, as have those of the ROK Forces. This chapter focuses on the participation of the other contingents – from the largest (United Kingdom) to the smallest platoon (Luxembourg).

KIWIS FIRST TO ANSWER THE CALL: NEW ZEALAND

New Zealand's response to the UN request for support in Korea came quickly. On July 3, 1950 two Royal New Zealand Navy (RNZN) frigates, the *Pukaki* and *Tutira* were despatched to the Korean War zone, and for the duration of the war two New Zealand vessels remained on duty with the Seventh Fleet. Their duties included essential patrols, defence of ROK-held islands, supply operations and coastal bombardment – in short, the multitude of tasks which have been assigned to smaller vessels for centuries. Over half of the RNZN's members eventually served in the Korean War.

When United Nations members were asked to provide ground forces, New Zealand was the first Commonwealth member to respond. On July 27, 1950 recruiting began for "Kayforce." When recruiting ended 10 days later almost six thousand had volunteered for the New Zealand artillery regiment.

By the end of the year the guns, vehicles and 1,231 New Zealand soldiers had arrived in Korea.

Before going into action 16 NZ Field Regiment moved to Myriang-chon, about 65 kilometres north of Pusan. One jeep apparently turned off the well-travelled main supply route and was ambushed by enemy guerrilla forces. The occupants, WO R.G. Long and Gunner R. MacDonald, were brutally clubbed, bayoneted, shot and stripped of their uniforms.

The regiment was attached to 27 Commonwealth Brigade and the U.S. 2nd Division. On February 15th the Middlesex Regiment came under heavy attack and while holding off the enemy, the Peter Battery observation post crew had to fight them off with rifle fire. The FOO and radio operator were decorated for their part in the action.

On the night of April 22, 1951, 16 NZ Field Regiment was enjoying a relatively peaceful existence in support of the 6th ROK Division. Then the Chinese struck – an intensive enemy artillery effort was directed against the South Koreans, who had only the 25-pounders of the New Zealanders available to respond. The South Koreans fled, leaving the New Zealand gunners unprotected against a mass of Chinese troops. The Middlesex Battalion was sent forward for local support and the Kiwis were ordered to disengage. As the ROK troops continued to withdraw the New Zealanders continued firing, at almost point-blank range, eventually pulling back troop by troop as the British infantry covered their withdrawal.

The withdrawal was a nightmare. The roads were clogged with refugees and retreating South Korean troops. Meanwhile, the Australians and Canadians had been rushed into position on either side of the route. The move raised additional problems. The CO, Colonel Moodie, was ordered to open fire on the retreating refugees if necessary to clear his route, but refused to pass on those orders.

By nightfall on the 23rd, the Regiment had rejoined the rest of 27 Brigade and established its position at Kopkwang-ni, northeast of Kapyong. That night the Australian battalion came under attack, and 16 Field Regiment moved up into range to support them. The gunners suffered an accidental napalm attack by U.S. aircraft, causing casualties and loss of equipment.

The Aussies were forced to withdraw, despite heavy supporting fire from their Anzac allies. On the 24th it was the turn of the Canadians to hold firm, again strongly supported by the New Zealand gunners. One Canadian veteran recalls that over a few hours, more than 10,000 rounds were fired by the Kiwi gunners – the piles of empty shell-cases were described as "mountainous." They were in action continually with little or no sleep for 72 hours.

16 NZ Field Regiment's next major role was in Operation COMMANDO. During the six days of Operation COMMANDO, 16 NZ Field Regiment fired 72,000 rounds.

With the consolidation of the Division on the Jamestown Line, the regiment went on to the defensive. When the radio of Captain Peter King MC, the FOO, was destroyed, he and his operator, Gunner Rixon, fought as infantrymen, restoring a critical situation. Captain King was wounded three times and Rixon, although wounded, carried his officer to safety and was wounded a second time while doing so. This gallant soldier was justly awarded the Distinguished Conduct Medal for his part.

In 24 hours of hard fighting, 16 NZ Fd. Regt. expended 10,387 rounds. On November 7 they sent their 200,000th round on its way, followed by the quarter-millionth on the 24th of that month.

In November 1952, the Divisional Commander, Major-General West, fired the Kiwis' 500,000th round, while in June the following year the total had reached three quarters of a million.

Their final rounds were fired at 0530 hrs on the morning of July 27, 1953 — the day of the ceasefire. Their total expenditure of almost 800,000 rounds was the highest of any field regiment in the Korean War.

Meanwhile, the support units performed yeoman service. The Signals were challenged by the extreme cold which corroded batteries and terminals, and the constant moves in the early months was a challenge to the telephone line-layers. The RNZEME Light Aid Detachment kept the guns and vehicles in action, while Kiwi sappers augmented the Commonwealth engineers, and sometimes were called upon to fight with the infantry. The transport company performed well too, with their British four-wheel drive Bedford 3-ton vehicles, which were not always wholly suitable for the poor Korean roads.

A total of 3,794 New Zealanders served in the Korean War, with its army members receiving a total of 4 DSOs, 11 Military Crosses (one of them to Captain King, DSO), one DCM, 7 Military Medals, and numerous other awards. Forty-nine were Mentioned in Despatches, while several foreign decorations were awarded as well as the ROK Presidential Citation. The Navy, whose role, if less spectacular, was just as vital, received eight gallantry awards and 18 MIDs. All this was not achieved without cost; the New Zealanders suffered 118 casualties, including 29 killed in action.

In 1956 General West, visiting New Zealand, stated: "If there is a better unit than the New Zealand 16th Artillery Regiment, I'd like to see it!" Commonwealth Division veterans, and 28 Brigade members in particular, would endorse those comments.

~ ~ ~ ~ ~ ~ ~ ~ ~ ~

THEY CAME FROM DOWN UNDER: AUSTRALIA

When the United Nations called for assistance in June of 1950, Australia responded quickly. The 77th Fighter Squadron, based in Japan, was soon in combat as a part of the U.S. Fifth Air Force. In June, too, HMAS *Bataan* and the frigate HMAS *Shoalhaven* were placed under command of the U.S. Far East Fleet; these were followed by six more vessels before hostilities ended.

On June 25, 1950 the Third Battalion, Royal Australian Regiment (3RAR), on occupation duty in Japan, was selected for service in Korea, and landed at Pusan on September 28. The Australians joined the 1st Middlesex and 1st Argyll and Sutherland Highlanders in what became 27 Commonwealth Brigade (later augmented by 2PPCLI, 16 New Zealand Field Regiment, and 60th (AB) Indian Field Ambulance).

After a brief encounter with North Korean troops at Waegwon, the battalion joined the UN advance northwards. At Sariwon, they captured almost 2,000 prisoners (the largest single capture by UN troops during the entire war). Pushing on beyond the North Korean capital of Pyongyang they took a further 225 prisoners at Pakchong and neared the Yalu River and the Manchurian border.

Then the Chinese entered the war and by the new year the Commonwealth Brigade had retired south of Seoul. 3RAR carried out dogged defensive and delaying actions and counterattacks despite bitter winter conditions. In April, the brigade moved into corps reserve at Kapyong.

On April 22 an enemy counter-offensive began, culminating in the battle of Kapyong. Thirty-two Australians were killed in action or died of wounds in this engagement.

Following Operation COMMANDO, the battle for Maryang San (Hill 317), the battalion was awarded the battle honour "Kowang-San" as well as two DSOs, nine Military Crosses, two DCMs and nine Military Medals.

Once the Jamestown Line was established, the rest of the war was spent in holding firm and patrolling activity. In June 1952, the First Battalion RAR arrived and there were now two Australian battalions in 28 Brigade. In 1953, the Third Battalion was relieved by 2RAR and later went home. During its nine years of existence, this unit had never served in Australia.

Meanwhile, the Royal Australian Air Force was not idle. Although the P-51 Mustangs proved no match for the enemy MiG jets, they performed an important function in ground support. They later received Gloster Meteors, which continued to serve well in the ground-support role. The intensity of their efforts can be judged by the fact that 67 of 77 Squadron's pilots received the Distinguished Flying Cross or Medal. Besides the fighter squadron, 30 Transport Squadron RAAF also provided yeoman service.

Nor was the Royal Australian Navy idle. Seven vessels served in Korean waters. Twenty-seven members received gallantry decorations, as well as a number of Mentions in Despatches.

William Rowlinson was the only soldier awarded two Distinguished Conduct Medals in Korea. The first award was for Kapyong in April 1951, the second was won less than five months later when Sergeant Rowlinson earned a bar to this award during the battle for Hill 317.

Private H.W. Madden was captured near Kapyong. He was subjected to continual beatings, torture and starvation for six months while his captors tried unsuccessfully to obtain his co-operation. He died of his ill treatment six months later, and was posthumously awarded one of the three George Crosses for Korean service.

Finally, Major E.C. Robertson. This officer gained the respect of the troops by evacuating casualties under heavy enemy fire during the Kapyong battle. Major Robertson was a Salvation Army officer, whose official duties were to provide comforts to the troops in rest areas.

Altogether, 3RAR received 11 battle honours for Korea – more than any other Commonwealth unit. While, admittedly, their tour of duty was much longer than other units, they deserve a heartfelt "Good on yer!" In the words of British Brigadier B.A. Burke: "For the Australians, I can find no words to express my admiration for what they have done."

~ ~ ~ ~ ~ ~ ~ ~ ~ ~

THE FLYING CHEETAHS: SOUTH AFRICA

No. 2 South African Air Force Squadron was in action early in the war, flying F-51 Mustangs in a close ground-support role. However, one incident deserves special mention.

On December 5, 1950, Captains Davis and Lipawsky were given the task of destroying 10 captured UN railroad cars, carrying explosives which were held north of Pyongyang.

Captain Davis attacked the cars with rockets, but to ensure complete accuracy he attacked low and close. He was only too successful – one of the cars exploded and his Mustang was struck by debris which, coupled with the force of the explosion, rendered Davis briefly unconscious and severely damaged the aircraft. He recalled, "Something big tore a hole in the cockpit, passing right between my legs."

Luckily the aircraft had been trimmed "tail heavy" which enabled it to climb and clear hills in the vicinity. The aircraft was a virtual wreck, controls almost inoperative. Davis was able to effect a crash-landing, demolishing two large trees in the process.

Meanwhile, Captain Lipawsky continued to fly cover, but no rescue facilities were available.

Luck was with Captain Davis. A light L-4 spotter aircraft piloted by USAF Captain Lawrence, with Captain Lewis Millit as an observer, was in the area on a reconnaissance flight, and spotted the remains of the downed Mustang. Skilfully landing the light aircraft on a narrow road, Lawrence picked up Davis, who, although badly shaken, was uninjured. Davis took the seat vacated by Captain Millit, who volunteered to stay behind, although he was unarmed and in enemy territory. Fortunately, after returning the South African to safety, Captain Lawrence was able to pick up his gallant observer, although the latter had come under enemy artillery fire.

~ ~ ~ ~ ~ ~ ~ ~ ~ ~

THE NATIONAL SERVICEMEN: UNITED KINGDOM

In the 1950s, 18-year-old British youth were called upon to perform two years of National Service in the armed forces. Many of them found themselves in Korea. Here are the stories of two of these teenagers, taken from *Morning Calm*, the newsletter of the British Korea Veterans Association, courtesy of the editor, Reuban Holroyd, and the author, Jim Jacobs.

William Purves was a bank employee in a small Scottish town when he was called up in 1950. After basic training, he was sent to Officer Training School and passed out as a Second Lieutenant. He joined his regiment, the King's Own Scottish Borderers (KOSB) in Hong Kong, but had little time to enjoy the delights of that colony as 1KOSB soon went to Korea to join the King's Shropshire Light Infantry and 3rd Royal Australian Regiment in 28 Commonwealth Brigade.

He participated in defensive and patrolling activities until the major advance north in Operation COMMANDO. On November 4, 1951, when the Chinese attempted to recapture Hill 355, an estimated 10,000 Chinese shells fell on the Commonwealth division front – 6,000 of them on the KOSB positions. A major attack by about 6,000 Chinese ensued, accompanied by the usual bugles, whistles and shouts, and a loudspeaker telling the Scots to "go home or this hill will be your grave."

The enemy advance, like flies on a mules back, headed directly for "C" Company and 2nd Lt. Purves's platoon, which was in grave danger of being overrun. By 0200 hours on November 5th, "C" and "D" Companies were cut off and being attacked on three sides.

With 13 wounded, Purves, shot through the shoulder and losing a lot of blood, asked, "Where are the orders?"

His CO did not know then that for the previous five hours the wounded subaltern had been moving around in the open under withering fire, encouraging his men and hurling grenades at the swarming Chinese with his good arm.

"Get out of it!" was his CO's response. With pride in his voice Purves replied, "But we're holding them, Sir!" That drew the response, "You heard the order, get back here." Just before 0230 hours, Purves, his wounds still untended, ordered the remaining 40 men of "C" and "D" Companies who were still on their feet to fight their way out to Battalion HQ.

Every wounded man was to be carried out, as were all arms and ammunition. At 0300 hours, the battle still raging, Purves almost fell into the command bunker, his bloodied left arm limp at his side. With his good right arm he saluted his CO and reported, "Two platoons of "C" and "D" Companies are ready for action, Sir. What are the orders?" His orders were to get himself taken to the Battalion Aid Post and have his wounds dressed.

1KOSB lost seven killed, 87 wounded, and 44 missing in the battle. Chinese losses, uncountable, were recorded as enormous. Second Lieutenant William Purves was decorated with the Distinguished Service Order, the only such award given to a National Service officer, and one that is very rarely awarded to junior officers; in those cases it was considered almost equivalent to a Victoria Cross.

Two other notable awards were earned during this battle. Private "Bill" Speakman of the Borderers became the only other rank to receive the Victoria Cross in Korea, while the Forward Observation Officer, Captain P.F. King of 16 New Zealand Field Regiment, also received the DSO for his bravery during the close-quarter fighting.

George Hodkinson was a Londoner, called up into the East Surrey Regiment. He volunteered to serve in Korea and became Fusilier Hodkinson of the First Battalion, The Royal Fusiliers.

In the early hours of November 25, 1952 – two days after 1RCR's hard-fought battle on Kowang-San – "D" Company of the Fusiliers took part in Operation PIMLICO, a company-size raid designed to take prisoners, hurt the enemy, and destroy enemy strong-points. Hodkinson was the 10 Platoon signaller.

12 Platoon was attacked by about 60 Chinese while crossing a stream, and had to fight its way back to Company HQ. This alerted another large body of Chinese who were laid up nearby, and attacked 10 Platoon. Heavy casualties were incurred, including the platoon commander and all the platoon's NCOs.

Hodkinson, although badly wounded in the leg and face, took control of the direction of the ensuing battle. He continued reporting concise details of the platoon's predicament, pausing occasionally to fire his Sten at the nearby enemy. To ensure the clearest transmission of his radio signals, he stood, exposed, upon a small mound.

He continued to direct artillery, mortar and tank fire, calling down rounds ever closer to his own position. His example inspired the platoon survivors, who fought on with the wounded at their feet. At 0250 hrs, Hodkinson received the order to withdraw. He replied that as they could not carry out all their wounded they would remain in position. He refused attempts by a comrade to apply a dressing to his own facial wound, as he said that it would hamper the use of his radio.

A final rush by the enemy elicited this final transmission: "This is it. They are coming in strength. We shall be overrun this time. They are coming up the hill. We are being overrun, we are being overrun…"

Of the 22-man platoon only six walked out, all wounded. "D" Company casualties were 14 killed, 19 wounded and eight missing. Two of the missing, including Hodkinson, became POWs. His leg wound eventually healed, but the facial one did not, and he lost the sight of his left eye.

For his outstanding courage and devotion to duty, showing complete disregard for his own safety, Fusilier George Hodkinson was decorated with the Distinguished Conduct Medal, the highest bravery award ever made to a National Serviceman at other rank level.

William Purves returned to his job as a bank clerk, but seeking a more adventurous life and hoping to renew his acquaintance with Hong Kong, took a job with the Hong Kong and Shanghai Banking Corporation. After more than 40 years, Sir William Purves, KB, CDE, DSO, retired as chairman of that prestigious organization.

A LITTLE TRIVIA: Another member of the Royal Fusiliers who served in Korea was Fusilier Michael Micklewhite. He is now better known as Michael Caine (the actor).

~ ~ ~ ~ ~ ~ ~ ~ ~ ~

THE BROWN BERETS OF BELGIUM

On July 22, 1950 the government of Belgium responded to the UN request for assistance, and decided to dispatch an infantry battalion. A call went out for volunteers, and over 700 were selected from the many applicants from regular and reserve units.

The battalion was organized into three rifle companies and one heavy-weapons company, and intensive training was soon well underway. The volunteers were gathered from all over the country and spoke two languages. Those who survived the rigorous training program were awarded a brown beret with the Battalion's distinguishing badge.

On November 6, 1950 the new battalion was presented with its colors, and a little over a month later sailed for the Far East. Following their arrival in Pusan on January 31, 1951, the Belgians (less their transport, which arrived in late February) were assigned to protect the lines of communication north of Taegu. Forays against reported concentrations of Communist guerrillas proved fruitless, and the Belgian commander, Lieutenant Colonel Crahay, constantly visited EUSAK seeking a more active role.

In March 1951, the Belgian Battalion was assigned to a defence position on the Han River, suffering its first casualties when two officers accompanying a U.S. reconnaissance group encountered a mine (one was killed and the other seriously wounded).

On April 3 the unit came under command of 29 British Brigade and took its place on the right flank of the Imjin. On April 22 the Chinese opened a large-scale offensive. The 29th Brigade held a 10-kilometre front on the Imjin line, between 1ROK Division and 3rd U.S. Infantry. The first contact by the Belgians was made at 1500 hours, and by 2100 hours all three forward battalions of 29 Brigade were engaged.

During the night, the Chinese pushed forward and penetrated between the forward companies and battalion headquarters. Hand-to-hand fighting ensued and the situation became desperate as company positions were penetrated. A combat patrol was sent out to secure bridges over the Imjin and Hantan rivers, which would be vital in case of a withdrawal. The patrol was ambushed and six Belgians were taken prisoner.

By now the gallant Belgians were exhausted, almost out of ammunition and had suffered heavy casualties. They were ordered by the brigade commander to withdraw and took up a position between the Gloucestershire Regiment and Royal Northumberland Fusiliers. Efforts to relieve the Gloucesters were unsuccessful, and the Belgians were ordered to open up a withdrawal route for the remaining battalions, the Fusiliers and the Royal Ulster Rifles. All four battalions sustained heavy casualties in the battle and subsequent withdrawal.

Later, following the UN counteroffensive (where the understrength Belgian unit performed well) they took their place in the line with the 1st Cavalry Division. In March and April 1953, the Belgians were subjected to 55 days of continuous attacks ranging from small-scale sorties to battalion-strength efforts, together with heavy mortar and artillery fire.

In 1955, the Brown Berets returned home bearing Korean and U.S. Presidential Citations for their performance. But the cost was high: 106 were killed in action (including five initially reported as missing) and 349 wounded.

BELGIAN BATTALION HOLD ITS OWN

Raphael Dael served with the Belgian Battalion in Korea and later immigrated to Canada. This is his story:

"Upon arriving in Korea I was assigned to the Reconnaissance Platoon of the heavy weapons company and was given the job of second gunner in a machine-gun squad manning a .30-calibre air-cooled machine gun.

"On October 24 (my 20th birthday) we took up our position in the Chorwon Valley area. This line was very uneventful except for the fact that we felt like sitting ducks, at the mercy of an enemy that was looking down on us from a 400-meter mountain range. Keeping your head down was the order of the day. And to add to the misery, it seemed as though all the rats had chosen this valley for residency.

"The Battalion was assigned a new position on White Horse Hill, which had seen a ferocious battle at the end of September. By the beginning of October, winter had set in. I remember it to be extremely cold and, living in small foxholes dug out of the side of the mountain, we were hard-pressed to keep ourselves warm.

"However, the heavy frost and substantial layer of snow reduced the odors from the hundred bodies of dead Chinese soldiers that had been left behind from the earlier battle for the hill. The Communist forces tried, via loudspeakers, to persuade us to surrender. It was quite eerie to hear those voices in the middle of the night.

"Just before New Year 1953 we were relieved and spent a number of weeks doing maintenance and hard training. In late February or early March we took up positions on Chat-kol Hill. My squad was assigned to support "C" Company. We were a busy bunch, improving our positions but under constant shelling. The Reds never let up, bombarding us day and night. They attacked our lines nearly every night; we lost a significant number of dead and wounded. As the nights grew shorter the attacks became more frequent.

"Despite the constant barrages and assaults by the Chinese we were able to hold our important position to the very end. This could only have been achieved by the true *esprit de corps* of the rank and file of the Belgian Battalion."

~ ~ ~ ~ ~ ~ ~ ~ ~ ~

LUXEMBOURG

Despite its small size, Luxembourg was quick to respond to the UN's call, and asked for volunteers to serve in Korea. Following an overwhelming response, on November 1, 1950 the Korea-bound platoon was activated, with a total of one officer and 47 NCOs and men.

The platoon was assigned as an integral part of the Belgian battalion and, on December 18, 1950, sailed with the Belgians on the SS *Kamina*. In March, the Belgians and Luxembourgers participated in the general offensive under command of the U.S. 3rd Infantry Division. They later came under command of British 29th Brigade, relieving the Philippine Battalion. After a couple of fairly quiet weeks, a patrol under Lieutenant Wagner was engaged in a firefight with the Chinese, breaking off without casualties. Things soon heated up.

On April 22 the platoon, together with the rest of the Belgian Battalion, was heavily attacked on the Imjin River. The unit was forced to withdraw but, as the enemy pressed on against 29 Brigade, the Belgians were assigned to the British right flank. After heavy fighting, during which the Luxembourgians came under fire from the dominating feature of Kamak-san, the unit was ordered to withdraw to the Seoul area. For their part in the crucial Imjin battle, the unit was recognized by a citation from their government.

In June, the platoon recrossed the Imjin and established a bridgehead to support a reconnaissance-in-force by two Belgian companies. Meeting heavy opposition, the Belgians withdrew, their retreat covered by the Luxembourg Platoon who suffered their first fatality. Sergeant Steffe and Corporal Mainz were decorated for their work in covering the retrieval of the Belgian wounded.

It was time for the Luxembourgers to go home and, on August 25, they left Inchon, proudly carrying the insignia of Presidential Unit Citations from the Republic of Korea and the United States. Meanwhile, a second platoon was preparing to take its turn in Korea. Leaving by air on March 16, 1952, they arrived in Korea 10 days later. Among the 52 infantrymen, were six members of the first shift who had volunteered for a second tour.

After three months of intensive training, familiarization with new weapons and rear-area duties, they went into the line in late June. By this time, the war was mainly in a static mode, although the Luxembourgers were engaged in intensive patrol activity. In August, the enemy became more aggressive, and one NCO was killed during one of many heavy mortar bombardments. The Chinese offense became more heated and on September 25, 1952, the positions – known as King Post – were heavily attacked. The platoon, inspired by platoon commander Lieutenant Lutty, held their positions. Lutty, although seriously wounded, refused evacuation and continued to lead his troops, personally rescuing a wounded soldier under heavy fire.

During their tour, the platoons had taken part in two major engagements – the Imjin battle and King Post. In addition to Korean and U.S. recognition they received a citation from their own country. Of the 94 Luxembourgers who served in Korea, two were killed in action and 10 were wounded. While these figures may seem insignificant, remember that, despite the fact that they were only in Korea for a little over 18 months, their casualty rate was twice our own.

~ ~ ~ ~ ~ ~ ~ ~ ~ ~

LE PITON: FRANCE ANSWERS THE CALL

French forces served with distinction during the Korean War. Less than a month after the North Korean invasion, France placed the frigate *La Grandière* at the disposal of the UN command. In August of 1950 the call went out for volunteers, and the following month the Forces Terrestres Françaises de l'ONU – a battalion-sized group of 39 officers and 978 enlisted men – was activated. While over half of the officers and NCOs were from regular units, about 90 per cent of the soldiers were volunteers from the reserves.

Their CO was already a legend in his own army. Colonel Monclair was severely wounded 17 times in the First World War, and held every military decoration for valour that his country had to offer. In World War II, he took command of a Legion demi-brigade in the Free French forces. After distinguished service in both North Africa and Italy, Monclair was eventually promoted to the three-star rank of général de corps d'armée. In 1950, he voluntarily reverted to the rank of lieutenant colonel in order to command the Korea-bound battalion.

The French battalions arrived in Korea in November of 1950 and within a month were in the line under command of the U.S. 23rd Infantry Regiment. On January 10, 1951 they withstood several heavy attacks and sustained their first casualties. Later, their tenacity, coupled with the effective use of the bayonet, played a major role in halting the enemy advance.

The next major action was near the centre of the Eighth Army front. On February 1, the battalion was engaged by strong enemy forces on three sides, but aided by an airdrop of much-needed ammunition, held their ground. For a loss of 30 killed or missing and 97 wounded, the French counted 1,300 enemy dead in front of their positions. For this action, the battalion received its first U.S. Presidential Citation. At Chipyong-ni, they earned a second American citation.

In March the allies advanced, and the French Battalion was engaged in a stubborn fight when they captured and held Hill 1126 in atrocious weather, at a cost of 143 killed and wounded.

On May 10, a French medical officer, Commandant Jean-Louis, lost his life in a patrol sent to rescue two wounded ROK soldiers. A monument is erected to his memory in Hong-Chon area. The French Battalion lost 112 killed and wounded during the month of May 1951.

Other major actions were still to come. For several weeks the 23rd Regiment, including its French Battalion, was heavily engaged in the Heartbreak Ridge battles, where close-quarter combat against determined North Korean formations was the norm. The key objective – Hill 851 – was finally secured on October 13 by the French unit.

The battle-weary members of 2nd Division spent 50 days in a rest area near Kapyong (fortified by generous donations of wine from the Paris newspaper *Figaro*). The 59-year-old Colonel Monclair left from home (where he received yet another Médaille Militaire). During the battles, 260 Frenchmen had been killed or wounded.

Other fierce defensive actions took place before the ceasefire at the Iron Triangle (again), T-bone Hill and Arrowhead Ridge. There were many individual heroic exploits. The Pioneer Platoon was twice wiped out and received the rare distinction of becoming one of the few sub-units of its size to receive two presidential citations. One *poilu* was captured and was able to sneak a grenade into one of his captors' armpits with the striker lever down. When the Red Chinese moved his arm, the Frenchman made his escape while the enemy were taken out of action.

In all, the Bataillon Français lost 271 killed or missing and 1,008 wounded. Besides two Korean and three U.S. presidential citations, they were awarded four more by the French Army, which are proudly borne on the unit colours.

However, this story does not have a happy ending. While most of their allies returned home, to varying degrees of welcome, the Forces Terrestres Françaises de l'ONU was shipped to Indo-China, where most became casualties to the Viet-Minh in the closing days of that colonial war.

~ ~ ~ ~ ~ ~ ~ ~ ~ ~

FROM BOGOTA TO OLD BALDY: COLOMBIA

In the United Nations Command in Korea, South America was represented by a country, which, despite internal conflicts, provided both military and naval forces. When the appeal went out for assistance Colombia answered the call.

On November 1, 1950 the frigate *Almirante Padilla* set sail and on May 8, 1951, the *Padilla* joined the Seventh Fleet's Task Force 95 and was immediately assigned to patrol duties on Korea's west coast. Her comparatively shallow draught enabled the vessel to work close inshore.

The *Padilla* was transferred to the East Coast on June 14, and was engaged in constant interdiction of Wonsan, a North Korean communication centre. The Colombian vessel's principal role was participation in PACKAGE and DERAIL programmes, to disrupt enemy communications over a 100-mile stretch of coastline south of Songjin. Risks were ever present, as the ships would close to within 2,000 yards to open fire.

On January 19, 1952, *Padilla* left for Yokosuka, where she was relieved by ARC *Capitan Tono* and later *Almirante Brion* (having undergone major repairs) arrived in the theatre on June 29, 1953, and remained on station after the ceasefire, returning in April 1954.

Meanwhile, on December 26, 1950, the 1st Colombian Infantry Battalion was activated and on May 21, 1951 the battalion sailed for Korea.

On August 6, they received their first casualties when a combat patrol, advancing five kilometres north of the main defended positions, encountered heavy Chinese opposition. They soon proved their aggressiveness by a continuing series of patrols and small-scale attacks. On October 13 they joined the 21st Infantry Regiment.

The Colombian troops seized and held a company-strength outpost on a hill, Hoegogae, which effectively checked enemy intrusion and provided a firm base for patrol. This was held against strong opposition until handed over to ROK units on November 15.

By now winter had set in and the Colombian troops suffered severely from cold and frostbite. Despite this, they continued to keep up the pressure on the enemy with daylight patrols and small-scale attacks. During 1952 the Colombian Battalion maintained its place in the line. On December 9 their service was recognized by the award of the U.S. Presidential Unit Citation for their part in the Kumsong area.

The final major actions of the battalion included Operation BARBULA, a company operation to destroy two enemy positions. After heavy hand-to-hand fighting, Chinese reinforcements arrived. The Colombian medics were overwhelmed, and the Korean Service Corps stretcher-bearers fled. Two platoons were forced to withdraw – the third platoon returned at considerable risk to recover their wounded and dead comrades. This action cost the company 19 killed, 44 wounded, and eight missing.

On March 23 a company of the Colombian Battalion held the "Old Baldy" position, adjacent to Pork Chop Hill of movie fame. Here "B" Company resisted a battalion-strength attack while being relieved by "C" Company. Before withdrawing to the south-west slope of the feature, the Colombians had suffered 60 per cent casualties. The battle had cost the Colombians 95 dead, 97 wounded and 30 captured. One irony of the battle is that some Colombians seeking shelter from the heavy shelling in the bunkers on the hill were greeted by a group of Orientals already there. Their hosts even gave them cigarettes. When the fire was lifted, the former inhabitants left; it was only later that the South Americans found that their involuntary hosts were not friendly ROK troops, but Chinese.

During operations LITTLE SWITCH and BIG SWITCH 28 Colombian POWs were returned from captivity. Total casualties were high, including 163 who died in action and 448 wounded (including their first CO, Colonel Puyo). Most of these were incurred in patrol actions. Too little has been written of this gallant band whose country, although undergoing internal strife readily answered the UN call.

In one respect many U.S. troops will remember the Colombians. While the unit was in rest they often formed a nine-man Latin-American band to augment to the movies shown in reserve locations.

~ ~ ~ ~ ~ ~ ~ ~ ~ ~

THE VAN HEUTSZ BATTALION: THE NETHERLANDS

When the Netherlands responded to the United Nations' call for assistance in Korea, the request came at a bad time. Although naval forces could be and were dispatched immediately, the army was in a state of disarray. The conscripts that had been recruited for service in Indonesia had been released when the Dutch left that area and the Netherlands was, at that time, engaged in raising a land force for NATO.

Nevertheless, volunteers were called for. In view of the urgency, only regular or trained personnel could be accepted. This led to a unit of various backgrounds. Some volunteers had served with the Resistance or Free Dutch forces, while many were former members of the Waffen SS whose prison terms were remitted and citizenship restored for volunteering. The new unit was designated the Van Heutsz Regiment in honour of a 19th century general.

The battalion left Rotterdam on October 26, 1950 and arrived in Pusan on November 23. The Dutch were assigned to the 2nd Division's 38th Infantry Regiment.

On the night of February 12-13, 1951, Chinese troops, who had infiltrated among retreating ROK forces, launched a heavy attack on the Dutch positions. Rallying his headquarters personnel, the commanding officer, Lt.-Col. M.P.A. den Ouden and four of his officers were killed. Following fierce hand-to-hand fighting, the enemy was finally repelled.

By the evening of February 14, the enemy controlled Hill 325, a feature that dominated the UN positions. The under-strength "A" Company, reinforced by personnel from "B" and heavy weapons companies, was ordered to recapture Hill 325. Just before dawn, after being repulsed twice, the exhausted Dutch, their ammunition almost expended, fixed bayonets and, shouting their battle cry, gained their objective. For these actions the Van Heutsz received its first U.S. Presidential Unit Citation at the cost of over a hundred casualties.

Following their first rotation in July the Dutch participated in the recapture of a number of enemy-held features, including the notorious Heartbreak Ridge.

In April 1952, the Battalion was pulled out of the line to assist in quelling the Koje-do prison camp disorders. For the remainder of hostilities, the Netherlands' experience was similar to that of most of us – holding the line and undergoing miserable living conditions, frequent interruptions by enemy artillery and mortar fire, and, at times, by assaults of various strength by an always-aggressive enemy. Patrols and counter-patrols were routine. Their final action was the defence of Hill 340, near Kumhwa, during the Chinese truce offensive between July 14-27, 1953.

The Van Heutsz suffered 123 killed or missing in action and 645 wounded. Altogether 3,972 served in Korea – some of them two or three times. The Van Heutsz Regiment received a Republic of Korea Presidential Unit Citation, 31 Dutch gallantry decorations, and 120 U.S. and 43 Korean awards.

The Royal Dutch Navy, meanwhile, performed yeoman service. Each destroyer, from HMNS *Evertsen* (on station in July 1950) to HMNS *Van Zijll* (which left for home in January 1955) served for about eight months under the command of the U.S. Seventh Fleet. *Evertsen* took part in the Inchon invasion while HMNS *Piet Hein*, like many of her Canadian counterparts, became a member of the exclusive train-busters club.

~ ~ ~ ~ ~ ~ ~ ~ ~ ~

STHASEN I TURKI!: REPUBLIC OF TURKEY

Turkey had been quick to respond when called on to provide support to the United Nations in Korea. The Turkish Brigade group, of almost 5,500 men, was one of the first allied contingents to arrive in Korea, reaching Pusan in October 1950. The formation was commanded by Brigadier General Tashin Yazici, who had been a divisional commander at Gallipoli.

The Brigade was first in action in the Tokchon area in late November. It was not an auspicious baptism of fire. They engaged what appeared to be advancing enemy troops, claiming a victory when, in fact, they had killed a number of retreating ROK soldiers.

More communication difficulties arose later, when the Turks were twice ambushed near Kunu-ri, suffering heavy casualties.

In the battle to regain Seoul in January, the Turks regained their fighting reputation with a bayonet charge that overran the Chinese and inspired the commander of the U.S. 8th Army, General Ridgway, to order all units to operate with bayonets fixed in future.

During the static phase of the war, the Turks took part in the defence of the Iron Triangle, including the bitter fighting on Heartbreak Ridge. Again the Turks distinguished themselves with the use of cold steel during these operations. Their final major battle was in May of 1953, a few miles east of Panmunjom. The Chinese had successfully attacked and taken part of the allied line, but the bayonet-wielding Turks counterattacked and held the position until relieved four days later.

But perhaps the most significant characteristic of the Turks was their toughness. One of the Norwegian MASH doctors was exasperated when he was trying to determine a wounded Turkish infantryman's injuries. He kept asking the victim to tell him when his probing hurt. The stoical Turk refused to admit to any pain, merely replying, "No hurt – me Turk!"

Notably, not one of the 234 Turks held in Chinese prison camps died during captivity. According to Max Hastings in *The Korean War*, the only collaborator was "quietly killed by his compatriots."

Almost 15,000 Turks served in Korea and their casualty rate was among the highest in the UN forces: 741 died and 2,068 were wounded.

NOTE: The title of this article is a Greek expression which means (roughly) "we're in big trouble." It translates as "The Turks are here!"

~ ~ ~ ~ ~ ~ ~ ~ ~ ~

THE EVZONES: GREECE

Speaking of the Greeks, in December 1950 the Greek Expeditionary Forces (GEF) arrived in Korea with a force of one infantry battalion consisting of 851 men and one transport flight of seven C-47 aircraft. Once in theatre the Greeks quickly joined their American allies, with the battalion joining the 7th Calvary Regiment of the 1st U.S. Calvary

Division.

The 13th Flight was the first Greek unit to enter combat and from December 4 to 24 participated in keeping supplies going to American troops that were caught and circled by the enemy on the Hungnam bridgehead. For its work in this dangerous mission the flight was awarded an Honorary Citation from the President of the United States. During the war the flight transport completed 1,795 battle sorties with 8,288 combat flight hours carrying 34,640 men and 5,958 wounded men. Three aircraft were shot down and killing all those aboard.

The battalion participated with the Americans in several offensive operations from the early part of the war including the battle of Hill 381, Hill 402 and Hill 326. They then joined up with the 15th Infantry Regiment of the 3rd U.S. Infantry Division for the static part of the war.

In total 186 members of the Greek Expeditionary Forces were killed and 610 wounded. Overall the GEF was awarded honorary citations by both the presidents of the U.S. and ROK. The Americans decorated the Force with six Military Crosses for Distinguished Service, 32 Silver Stars, 110 Bronze Stars and 19 Air Medals. As well, the GEF was awarded a number of decorations by the ROK government.

~ ~ ~ ~ ~ ~ ~ ~ ~ ~

THE KAGNEW BATTALION: ETHIOPIA

In 1935 Mussolini's forces launched an unprovoked attack on Abyssinia. Emperor Haile Selassie's pleas for assistance from the League of Nations had little effect. Abyssinia remained under Italian domination until it was freed by the British in 1941.

In 1950, when a similar situation occurred in Korea, Abyssinia (since renamed Ethiopia), having been there, quickly answered the United Nation's call for help in suppressing the North Korean invasion of the South. Emperor Haile Selassie offered to provide a thousand soldiers.

The Ethiopian contingent was selected from the elite Imperial Guard and was designated the Kagnew Battalion. This unique designation was derived from the name of the warhorse of Ethiopian King Menelik, a warrior-king who had earlier defeated the Italians in the war of 1880. The only African ground troops, the members of the Kagnew Battalion were seasoned professional soldiers, every one of whom was over six feet in height. This was to stand them in good stead when they encountered the hilly Korean terrain.

On April 16, 1951, 931 members of the battalion sailed from Djibouti and arrived in Pusan on May 7. Following further training in the use of their new American weapons and equipment, the Kagnews were assigned to the U.S. Seventh Infantry Division, with whom they remained for most of the war.

The Kagnew Battalion gained a reputation as one of the toughest and most aggressive infantry units in Korea. Their valour did not go unrecognized. In one notable action on

January 24, 1953, two single platoons took a hill south of Old Baldy in the Pork Chop Hill area and defended it against overwhelming odds when the Chinese counterattacked. They held their ground under heavy artillery bombardment and abandoned the hill only when directly ordered to do so.

The United States, too, recognized the fighting ability of these African soldiers. The 2nd Kagnew Battalion (which had relieved the 1st Battalion in March 1952) was awarded a U.S. Presidential Unit Citation in September 1952. A Silver Star and 18 Bronze Stars were also awarded to the Ethiopians.

At their peak strength in 1953, about 1,200 Ethiopians served in the Korean War. A total of 3,518 served over the entire period, in three shifts (rotations were conducted on a battalion basis). Of these, 121 were killed in action. The Kagnew Battalion can proudly claim that it never gave up an inch of ground, and that not a single Ethiopian soldier was captured by the enemy.

Like some other national contingents, the Ethiopians encountered linguistic and cultural challenges. Few Americans spoke their language (Amharic), therefore it was necessary for them to take informal crash courses in basic English phrases and military terminology. Although the Kagnew Battalion had its own surgeon (a European doctor who spoke English), a contingent of Ethiopian medical aides, stretcher-bearers and (later) nurses also accompanied the battalion.

Sadly, while their comrades were fighting in Korea, an attempt by the Imperial Guard to overthrow the Emperor was hatched. More unrest followed over the next decades – uprisings and wars with Somalia and the break-away province of Eritrea as well as widespread famine took their toll. Today, Ethiopia's gross domestic product (GDP) is one of the world's lowest at $750 per year (compare this with our own $29,400 for 2003). Many of these proud soldiers have been reduced to begging in the streets.

Ethiopia awarded a Korean War Medal to those who served there. The inscription reads (in Amharic): "We support every nation's independence but we are always the enemies of aggression, Korea, 1943." A fitting comment.

~ ~ ~ ~ ~ ~ ~ ~ ~ ~

FOXHOLE TO PRESIDENTIAL PALACE: THE PHILIPPINES

> *"You ... will be the first to carry the flag of your own sovereign nation abroad in the war for freedom."*
>
> ~ *President Elpidio Quirino, as the Philippine contingent departed for Korea*

When the Korean War broke out, the Republic of the Philippines was barely four years old, weakened by Japanese occupation and suffering from severe internal unrest. Nevertheless, when the call went out for support of the United Nations' effort in Korea, the Republic responded quickly.

The Philippines acceded to the U.S. request for a formed unit. The only effectively trained unit was the 3rd Infantry Battalion, reinforced by two tank squadrons, an artillery battery and support units to form the 10th Battalion Combat Team (BCT). On September 15, 1950, 10 BCT left Manila and arrived in Pusan four days later. On October 14 they had their first clash with North Korean troops. Unaccustomed to the bitter cold weather – as low as -22° C – they suffered badly from frostbite and hypothermia. The so-called winter clothing they were issued proved inadequate for the conditions. Many troops were so chilled that they could not even squeeze their triggers.

10 BCT found itself in Sam-go Ri on April 10, 1951, face-to-face with two Chinese battalions. After an all-day battle the enemy retreated, leaving 28 dead behind, while the Filipinos sustained the loss of only two killed.

On April 22, 10 BCT was the first unit to face the heavy Chinese onslaught at Yultong Ridge. The unit held firm against overwhelming odds. Cooks, clerks and drivers took their places in the line. Three rifle companies left over 600 enemy dead before finally receiving orders to pull back. The Filipinos were called on to try and effect a break-through to the beleaguered Gloucestershire Regiment. Facing heavy opposition, the Battalion team was unable to reach the British unit, although they came within 2,000 metres of the Glosters – the closest of any unit in the relief force.

In May 1951 the first group returned home. The unit was only half of its original strength. One hundred and fifty had been killed, wounded or missing, while another 104 disabled troops had been returned to their homeland. Of the remainder, 182 had been rendered unfit for combat due to combat exhaustion or winter conditions.

They continued to serve with distinction in the "Iron Triangle." On May 8, 1952 the unit was engaged in nine separate skimishes, while the enemy had their final fling in the closing hours before the ceasefire. The Filipinos, on Heartbreak Ridge, received over 1,000 artillery rounds between 1100 hours and 2200 hours on July 27, 1953. Not to be outdone, the artillery battery which formed part of the Combat Team retaliated, and by 1800 hours that day the hill in front of A Company was a shambles.

When the smoke had settled, the enemy had been routed and more than a dozen bunkers destroyed. The Filipino unit's only casualty was one soldier who acquired some mortar fragments in his nylon protective vest.

One young officer went on to greater things. Second Lieutenant Fidel "Eddie" Ramos became chief of the Philippine defence staff and, later, president of his country.

In May of 1955 the final Philippine unit left Korea. Casualties had been high, with many due to the impact of the cruel Korean winter on the unprepared Filipinos. Honours and awards from South Korea, the United States and their own government were showered on 10 BCT and their successor units in Korea. General James Van Fleet, commanding general of the Eighth U.S. Army, summed it up well: "Many foreign armies have proven their worth here in Korea, and the Filipinos are among the bravest."

~ ~ ~ ~ ~ ~ ~ ~ ~ ~

THAILAND

The Kingdom of Thailand was prompt to respond to the United Nations call for assistance in 1950. On August 21, 1950 the Royal Thai Army's 1st Battalion, 21st Infantry Regiment was activated and on October 3rd of that year the advance party landed in Korea. On November 7 the main body had arrived and moved to Taegu prior to integration into the First Cavalry Division. The same month, Thai naval vessels arrived; two of them, HMRTN *Bangpakon* and HMRTN *Prasea*, would serve with the U.S. Naval Command's Far East Blockade and Escort Force. Two transport flights from the Royal Thai Air Force were also committed to the UN Command in October 1950 (some of our members may recall travelling on R&R leave on Thai C-47s).

Unfortunately, the experiences of the Thai Battalion in Korea are not as well recorded as those of many other contingents. We do know, however, that they were active in two major battles in the Pork Chop Hill area. Before their actions in that area, they were neighbours of the First Commonwealth Division while under command of the First Cavalry.

Records show that the battalion fought with distinction defending Pork Chop Hill in November of 1952. At that time the battalion was attached to the U.S. Second Division. Despite heavy ground attack by superior Chinese forces the unit tenaciously held its ground for two long days. The Thais were awarded one Legion of Merit, twelve Silver Stars and 26 Bronze Stars by the United States for their part in the action.

The Republic of Korea honoured the unit with two Presidential Unit Citations – one was for the overall period of service and the other for their part in the closing days of hostilities, on Hill 351 in the Kunwha area between 14-17 July, 1953. Besides a total of 37 Distinguished Service Medals awarded by Thailand, the unit received an impressive total of 144 decorations from the U.S., South Korea and Belgium. The navy, air force, and medical detachment received another 17 awards.

A total of 3,142 Republic of Korea War Service Medals were also awarded by (then) President Syngman Rhee. In all, a total of 6,180 Thai soldiers served in Korea before the ceasefire – at their peak 2,174 of them were serving in 1952. The battalion finally completed its tour of duty and left Korea in March of 1955.

Their legacy lives on. Today, the 21st Regiment forms the personal guard for H.M. Queen Sirikit.

~ ~ ~ ~ ~ ~ ~ ~ ~ ~

THE RED CROSS OF ITALY

Although as a non-UN participant Italy was unable to send armed forces to Korea, the nation responded to a request from the International Red Cross to provide medical assistance. In November 1951, Italian Red Cross Hospital 68 arrived in Korea, with a complement of seven doctors, six nurses, a chaplain and 50 non-commissioned ranks. A total of 67 volunteers, including administrative staff, served in Korea, with one contingent rotation during the three years Hospital 68 spent in theatre.

A 50-bed field hospital was established in Yongdongpo. A year after the Italians' arrival, the hospital burned down, probably by the action of Communist partisans. However, due to prompt action by the staff, not a patient was lost. By February 1953 the reconstructed hospital was expanded to 145 beds, 80 of them for surgical cases.

Despite the bitter cold of the first winter, the surgeons operated on a 24-hour basis, often desperately short of rest. Although the war had developed into a more static nature, the number of battle casualties continued to mount. During the first eight months of operations, the Italian hospital treated over 40,000 patients, over 1,000 of them as in-patients. The Italian medics were further put to the test when a serious rail accident occurred. The hospital dispatched emergency teams, and were credited with saving about 150 injured.

As the wounded soldiers were evacuated to their home countries, the Italian hospital shifted its primary role to the providing of medical and social assistance to Korean civilians. By the ceasefire, they had treated 1,639 in-patients with a mortality rate of less than four per cent. Their surgeons had performed 3,297 operations. When they left Korea they took with them the heartfelt thanks of the UN Command and the Korean people plus two Republic of Korea Presidential Citations.

SCANDINAVIAN SUPPORT: SWEDEN, DENMARK & NORWAY

First on the scene was Sweden. A 160-member Red Cross team left Stockholm in August of 1950 and set up a 200-bed hospital in Pusan at the start of October. The urgent need for medical facilities resulted in its eventual expansion to a 450-bed unit. The heavy fighting imposed a tremendous load on the overworked 10 doctors, who, together with a complement of 30 nurses, had little opportunity for rest.

Besides the thousands of battle casualties, the Swedish medical staff gave support, treatment and comfort to the many refugees in the area, often in what should have been their off-duty hours. In addition, due to a critical lack of supplies and trained medical staff in Pusan's two major civilian hospitals, the Swedish medical unit supported them with medical personnel and supplies. In April 1957, the Swedish hospital closed, after providing five and a half years of medical service to military and civilian patients.

Next to arrive in Korea was Denmark's contribution. This took the form of a hospital ship, the *Jutlandia*, which arrived in Pusan on March 7, 1951, with a total of a hundred medical personnel. The vessel had a two-fold role: Casualties transferred from the front could be treated in the well-equipped wards and operating rooms aboard, while critical cases were evacuated to base hospitals in Japan. Although based in Pusan, the hospital ship often sailed to other (sometimes dangerous) areas, to move closer and provide more effective medical care to the wounded. One concern was the matter of lighting. For security reasons the Seventh Fleet wished to have the ship blacked out yet, to conform to the Geneva Convention, the vessel was supposed to display an illuminated Red Cross symbol. A "lights on, lights off" compromise was finally reached.

Jutlandia missed out on one possible claim to fame. When the Korean War truce talks began in 1951, the ship was offered as a possible location for the meetings. Instead, Kaesong, close to the 38th Parallel, was selected. During her final tour, *Jutlandia*, as well as the British *Maine* and three U.S. hospital ships, which had been de-mothballed for the Korean War, were equipped with helicopter landing facilities, thereby facilitating rapid casualty evacuation from the front lines.

The *Jutlandia* finally left Inchon on August 17, 1953, after the ceasefire. The remaining supply of medical stocks and materials were handed over to Korean civilian hospitals.

One of the crew members found herself with two officially appointed guardians. Edith Jytte Skov was only 21 years old when she arrived in Korea. UN policy was that "no female under the age of 24 years should serve in Korea." Eventually, by special decree, the ship's captain, Commodore Kai Hammerich, and the chief surgeon, Otto Kapel, were appointed official guardians of the determined young lady, who served in the Korean theatre from September of 1951 to June 1952.

An estimated total of 15,000 patients were examined and treated on the Danish ship. During her change over return trips to Europe, wounded soldiers were repatriated to Belgium, Ethiopia, France, Greece, the Netherlands, Turkey and the United Kingdom.

However, perhaps the Scandinavian medical unit best known to members of the Commonwealth Division was the Norwegian Mobile Army Surgical Hospital – the NORMASH.

The first contingent of Norwegian medical staff arrived in Korea in June 1951. The 83-strong group, consisting mostly of army reserve volunteers, was equipped with material purchased by Norway from U.S. stocks in the Far East. It was agreed that NORMASH would operate under command of I Corps. The facility officially opened on July 19, north of Seoul and some 14 kilometers from the front lines. As the normal strength of a U.S. MASH was over 120 personnel, some 40 U.S. medical staff were loaned until a further draft arrived from Norway, when the Americans left and about 70 Koreans were taken on as guards and civilian workers.

During periods of heavy fighting in the Corps area, the original 60-bed capacity of NORMASH was often expanded to up to 200 in-patients. The role of the MASH was to provide urgent surgery to casualties before they were moved to base hospitals. The average duration of a patient's stay in NORMASH was three days before being evacuated.

Most of the Commonwealth Division's serious casualties passed through the Norwegian hospital; in fact, 27 per cent of all patients came from the Division. They included a total of 1,241 Canadians in a total of almost 15,000 members of all of the UN participants and even 172 Chinese and North Korean prisoners of war.

In addition, over 75,000 out-patients were treated or examined for minor injuries. Over 36,000 were X-rayed, including thousands of Korean civilians and UN soldiers who were examined for tuberculosis. The low fatality rate of 1.2 per cent is indicative of the quality of care, especially as this figure includes those who arrived and died before they could be treated.

There was a strong empathy between the Norwegians and the Commonwealth troops, and many of them owe their lives to the high standards of care received in NORMASH. Even today, the Norwegians keep in touch with many of their former patients in the U.K. One of these was Padre Lorentz Pedersen, who hired (and personally paid for) a substitute pastor to care for his flock in Norway when he volunteered for Korea. Padre Pedersen has recorded the story of NORMASH. In addition to his religious duties, he served as welfare officer, editor of the NORMASH newsletter and had the onerous task of "escort to the very pretty nurses when they visited army camps."

Because of its proximity to the sharp end, it was necessary to employ a South Korean guard force – enemy guerrillas were a constant threat to be reckoned with, although fortunately no attacks took place.

The unit finally left Korea in November 1954. NORMASH received two Korean and one U.S. citation, as well as 18 U.S. and South Korean decorations. Major General West, Commander of the Commonwealth Division, wrote: "NORMASH and its personnel were highly respected by all units involved. The organization of the hospital is perfect both with respect to the medical and military aspects, and even a non-professional could see how useful and efficiently they carried out their missions... I do not believe that Norway could have provided a more valuable contribution to the United Nations in the Korean War."

~ ~ ~ ~ ~ ~ ~ ~ ~ ~

AIRBORNE MEDICS: INDIA

During 1951-52, maroon berets and jump wings were common sights throughout the First Commonwealth Division, especially in 25 Canadian Infantry Brigade, which included the First Battalions of the three major infantry regiments. However, comparatively few Korean War veterans remember that the only Commonwealth unit to take part in a combat airborne operation was from India.

The story begins at the United Nations Security Council, where the Indian representative, Sir Bengal Rau, was instructed by his prime minister, Jawaharlal Nehru, to support the motion denouncing North Korean aggression in Korea.

Because of the delicate balance of Far East politics, India would not offer combat forces. While morally supporting the UN, Nehru was limited by a small army and domestic military commitments. However, despite India's neutral position, he committed a field ambulance and surgical unit as a humanitarian gesture.

The 60th Indian Field Ambulance, a unit of the Indian Airborne Division, was selected. They came from all parts of India, and most were veterans of the Second World War.

Under their commanding officer, Lt.-Col. A.G. Rangaraj, the 346-man unit arrived in Pusan on November 20, 1950. It was decided that a part of the unit would serve 27 British Brigade (which had no medical unit of its own) in the forward areas while the remainder would meet a critical need in Taegu. The unit immediately entrained to join the British in the Pyongyang area, dropping off the Taegu detachment en route.

Unfortunately, when they arrived in Pyongyang on December 4, the tables had turned and the city was being abandoned. It was here the Indians first showed their mettle. Colonel Rangaraj disobeyed orders to destroy his precious medical equipment and relied on the product of a century of Indian history.

The railways had been a major employer in India, and 60th Field Ambulance had a number of former railway men on strength. A dilapidated railway engine and a few trucks were discovered, a Bengali (who had been a fireman on the Deccan Mail and joined the army when he despaired of promotion to driver) took over the throttle, and the unit formed a chain to load the precious stores together with wood for fuel and water for the boiler.

With a jubilant note from the locomotive whistle, the train with its cargo and the men of the Field Ambulance rolled south, to the astonishment of the U.S. engineers who were about to demolish the last bridge on the Taedong river.

On December 14 the unit rejoined 27 Brigade (now, with the addition of Canadian, Australian and New Zealand troops, retitled 27 Commonwealth Brigade) at Uijongbu. They were soon kept busy dealing with both battle casualties and the effects of the bitter cold. As the Brigade withdrew southwards, the Indian Field Dressing Station was one of the last units to cross the Han River; the commander had refused to move earlier as he was still treating some casualties. Just as on their wild train trip, they crossed into safety before the last bridge was blown behind them.

The cold weather was a challenge. Water would freeze within eight feet of a stove; and medicinal solutions froze as did whole blood and diluted plasma. Eventually, hot water bottles were wrapped around the solution flasks to administer plasma. The dedicated crew worked day and night performing major surgery, and soon British, Australian and even American sick and wounded openly declared that they wanted 60 Field Ambulance to attend them. (They also found the curries served up by the cooks a welcome relief from C-rations.)

Meanwhile, United Nations Command had planned an airborne operation in the Munsan area to pave the way for an armoured advance. The U.S. 187th Airborne Regimental Combat Team was selected for this assignment, and medical support was provided by 60th Indian Field Ambulance. Led by the redoubtable Colonel Rangaraj, a detachment of the unit joined 4033 paratroopers of the 187th and jumped into hostile territory on the morning of March 23, 1951. At the assembly area the Indians found over a hundred patients who had been injured in the jump. Although enemy resistance was light, serious cases were evacuated by helicopter.

In June of 1951 the unit became part of what was truly an integrated formation. 28 Commonwealth Brigade now included British, Australian, New Zealand and Indian units, as well as a number of Canadian attachments. During Operation COMMANDO in October of that year, 60th Field Ambulance again acquitted itself well – they followed close behind the advancing troops and at times casualties being evacuated came under fire. Of the total of 262 wounded in that operation, about 150 were treated or evacuated by the Indians – all but three of them survived.

During the static period of the war, the unit continued to deal with the steady intake of casualties, with most of the battle wounded being victims of artillery fire. (The Indian Field Ambulance received enemy fire, resulting in a number of casualties.)

Colonel Rangaraj returned to India in early 1953, having served for 25 months in Korea. By the war's end the unit had performed 2,324 surgical operations and treated over 100,000 patients in the 28 Brigade and the Taegu detachments under Major N.B. Banerjee (which dealt with both military and civilian cases). Colonel Rangaraj and Major Banerjee were awarded the prestigious Mahar Vir Chakra decoration; the unit received four other high awards and 27 Mentions in Despatches, as well as several Korean and U.S. citations.

India had yet another role to play. With the ceasefire came problems associated with the repatriation of prisoners of war. Thousands of North Korean and Chinese prisoners did not wish to be returned, and became the responsibility of a Repatriation Commission. Command of the Neutral Nations Commission was entrusted to Lieutenant General Thimayya of the Indian Army and a 5,000-strong Custodian Force set sail from Madras in August of 1953. When the situation was finally resolved in February 1954, the Force returned home following a job well done.

To quote a senior Commonwealth officer, "Australians, British and New Zealanders would have nothing to do with any other field ambulance." While this is perhaps an exaggeration – if a soldier is wounded, beggars can't be choosers – it does perhaps reflect the admiration and respect earned by 60th Indian Field Ambulance. To 28 Brigade, the cherry beret of the 60th was a reassuring sight.

~ ~ ~ ~ ~ ~ ~ ~ ~ ~

THE "SECRET" ALLY: JAPAN

Ask any Korean War veteran which nations participated in the war on the UN side, and the chances are that he can rattle off the names of 22 countries which provided combat or medical support. Less known are the other UN members who offered help, which for one reason or another was not taken up. Five Latin American nations offered aid – Bolivia, Cost Rica, El Salvador and Panama, as well as Cuba (this was, of course, before the Castro regime).

What would have been the most significant contribution in numerical terms was offered by what was then Nationalist China. Generalissimo Chiang Kai-Shek offered the services of three of his infantry divisions and twenty C-47 aircraft. This offer was declined, no doubt to avoid an escalation into the Korean peninsula of the ongoing war between the Nationalists and Red China.

Perhaps our most unusual ally was a country with whom, technically, the United States and many of the other UN participants were still at war – Japan!

Much of the Japanese aid was offered overtly. Japan itself provided enormous technical support and supply resources. Textile factories were kept busy with the production of tentage and uniforms; repair and maintenance of military equipment and vehicles was in full swing. The post-war Japanese economy benefited from every form of activity ranging from the provision of female companionship and gallons of Asahi beer to the battle-weary troops on R&R, to the furnishing of merchant shipping to convey troops and supplies from the Japanese transit bases to the Korean mainland. Many Korea veterans remember the crossing from Kure or Sasebo to Pusan in an ancient "maru" which appeared to have been used to carry odorous but unidentifiable cargo before being pressed into service on the Korea sealift.

One undoubted advantage of General Douglas MacArthur's appointment to command the troops in Korea was that he was double-hatted. He was also the Supreme Commander Allied Powers in Japan – in effect, the military governor of an occupied enemy nation. This meant that, on his own authority, he could permit the use of naval and air bases in Japan for use in the Korean War. This was especially significant in the early days of the war as usable airfields on the Korean mainland were few and far between.

Beside these overt demonstrations of support from Japan, a less publicized form of assistance was requested and provided (in fact, this was not revealed until well after the war). Japanese Admiral Okubu Takeo, the director of the Maritime Defence Force, was approached by U.S. Admiral Burke with a request for assistance in clearing Russian-built mines off the East coast of Korea.

A number of Japanese vessels were dispatched to the area. Admiral Takeo recalls that they had to deal with three different types of mines; the moored contact mine, magnetic mines, and the pressure type which could be activated by a large vessel passing close by. To disguise their presence in the operational theatre, the Japanese vessels flew the International Code of Signals "E" flag at the masthead in place of a national ensign.

Captain Chiko Inoshi, in a television interview, remembers that having survived the Second World War, he was reluctant to risk his life and those of his crew to assist his former enemies. However, it was impressed upon him by his superiors that the operation would be a great thing for his country, and he took part. He recalls that while he was lucky enough to return with his ship to Japan, others were less fortunate and a number of his comrades lost their lives when their minesweeper struck a mine off Wonsan. (These casualties were apparently never included in the total of the Korean War fatalities.)

Admiral Takeo is convinced that this co-operation with the UN fleet was a key factor in the granting of Japanese independence and the extremely favourable peace terms the following year (a fact which may not be appreciated by, among others, our own Hong Kong veterans).

One serendipital effect of the Japanese war effort had beneficial results for a close friend of mine. Jeff Mulcock, a Vickers machine-gunner recalls: "We were laying down heavy fire on Hill 227. The Chinese had been very active and we'd been going through a lot of ammunition. I noticed that my tracer rounds were dropping short, a sure sign that the barrel needed changing.

"My Number Two was not really effective – we'd been getting a lot of arty fire ourselves – and I tried to change the barrel myself. This was bloody difficult as it's really a two-man job. All at once our Korean porter (who'd been bringing up ammo and water for our guns) grabbed a hold of the barrel and helped me change it. It was obvious that he knew just what he was doing, and he stayed with me as the Number Two for the rest of the action."

Corporal Mulcock subsequently found out that many of our Korean porters had been drafted into the Japanese Army during the Second World War and his "No. 2" had been trained to use captured Vickers MMGs.

There is little doubt that the Japanese participation had a great effect on the outcome of the Korean War. Not only was the logistical support essential, but the revitalizing effects of living for a few days under civilized conditions while on R&R leave in Tokyo did wonders for the mental and physical health of our troops (although it was generally conceded that the troops returning from five days in the Ginza Beer Hall and similar cultural haunts looked in far worse shape than those they met at the airport going out!).

It has been said that there were no victors in the Korean War. In a military sense, this may be true. However, in *The Korean War*, Max Hastings suggests that, in fact, the Japanese came out as real winners. Their economy got a much-needed kick-start, the influence on their peace treaty terms was evident, and perhaps most of all, the hundreds of thousands of United Nations troops who passed through Japan brought a new conception of Japan and the Japanese to the outside world.

Meanwhile, at the United Nations cemetery outside Pusan, the flags of 22 participating countries fly in memory of those who died in the War, including 516 Canadian servicemen. There is no flag to remember the Japanese sailors who gave their lives – not even an "E" flag.

The Canadian memorial in Naechon (Kapyong area). (VAC PHOTO)

❧ EPILOGUE

In 1935 the League of Nations turned a blind eye when Abyssinia asked for help against an Italian invasion. This encouraged the Axis partners to continue their exploitations, culminating in the Second World War.

In 1950 the United Nations were more resolute. The show of unity may well have given the Communist bloc second thoughts about its plans for world domination. It might not be an exaggeration to say that the forces of the 22 allied nations who fought in Korea were, in a way, saviors of democracy.

When they came home from Korea most of our veterans simply returned to their communities with no parades or fanfares. Indeed, some were not accepted as veterans by local Royal Canadian Legion branches (these were isolated incidents – the Legion, as a whole, has long supported Korean War veterans' concerns).

It was not until 40 years later that the Korean War was finally accepted officially as a "war," although over 27,000 Canadians participated and 516 lost their lives. In 1991 Canada finally awarded a Canadian Volunteer Service Medal for Korea to qualified veterans.

Some Korea veterans achieved a modicum of fame. Of the many regulars who remained in the forces, two became chiefs of the defence staff. Others were successful in politics or business. Most however went on to live normal, productive lives.

Some of our allies continued successful careers. Fidel "Eddie" Ramos became president of the Philippines, while South Korean General Park was well-known as his country's ambassador in Ottawa. Others were less fortunate. Once-proud Ethiopian veterans have been reduced to begging in the streets, while many of the gallant French battalion lost their lives later at Bien Den Phu in Indo-China.

Our numbers are decreasing – probably 14,000 Canadian Korea vets are still active. However, we all agree on one thing – Korea was indeed a WAR!

Index